Drawing and Looking

THE DEVELOPING BODY AND MIND

Series Editor:
Professor George Butterworth, *Department of Psychology. University of Sussex.*

Designed for a broad readership in the English-speaking world, this major series represents the best of contemporary research and theory in the cognitive, social, abnormal and biological areas of development.

Drawing and Looking

Theoretical approaches to pictorial representation in children

Edited by

Christiane Lange-Küttner
Free University Berlin

Glyn V. Thomas
University of Birmingham

HARVESTER
WHEATSHEAF

New York London Toronto Sydney Tokyo Singapore

First published 1995 by
Harvester Wheatsheaf
Campus 400, Maylands Avenue
Hemel Hempstead
Hertfordshire, HP2 7EZ
A division of
Simon & Schuster International Group

Typeset in 10/12 pt Ehrhardt
by Photoprint, 9–11 Alexandra Lane, Torquay

Printed and bound in Great Britain by
T. J. Press (Padstow) Ltd

British Library Cataloguing in Publication Data

A catalogue record for this book is available from the British Library

ISBN 0–7450–1571–9

1 2 3 4 5   99 98 97 96 95

To those defining parts of the family whose world became invisible during the Second World War

C. L-K

Contents

Preface

Children's drawing is a topic of considerable theoretical and practical significance to students and professionals in a range of specialisms, including art education, nursery and primary school education, as well as the psychology of perception and cognitive development. In recent years, the work of experimental psychologists has given us a much clearer understanding of the role of production factors in determining the finished product. At the same time there have been developments in the fields of visual perception and in children's understanding of mental representation (for example, their acquisition of a 'theory of mind') which have led to new research on children's perception and understanding of pictures. Cognitive psychologists are also now becoming more aware of the importance of social and cultural factors in children's drawing.

In sum, in recent years there has been a number of new and interesting empirical and theoretical advances which, as is usual for this topic, are scattered across a very wide range of journals and other sources. The aim of this book is to bring together accessible accounts of these developments in a single volume for anyone with interests in children's drawing and their cognitive development.

We have tried to include accounts of all the theoretical approaches that are currently important. Inevitably, there are some gaps in the coverage; we regret, for example, that expressive aspects of drawing and the contribution of Arnheim and his followers are not fully represented.

It has been our principal aim to present readable and interesting accounts of the main theoretical approaches in the field. Contributing authors were asked to relate their theories to empirical studies and to specific examples, but the book was never primarily intended as an outlet for new research findings; refereed journals do a better job of that. We intended to take the interested reader deeper into psychological theories of children's drawing than is the case in the currently available introductory texts. The book also brings together work on children's drawing and on understanding about pictures as representations. These two areas of research are normally rather independent of each other; it was our intention to bring them into closer contact.

Although the focus is on pictorial representation, it will be clear that many of the issues raised are of more general significance. Consequently, the book could well serve as a useful supplementary text for courses on cognitive development.

We, as editors, have been helped by a great many people. We particularly wish to thank Harry Beilin, George Butterworth and Farrell Burnett for their early support and encouragement for the idea of the book at all. Further, we are obliged to Wolfgang Edelstein, Max Planck Institute for Human Development and Education, Berlin and to Angela Friederici, Cognitive Science Lab Berlin, Free University Berlin for their constant support and encouragement. We are also grateful to Helen Jones in Birmingham for her help in preparing the manuscript, and to Clare Grist as well as Janet Clayton of Harvester Wheatsheaf for taking over at short notice the responsibility for the production of the book.

Finally, but most importantly, we wish to thank the authors who responded so promptly to our invitations to contribute to this volume. We are grateful for their patience and tolerance of our editorial requests and timetables.

Acknowledgements

The chapter authors and editors acknowledge the permission to use the following material:

Franklin, S., van Sommers, P. and Howard, D. (1992) 'Drawing without meaning? Dissociations in the graphic performance of an agnosic artist', in R. Campbell (ed.), *Mental Lives: Case studies in cognition*, Basil Blackwell, Oxford.

Kennedy, J. M. (1983) 'What can we learn about pictures from the blind?', *American Scientist*, vol. 71, pp. 19–26.

Lorant, G. and van Eekhout, P. (1980) *L'Homme qui ne savait plus parler*, Nouvelles Editions Baudinière, Paris.

Luquet, G. H. (1927/1977) *Le Dessin enfantin*, Alcan, Paris. (Third edition reprinted by Delachaux and Niestlé, Lausanne and Paris, 1977.)

Mooney, C. M. (1957) 'Age in the development of closure ability', *Canadian Journal of Psychology*, vol. 11, pp. 219–26.

Piaget, J. and Inhelder, B. (1966/1971) *Mental Imagery in the Child*, Routledge & Kegan Paul, London.

Reith, E. (1988) 'The development of use of contour lines in children's drawings of figurative and non-figurative three-dimensional models', *Archives de Psychologie*, vol. 56, pp. 83–103.

Silk, A. M. J. and Thomas, G. V. (1986) 'Development and differentiation in children's figure drawings', *British Journal of Psychology*, vol. 77, pp. 399–410.

Silk, A. M. J. and Thomas, G. V. (1988) 'The development of size scaling in children's figure drawings', *British Journal of Developmental Psychology*, vol. 6, pp. 285–99.

Thomas, G. V. and Tsalimi, A. (1988) 'Effects of order of drawing head and

Acknowledgements

trunk on their relative sizes in children's human figure drawings', *British Journal of Developmental Psychology*, vol. 6, pp. 191–203.

van Sommers, P. (1991) 'Where writing starts: the analysis of action applied to the historical development of writing', in J. Wann, A. Wing and N. Sovik (eds), *Development of Graphic Skills*, Academic Press, London.

Willats, J. (1977a) 'How children learn to draw realistic pictures', *Quarterly Journal of Experimental Psychology*, vol. 29, pp. 367–82.

Willats, J. (1977b) 'How children learn to represent three-dimensional space in drawings', in G. Butterworth (ed.), *The Child's Representation of the World*, Plenum Press, London, pp. 189–202.

Willats, J. (1992) 'The representation of extendedness in children's drawings of sticks and discs', *Child Development*, vol. 63, pp. 692–710.

Chapter 1

Introduction

Christiane Lange-Küttner *Free University Berlin*
Glyn V. Thomas *University of Birmingham*

This book is about theoretical approaches to pictorial representation in children, and at the same time it is an international book. The idea for it emerged from a symposium on 'Theoretical approaches to pictorial representation' at the 5th European Conference on Developmental Psychology in Seville, Spain, in September 1993. The contributors to the symposium were Glyn Thomas and Liz Robinson, United Kingdom (Reflective understanding about pictures), Anna Stetsenko, Russia (Social origin of thought), John Willats, United Kingdom (Information processing) and Emiel Reith, Switzerland and Christiane Lange-Küttner, Germany (Genetic epistemology); the discussant was George Butterworth, United Kingdom. A key issue was the link between perception and production processes in relation to children both responding to and producing pictures.

It seemed to us at the symposium that there was a need for a book to bring together the various psychological theories relating to pictorial representation – and so the idea for the present volume was born. Subsequently, other authors were invited to write chapters on further theoretical approaches to depiction in children: Sergio Morra, Italy, joined us to explain the neo-Piagetian approach; Alan Costall, United Kingdom, to explain the Gibsonian ecological model of perception and its implications for drawing development; John Kennedy, Andrea Nicholls and Mary Desrochers, Canada, and Peter van Sommers, Australia, to present the biological and neuropsychological side of perception and production; and Norman Freeman, United Kingdom, to explain a framework theory of pictures. Additionally, Glyn Thomas wrote a chapter on the planning strategies approach which Freeman had put forward in 1980 and which has stimulated numerous empirical studies on children's drawings ever since.

The aim of this book is to elucidate each of the diverse theoretical approaches. The sequence of the chapters corresponds to a scale, with theories closer to natural science at one end and approaches closer to social science at the other. However, this classification is founded neither on methods nor on *Weltanschauungen*. Rather, it relates to the different aspects and processes that the acts of perceiving, judging or graphically constructing a picture entail. Furthermore, this scale is not metrically defined but constituted out of local theoretical neighbourhoods. As neighbourhoods are more intuitive we could have found a different order: there are many more possible links between the theoretical approaches than we shall be able to comment on here.

Costall and Willats share references to the perceptual theories of Marr and Gibson, to whom Kennedy also refers. Kennedy's contribution is also close to van Sommers': both share the consideration of human physical reality, i.e. a neuropsychological view on graphic depiction. The chapters by Lange-Küttner and Reith and by Morra have common roots in the work of Piaget; for this reason they may be perceived as a grouping. The role of drawing strategies discussed by Thomas overlaps with the neo-Piagetian theories discussed by Morra, and so these chapters are placed together. The contributions of Nye, Robinson and Thomas as well as of Freeman share their view on pictures as being a special medium: they try to define what a full reflective understanding of pictures might entail, and report on studies that map children's emerging understanding of this domain of representation. These chapters were consequently grouped together. Finally, social and cultural factors on drawing are considered in the contributions of Stetsenko as well as of Lange-Küttner and Edelstein and, therefore, these chapters form a neighbourhood.

To familiarize the reader with the theories explained in this book all chapters are summarized briefly following the sequence listed in the Contents. Some introductory remarks are made about earlier theories and on general tendencies in current theorizing that provide a background to psychological models about drawing and looking.

The very act of drawing involves many interacting processes, sensorimotor coordination, perception of the external model when there is one, consulting an inner image or schema or representation in memory when no external model is present, production of a graphic form and its correction, understanding of pictures as a medium of representation and communication. The separation of these diverse processes which already occur within a constrained time window represents a challenge to the psychologist.

Scientists' predictions about the relation between perceptual and conceptual processes sometimes implicitly take up earlier philosophical theories. For instance, Kant (1787/1926, p. 66) thought that we have to become aware of the fact that space and spatial objects can never be understood completely when we make ourselves dependent on their appearance. Instead, we would have to define space *a priori*. A different theory about our perceptual and conceptual understanding was developed by Hume (1878). He was not so much concerned with our being cheated by appearance, but stressed the danger of unexperienced reasoning leading to logically correct but nevertheless false conclusions. Thus, the optimal proportion of perceptual and conceptual processes for reasoning was an issue already in the past.

Chapter 2: Ecological theory

Given that pictures are easy to see, it sometimes comes as a surprise to discover that they are hard to explain. More strictly, there is as yet no agreement among experts on how pictures should be conceptualized and on how they 'work'. Although there are some aspects of pictures and their perception which seem to depend on convention and experience, most theorists agree that there is a close link between picture perception and perception of the real world. This argument is based on the general finding that even very young children seem to be able to identify the subject-matter of many pictures without special training. It follows from this starting point that what you think picture perception involves depends on what you think perception of the real world entails.

In Chapter 2, Costall argues that most traditional theories of drawing and pictures have been committed to the idea of a 'sensory core', which assumes that drawing in perspective ought to be a purely physically determined process. Being physical again seems to be synonymous with being innocent: Costall records that both Sully (1895) and Bühler (1930) were similarly convinced that early innocent perception of the visual world soon becomes 'corrupted' by intelligence and concepts. These perceptual models of drawing can be characterized as theories of loss and repression, and compared with more modern efforts to find conceptually uncontaminated graphic performance in the drawings of special populations, such as the autistic children described by Selfe (1983). Costall notes that information about the infancy of these autistic children has seldom been seriously considered to be of value, although it would be of importance to the current debate about the nature of perception.

The chapter then develops Gibson's criticisms of theories of perception based on the notion of a stationary eye taking in a single view. We should note that Gibson distinguished sharply between the concept of the visual field and that of the visual world. Theories based on the stationary eye and the visual field, Gibson argued, neglect the important information about the visual world gained via the natural interaction processes between a moving observer and his or her environment. Costall is particularly critical of current notions about visual realism and of viewer-centred perspective. In Marr's perceptual theory the viewer-centred specification comes first and is followed by a complex set of operations reworked into a structural description of the visual scene. In contrast, visual realism in children's drawings is often defined by investigators only by very loose and simple criteria. In particular, Costall suggests that these criteria for classifying young children's drawings as being in perspective (providing view-specific information) are inadequate.

Costall concludes that there is no reliable evidence that true and innocent perception really exists, and thus drawing in perspective need have nothing to do with access to a sensory core. He introduces Gibson's notion of the extraction of formless invariants from visual input to the eye. Forms *per se* are supposed to be only 'unhidden', but formless invariants are perceptual abstractions that are conceptual. Modern conceptual art, for example, illustrates how artificial the distinction is between conceptual and perceptual processes.

Chapter 3: *Human information processing*

In contrast to Costall, the approach presented by Willats *is* based on the assumption that the visual input to the eye provides view-specific information (the sensory core) out of which interpretations of the shape and positions of objects are extracted. We are introduced here to Marr's information-processing approach, and to the postulation of technical devices designed to simulate mechanically the processes involved in perception.

Willats' account of the human information-processing approach starts with a comparison between input and output processes as well as their transformation algorithms in machines such as cameras and computers. An analogy is made with the systems of rules and transformations that children might apply when they draw a picture.

Willats introduces the notion of a denotation system which relates two-dimensional graphic constructions to objects that are three-dimensional in reality. The description of the various graphic construction systems for depicting geometric spatial objects such as tables is extended to natural and organic objects such as the human figure. He prepares the reader for a model which is derived from linguistics. The relevant point is that linguists (for example, Quirk *et al.*, 1985) differentiate between the syntactic structure of language (the grammar or the constructedness of speech out of units), the semantic dimension of language (its meaning), the morphological form of a unit of language (its global shape), its phonological form (its pronunciation) and its graphical form (its spelling). In Willats' chapter these linguistic differentiations are not referred to in full. In considering how a picture can be constructed, the degree of dimensionality and angularity is described within a framework of drawing and denotation systems. One could say that Willats is interested in the semantics of drawing. The starting point for this analysis is the question of whether children use views or descriptions, i.e. whether their internal model of the to-be-depicted object is visual or verbal. Willats describes the development of graphic competence as proceeding from expressing nonaccidental properties of objects to drawing the most likely views of objects. Referring to Witkin and Tennenbaum (1983) and Biederman (1987), Willats explains that young children present graphically only what is true for both the view and the physical properties of the object: the extension of an object and its topological relation with others. Later, they start to differentiate between likely and unlikely, possible, true and impossible views. Willats' study of drawing a foreshortened disc taps the conflict between producing a graphic form that looks right, and is acceptable in terms of making sense of an object, and reproducing a visually correct though ambiguous graphic form.

Willats' approach to children's rules for transforming visual perception of objects into graphic denotations concludes with the statement that drawing is extremely complex. How complex even fast automatic processes can be is shown by neuropsychological accounts of perception and production. In the past, most philosophers were eager to demonstrate that thought really exists, even though we cannot see it. Because of its invisibility, it can be difficult to believe in the existence of thought, and even more so in its effects. The freedom of thought was a most important notion for modern societies as the secrecy of these mental processes provided for a sense of individuality, which seems to be unique and still not wished for in all cultures because individual conceptions may tend to become uncontrollable and threatening for a community. Modern philosophers like Habermas (1981), therefore, changed their mind about the salvatory effects of intelligence as such on the state of a society, and instead claimed that only the interaction of minds, the sharing of thoughts and concepts in discourse could lead to a true change for the better. But this view still ignores the physical side of life. Modern French philosophers like Bataille (1963) or Foucault (1979) claim that it is precisely the predominance of thought and the disregard of the significance of the physical body that create distorted perceptions of the possibility of progress and change.

Neuropsychological accounts of cognition provide knowledge about the necessary but also vulnerable and transitory physical basis of thought. Neuro-psychologists give us an idea of what can happen when the brain or the peripheral sensory organs are damaged: processes become selectively disrupted and draw our attention to matters that we had taken for granted. Especially the dysfunction of certain groups of specific processes indicates that the brain has a structure that corresponds to cognitive processes in a nonaccidental fashion.

Chapter 4: The modular model

Van Sommers presents a modular information-processing approach to this field. The basic assumption of modular models of the mind is that cognition is not a monolithic process, but consists of fast, automatic and encapsulated subprocesses (Fodor, 1983). The physical bases for these processes can be localized in particular regions of the brain, although we must assume that these locations might change during development (Friederici, 1990). Van Sommers reports evidence that supports a modular account of drawing. He shows that selective neuropsychological impairments lead to selective deficits in graphic performance.

This chapter starts with a description of the 'natural' logic of action and also of common errors that occur when drawing, for instance, a flower or a bicycle. The robust common mistakes and graphic misconceptions frequently found in normal subjects lead to the methodological conclusion that it would be unproductive to compare the performance of patients with brain lesions with that of most normal subjects, as both draw comparably poorly. For this reason, van Sommers considers only the drawing of experts and skilled amateurs who have suffered brain lesions.

The evidence presented in this chapter shows, first, that lesions which impair *motor skills* can cause superficial output problems but not the loss of underlying ability to plan and execute a complex drawing. A previously right-handed patient with a left hemisphere lesion, for example, was able to transfer quite successfully to drawing with his left hand.

The ability to form an *internal image* is one of the basic requirements when drawing without an external model. Van Sommers describes the drawing of patients who appear to lack visual imagery; they produce very sketchy and recognizable figures but are not able to describe them adequately. The reader could infer that in some ways imagery and verbal explanation are linked. In fact, van Sommers draws the conclusion that imagery may not be just a simultaneously present visualized picture, but is constituted as a sequential and heterogeneous assemblage of iconic or abstract, static or procedural processes.

With regard to *memory*, van Sommers reports that selective memory deficits which have occurred as a result of strokes or ageing can cause extreme dependency on an external model. This evidence indicates that memory capacity is of major importance for the drawing process. That this is also true of children's drawings is explained in Chapter 7 on neo-Piagetian approaches. We should note that visual agnosia – the inability to recognize visual objects as meaningful – does not necessarily lead to a complete deficit in graphic depiction. Errors occur mainly in shapes and their connection. It seems that the outline construction of the graphic object especially is impaired. Van Sommers uses this evidence, and the fact that it is difficult to devise computer-driven pattern recognition programs, to make sense of photographed landscapes to argue against the view that elaborate graphic constructions require the analysis of visual input into a meaningless array of colour and shades. The reader might note a possible link between this line of argument and the distinction between the visual field and the visual world made by Gibson (Chapter 2), and also the suggestion made by Piaget and Inhelder that figurative thought may be transformed but never dismissed completely (Chapter 6).

In the domain of *depth perception* van Sommers shows that the process of abstracting depth from a 2½ D picture of an unfamiliar object places considerable demands on the subject. Once acquired, this faculty can be lost again as a result of neurological disease or ageing processes even in experts in drawing and painting. To sum up, this chapter shows the reader that the selective dysfunction of certain subprocesses owing to neurological impairment does not necessarily cause a complete breakdown of drawing skill, but produces patterns of impairment and sparing, which suggest that graphic competence is in fact organized in a modular way.

Chapter 5: Neural networks

Kennedy, Nicholls and Desrochers also use a neuropsychological model for conceptualizing perception and production processes, although of a rather different sort. In their model firing cells in a layered network perceptually extracts an axis from a line. Their principal purpose is to account for how a picture which literally consists of a network of thin lines can be 'read' so easily as a representation of a three-dimensional object. Hochberg and Brooks (1962) had already found that line drawings of common objects were instantly recognized by a child with no prior training on pictures. Kennedy *et al.* suggest that there is a universal tendency to perceive thin lines as outlines of solid objects. This capacity may be innate, however, it seems unlikely that it could have evolved specifically because it allowed our ancestors to perceive pictures. Kennedy *et al.* set out a neural network model to explain how our sensory systems of vision and touch might be constructed to detect contours in normal sensory input from the world, but which as a byproduct will also respond to thin lines as contours.

Neural network models are based on the principle that real neurons communicate information via interactive processes which can be described chemically and electromagnetically. The notion that a network of modifiable inhibitory and excitatory connections can store and process information is at the heart of connectionist (neural network) approaches.

To link perceptual and neurological models Kennedy draws on Gibson's assumption that perception depends on perceiving surfaces. However, Kennedy *et al.* explain that surfaces have contours, even when it is what we perceive as a line. Pictorially, lines can be interpreted in several different ways. First, lines may be seen as surfaces, although this may not be a common interpretation; second, lines can be boundaries and outlines of graphic objects; third, especially in young children, lines can denote all sorts of properties of objects such as corners of a cube, or objects themselves, as snakes; fourth, lines can be spatial axes that constitute a spatial system. Kennedy *et al.* stress that spatial axes are not perceptions of brightness, colour or pressure, and thus perception of axes is not a visual or tactile phenomenon but an amodal abstraction, a statement which the reader will also find in Chapter 2.

To summarize the connections between the different layers of the network: the activation goes from the input layer 1 through a hidden layer to layer 2, responsible for contour detection. More sophisticated processes which ambiguous objects require are executed by the additional layers 3 and 4. Kennedy *et al.* describe the interplay of inhibition and activation that is necessary for effective functioning. In this way, they describe more dynamic processes than implied in the modular model which implicitly places greater stress on the importance of encapsulation of cognitive modules for effective functioning. It is assumed that the neural hierarchical network supporting perceptual processes is fully functioning from early on in life.

Chapter 6: Genetic epistemology

This assumption of early perceptual abilities is also shared by the approach of Piaget and Inhelder, which is described by Lange-Küttner and Reith. However, they suppose that perceptual activity is either passive registration or active conceptualization of reality in changing proportion. Lange-Küttner and Reith introduce the late work of Piaget and Inhelder, and not their stage concept of development which Piaget thought not to be valid in perception. Wohlwill (1962) distinguished between two Piagets – the psychologist of the development of intelligence who describes stages of development, and the psychologist of perception who published an equally impressive series of studies about perceptual phenomena. It seems that in their later work Piaget and Inhelder (1966/1971) were trying to synthesize these two sides of Piaget's work. To describe their theory in Costall's terms (Chapter 2) one could say that in the young child an active sensory core leads the child to conserve the visuosensory identity of objects, be they geometrically regular or naturally irregular in shape.

Piaget and Inhelder called this process of focusing exclusively on ready-made forms 'figurative thought'. The point about this process is that it conserves the Gestalt-like perceptual impression of the object. The emergence of the ability to construct and supplement axes within and between objects so as to express spatial relations was seen as a transformation of primary figurative thought.

Lange-Küttner and Reith argue that we can observe this transformation of figurative thought taking place simultaneously when systematic reasoning emerges. In children's drawings this change has an effect on both visual forms and spatial relations. For instance, spatial relations become graphically explicit, based on axes that structure the whole page and not only local areas. Lange-Küttner and Reith presume, however, that this process involves an *a priori* definition of space as indefinite, which disregards the significance of any spatial object. Space becomes conceptualized hierarchically; the object loses its status as a constituent of space and becomes an object that can be imagined at various possible places.

Thus, Lange-Küttner and Reith hold the view that rather than looking (visual perception) enhancing drawing development, on the contrary, looking away and distancing oneself from one's own visuosensory information facilitates active definition and conceptualization of visual reality. This approach points out that perceptual processes may actually hinder efficient conceptualization of spatial objects and places in drawings.

Chapter 7: Neo-Piagetian theory

Morra argues that Piaget's idea of the mind as a structure of schemes that changes over time is taken up by neo-Piagetians (Pascual-Leone, 1970; Case, 1985). They specify different types of schemes as well as diverse cognitive factors and mechanisms responsible for cognitive performance of specific tasks. Qualitative change in development is no longer assumed, but instead, a quantitative increase in information-processing capacity.

Morra describes a two-level architecture of the mind. The basic units of cognition are two types of schemes: figurative schemes which refer to objects and operative schemes which refer to spatial relations. These schemes can be simple or aggregated into complex ones. Individual differences at this level are assumed to be large; therefore, these structures are called subjective operators. The metasubjective or silent operators are situated on a second level of cognition. They are responsible for scheme creation and activation, and thus are supposed to be the regulators of dynamic processes of the mental structure. The silent operators are learning operators (C, LC and LM), a central attention or working memory operator (M), a central inhibitory operator (I) and a field operator (F). These are the factors referred to by the abbreviation for the theory of constructive operators, TCO, in the text.

In neo-Piagetian theory it is assumed that M capacity develops from 1 unit at age 3 years adding one extra unit at each year up to 7 units. The increasing size is indicated as $e+1$, $e+2$, ... $e+7$. The upper limit reminds us of the magical number 7 in short-term memory, which Miller (1956) described. In Morra's study on planning capacity in children's drawings, measures of M capacity and field dependence were taken from different groups of subjects. Subjects were also given drawing tasks which involved the explicit assessment prior to drawing of the children's plans with regard to the number and the location of graphic items to be drawn on the page. It showed that M capacity was clearly age-related, and significant correlations with graphic spatial planning scores were found.

Thus, this theory implies both a formal conceptualization of cognitive processes and, at the same time, a more individual description of the subject. Indeed, the aim of this theory is to make precise predictions about both individual differences and cognitive functioning.

A prediction about individual performance according to Morra would be that field-dependent subjects with a strong F operator would be more likely to differentiate well-structured Gestalten than a sophisticated spatial layout or composition as they do not have efficient M and I operators. As an illustration for a formal description Morra gives the case of two possible strategies for drawing overlap: strategy 1 requires $e+3$ M capacity units (visible object, invisible part object, visible part object) while an alternative strategy requires $e+2$ units (visible object, visible part-object).

In the neo-Piagetian model perceptual processes are just one factor in the TCO, varying in significance across individuals and across tasks.

Chapter 8: Strategies and skills

The theoretical position that children need planning strategies to elaborate a visual scene on a sheet of paper was put forward systematically by Freeman in 1980. The approach differs from Piagetian and neo-Piagetian accounts in its initial working hypothesis that children should be thought of as being in principle as capable at drawing as adults when provided with appropriate cues. In Freeman's hands, this challenging hypothesis was the starting point for an important programme of experimental research. Thomas argues the less radical position that children's drawing strategies and skills can play a crucial role in determining the final shape of the pictures that they draw. Consequently, it is not possible to derive reliable information from children's drawings about their underlying personality traits or mental structures without taking these production factors into account.

This chapter sets out arguments and evidence for the importance of a graphic schema in picture-making, although the use of the term 'schema' here refers exclusively to the graphic form on the page and should not be confused with the mental 'scheme' in Piagetian psychology. Instead, Morra uses the term 'items', Lange-Kuttner and Reith use the term 'graphic objects' for the graphic signs on the page.

Thomas draws on Gombrich's (1960) proposition that the schemata/formulae used by artists consist simply of patterns and marks which trigger a response in the viewer. This approach to picture perception requires that the perceiver constructs a perceptual interpretation out of essentially ambiguous input to the eye. The use of schemata is, on the one hand, essential for taking up traditions and cultural conventions but, on the other hand, schemata must also be considered as an internal constraint to drawing development. Thomas suggests that children rarely draw from an external model (reality), but that they build graphic constructions from a repertoire of graphic schemata. The argument advanced is that in making a picture, children and adult artists alike have to deploy already known graphic schemata, combining and modifying them by trial and error to create novel pictures.

This crucial role of the graphic schema nevertheless implies constraints on the development of the graphic repertoire. Thomas suggests that internal constraints are produced by two main factors. First, children have only a few schemata at their disposal; and second, such schemata as they do have consist of simple lines and shapes only. The emergence of new, more elaborated schemata may be a matter of personal discovery, or they may be copied from others. Sometimes established schemata for familiar objects are borrowed and adapted to new topics. The process of differentiation is always based on established forms which become modified for the new purpose. In this way, conservatism is not a personality trait of children but an internal constraint of development.

The second internal constraint on drawing is caused by the need to sequence the production of a drawing. Thomas draws on the numerous experiments that he has conducted with his collaborators in Birmingham, showing how the sequence in which the parts of a picture are drawn can influence its final form. There may, however, be limits to children's ability to vary the sequence in which a drawing is executed. Karmiloff-Smith has identified some intriguing constraints in children's drawing performance. Karmiloff-Smith (1990) found that when young children were asked to draw a human figure with two heads, they could not spontaneously prevent themselves from adding a second body to the second head. It would be an especially rewarding line of research to be followed if we could tease apart whether the change from a rigid execution plan to a flexibly ordered set of manipulable elements arises from habit or from cognitive capabilities.

Chapter 9: Reflective understanding of pictures

Becoming reflective about one's own habit of perceiving pictures as just either a referent or as a thing in itself, when in fact a picture is both, is at the centre of Chapter 9 by Nye, Thomas and Robinson. If allowed, one could reformulate their hypothesis in social terms: are pictures self-contained entities, or do they exist for others? It seems that young children think that some are self-contained and others are there for others. The important achievement is to understand that an individual, as well as a picture, can be conceptualized in more than one way. This point was made for pictures by DeLoache in her formulation of the dual representation hypothesis. To take one example, DeLoache (1991) found that young children may value an attractive model as an object in its own right and, in consequence, do not use it as a representation of a referent. They seem unable to treat an item such as a picture both as a symbol and as a thing in itself.

Nye *et al.* explain Beilin and Pearlman's (1991) specification of Piaget's childhood realism for the domain of pictures. Beilin and Pearlman introduced the term 'iconic realism' for errors about the physical and functional properties of pictorial objects. Some young children may think that pictorial objects are a kind of substandard version of the original object and might be uncertain about which properties they had in common.

Thus, the reader may note that young children may perceive a normal picture just as a substandard version of the real object it represents and not attend to the picture as an object in its own right. Nye *et al.* present evidence to suggest that the relation between object and referent is asymmetrical: young children were less likely to attribute visual properties of a picture to the represented object than vice versa.

Although even infants are able to differentiate between the original and the substandard (i.e. between a picture and a real exemplar of the thing it represents), nevertheless, to understand the dual identity of a picture is a late achievement in development. Nye *et al.* consider factors which may influence children's tendencies to confuse pictures and their referents. It is unlikely that there is one single cause for the various phenomena that have been called childhood realism. Some of the errors children make may be the result of cognitive factors; others may arise from the particular experiences children have had with pictures in a social context.

Chapter 10: *Children's theory of art*

The issues that Freeman considers can be linked with the emergence of 'folk psychology' and the child's development of a 'theory of mind'. From the latter, the term 'children's theory of art' can be derived. Children acquire an understanding of mental representation and of mind, it is argued, when they grasp the idea of false belief. With such a concept children are in a position to reason about other people's actions in terms of their intentions and knowledge about the world. The basis for this approach is to set out what is required for a mature understanding of mental representation (the key is understanding of false belief), and then study the emergence of this understanding in children.

Similarly, Freeman sets out to specify a framework theory of pictorial reasoning, which will adequately describe the goal towards which the development of a theory of art in childhood is directed. His approach is to specify a relational network of the artist (A) as the inventor/creator of the picture, thus introducing the source of originality of a picture, the picture (P), the beholder (B) and the world (W) for which the picture has been made. To put it another way, his model specifies the relations between the picture and the world, the artist and the world, the artist and the picture, the artist and the beholder, and the beholder and the picture.

This is the cultural framework for art production which children have to comprehend in order to judge the efficiency of the artist in realizing his intentions as well as the significance of a work of art within a social context and for individual members of a society. Freeman shows how children become art critics in middle childhood, a skill that finally results in folk psychological assumptions about the value of pictures, the beauty they convey and the impression they cause in the beholder.

One question posed in this approach is to ask children about the source of beauty in a picture. Freeman presents evidence that the younger children are straightforward in their opinion that the degree of beauty in the picture is a direct result of the beauty of the depicted object; thus an ugly object could never give cause to a beautiful picture. Freeman's older subjects, however, recognized the performance of an artist in using pictorial means to produce effects of beauty or emotional intensity. Similarly, younger children explained that only the feelings of the artist were necessary for a happy picture but not those of the beholder, while the older children were convinced of the reverse: only the competence of the artist would determine the quality of the picture while the emotional state of the beholder would have an effect on the beholder's perception. Freeman's psychological model extends the scope of existing approaches to how graphic competence develops or how pictures or visual reality are perceived to children's reaction to an adult world, where picture production does not only relate to the beholder but also to an anonymous customer and to tradition and innovation in art history. To the extent that it encompasses children's progress towards a specific adult world of social and cultural influences, Freeman's model has more ecological validity than most other theories that are restricted to a picture-producer or a picture-perceiver perspective.

Chapter 11: Drawing as a functional tool

The adult world, however, is also an indispensable part of the psychological approach of Vygotsky (1934/1962) and Luria (1971, 1983), which Stetsenko explains in her chapter. She describes how Vygotsky and Luria assumed that whether children develop language, draw pictures or learn to write, all these activities together would have the function of facilitating communication between the adult world and the child, thus preparing the child to share it in the future.

Within this functional context all cultural tools for communication develop as a unified semiotic system. Stetsenko points out that from this perspective very few experiments have been carried out investigating the relation between language, drawing and writing. She suggests that children may consider drawing pictures and writing as similar, although this need not mean that they are unable to distinguish between the two. She explains that young children frequently judge their scribbled signs as handwriting and even take pains to match the space the signs take to the one the model handwriting filled.

Thus, it seems that children perceive an important functional similarity between their graphic constructions and what they think writing is supposed to be for. A study by Obukhova and Borisova (1981) indicates that the development of speech and of drawing is interrelated. Children of various ages were observed while making drawings, and any spoken commentary the child made was recorded. In the youngest children, single words about depicted objects were just 'uttered'. Older children progressed to a second stage where comments accompanied drawings and, finally, at a third stage language anticipated the making of the drawing. In a separate study, Obukhova compared normal primary school aged children with language-impaired children. The study indicated that their graphic ability as such was similar, but that differences between the samples emerged whenever the task required that language and drawing be connected (for example, using pictures to aid verbal recall, providing a verbal description of a depicted scene or illustrating a word or an idea were all tasks on which the language-impaired clinical group performed less well than the normal children).

The function that drawings have in everyday life and development was examined in research by Leontiev (1931/1983). Again, three stages were identified in an experiment asking young and older children as well as adults to use pictures as an aid for recall. The youngest age group did not use pictures at all; for older children pictures facilitated recall; but adults showed no differences in performance whether they used this aid or not.

The conclusion Stetsenko draws is that the production of pictures might not only be a precursor for writing but also a preparation for the internalization of visual information and independent formation of cognitive functioning. In this model, drawing is not only seen in the broader context of cognition but also in terms of its function of adapting the child to an adult world. In this model, perceptual processes, like perceiving scribbles as handwriting, seem to be closely related to functional change of media.

Chapter 12: Development and style

The final chapter in the book also refers to the social dimension of the development of cognition in general and drawing in particular. Lange-Küttner and Edelstein propose an approach that considers individual differences as group styles. The repeated measurement of drawing space and the human figure was carried out within a comprehensive longitudinal project designed to tease apart the contribution of biological, psychological and sociological factors to the development of cognition. However, in their chapter Lange-Küttner and Edelstein are solely interested in the relationship between cognitive development and cognitive style. They describe how cognitive style emerges mainly in drawing the human figure: a constant gender effect and an emerging effect of the socioeconomic background of the child, which nearly replaces the influence of ability, are evidenced in their data-set.

Girls preferred to differentiate the human figure, while boys either selected the graphically easy task to reduce complexity or the difficult task of depicting movement. The effects of social class emerged from 12 years only, indicating that drawing is an intellectual challenge for the child but a matter of style for the adolescent. In cognitive tasks comparable effects of gender and social class could be found.

Lange-Küttner and Edelstein propose more than one interpretation for these phenomena but conclude that development of cognition in general and graphic competence in particular might also consist in overcoming primary social group biases and not only in developing a graphic repertoire by learning a technical device in a straightforward manner. Thus, Lange-Küttner and Edelstein join the Piagetian notion that development of intelligence has social origins with the traditional educational aim that challenging the personality might lead to better results in cognitive development than detached technical instruction.

Onward

We hope that the reader might form from this introduction a first impression and an overview of the chapters of this book. We have tried to suggest some links, but there are more to be made. It was always part of our purpose in preparing this collection to make it easier to build links between different areas of research and theory and thus facilitate improved understanding of the many aspects and complexities of children's production and perception of pictures. We have offered just one possible overview, admittedly; but then theories of depiction, just like pictures themselves can be seen – and conceptualized – in more than one way.

The myth of the sensory core: the traditional versus the ecological approach to children's drawings

Alan Costall *University of Southampton*

When Corrado Ricci 'discovered' children's drawings in 1882, these were not the charming efforts of well-behaved children drawn under the appreciative eye of a parent or enlightened teacher, or solemn copies of an actual object, such as a cup, a standard item employed in the modern experimental research. The drawings which excited Ricci's interest were 'undomesticated' graffiti scrawled over walls, where the images and any associated writing were 'crude' in every sense of the word.

There followed a frenzy of collection, with researchers commandeering hosts of 'volunteers', usually hard-pressed teachers, to collect their material. Karl Bühler blamed this obsession on the American 'tendency towards mass-production' (Bühler, 1930, p. 107) but it was an international affair. Kerschensteiner (1905), working in Munich, gathered as many as 300,000 separate drawings in this way, and somehow managed to analyze them with some degree of thoroughness. For others, however, the task of collecting became literally endless, the drawings being left largely untouched inside the boxes in which they had been delivered.

The purpose of this chapter is to present an 'ecological approach' to children's drawings. It will certainly question the value of the standard methods of study. The weakness of the early survey studies was their failure to provide information about the actual situations in which the children produced their drawings. The newer experimental research, in contrast, provides much detail of the controlled situations under study, but fails to relate those situations to the 'ecology of children's drawing', the actual contexts in which children normally draw. The primary focus of this chapter will, however, be on theory. The ecological approach provides a radical alternative to the traditional theoretical assumptions which continue to structure the study of children's drawings. My primary concern therefore will be to identify those traditional assumptions and explain their pervasive influence.

The sensory core and the innocent eye

A single issue has dominated psychological theorizing about child art. Why don't children draw in perspective? And regardless of the details, the majority of theories have provided a single kind of answer. Something must be *stopping* the child from drawing in perspective. Hints of this line of theorizing can be detected in Ricci's early account. Puzzled to find that children fail to reproduce their 'visual impression', he argued that their drawings are instead 'like a description they would make in words' (Barnes, 1894, p. 304). Here, in Ricci's answer, we find the beginnings of the formula which has dominated subsequent thinking about child art. Children draw what they know rather than what they see. In other words (words coined after Ricci's time), they are not *visual* but *intellectual* realists.

That Ricci, along with his many successors, regarded the nonperspectival art of the child as a 'puzzle', and formulated that puzzle in terms of a contrast between vision and knowing, stems from a commitment to two related assumptions. The first concerns the nature of vision; the second, the privileged perceptual status of linear perspective as a mode of pictorial representation.

Perceptual theory has, over many centuries, been committed to the hypothesis of 'the sensory core', a basic level of visual experience limited to a depthless and meaningless mosaic of lightness and darkness and corresponding to the perspectival appearance of things (Hatfield and Epstein, 1979).

With very few exceptions, *all* theories of vision subscribe to the hypothesis of the sensory core. Thus David Marr's theory of vision (Marr, 1982), celebrated as one of the foremost contributions to modern visual theory, has an ancient foundation. For, according to Marr, vision begins with a 'primal sketch', a low-level, depthless representation of the scene, which is then processed by the perceiver to reconstruct a spatial and meaningful world.

Theorists have certainly disputed whether the sensory core would normally be accessible to consciousness or introspection, many arguing that our habitual disposition of imposing meaning on our experiences could never be suspended, at least in the normal adult. It seemed possible, however, that the new-born child might be able to experience little else. As Preyer put it:

Many suppose that the infant, if he distinguishes at all any individual visible thing, sees 'all objects as if painted upon a flat surface' – that he has as yet no conception of anything external, existing outside of his eye. (Preyer, 1888, p. 60)

Why then do young children not draw in perspective as soon as they have the basic wherewithal to handle a pen or pencil? James Sully was one of the first to provide the 'obvious' answer. Children, he suggested, have already lost access to the sensory core by the time they begin to draw:

the child's eye at a surprisingly early period loses its primal 'innocence', grows 'sophisticated' in the sense that instead of seeing what is really presented it sees, or pretends to see, what knowledge and logic tell it is there. In other words his sense-perceptions have for artistic purposes become corrupted by a too large admixture of intelligence. (Sully, 1895, p. 396)

Karl Bühler, among many other theorists, repeated Sully's basic account, but placed greater emphasis on the corrupting role of linguistic symbolism:

As soon as objects have received their names, the formation of concepts begins, and these take the place of concrete images. Conceptual knowledge, which is formulated in language, dominates the memory of the child. (Bühler, 1930, p. 114)

Early accounts of the development of drawing such as Bühler's and Sully's are characterized in the modern literature as 'stage theories'. But are they? They do not propose that intellectual realism develops *into* visual realism; rather, they assume that a pre-existing and continuing disposition towards perspectival art is temporarily inhibited by intellectual factors. They are theories of *repression*.

The theoretical schema of how 'knowledge' (or 'linguistic symbolism', or 'tactile experience', or whatever) comes to suppress an inherent disposition towards perspective has proved a rich resource. It can explain almost anything and everything. This schema persists in current theory in two very influential forms, the first highly explicit and the second somewhat concealed.

The innocent autistic artist

Much interest has understandably been aroused by recent reports of remarkable artistic ability in autistic children. In the modern literature on children's drawings, such exceptional children have been taken to falsify the early stage theories. Yet the early theorists could hardly have been disconcerted by evidence that young children might sometimes draw in perspective, and many of the early writers made reference to such 'wonder children' (e.g. Kerschensteiner, 1905; Bühler, 1930). After all, the basic claim of the early theories was that there was something *stopping* the child from producing perspective, and if whatever was normally stopping the child were absent or removed, an intrinsic disposition towards visual realism would then be released.

Lorna Selfe is one of the few recent writers to appreciate the true logic of the repression theories. Indeed, she explicitly revives Bühler's theory in her own account of autistic artists. These children, she argues, are able to access a basic, perspectival level of visual experience (i.e. 'the sensory core') precisely because they are unable to abstract from, or make sense of, what they see; their artistic work is not an accomplishment but rather a symptom of their conceptual deficit (Selfe, 1977; 1983, p. 86). This explanation is now widely accepted (e.g. Arnheim, 1980; Pariser, 1981; Winner, 1982, p. 187; Thomas and Silk, 1990, p. 138; Cox, 1992, p. 201). A similar line of reasoning has been used throughout the twentieth century to explain away other awkward cases of fine artistic ability, such as palaeolithic cave art and the art of the Bushmen and Australian aborigines (Verworn, 1917; Bühler, 1930; Lowenfeld, 1951; 1952): 'the realistic drawings of these primitive peoples are not to be regarded as the result of long practice and a well-kept tradition, but as the expression of a mind whose original talent for drawing has remained unspoilt' (Bühler, 1930, p. 123). To close the circle, as it were, Howe (1989, p. 149) has even suggested (if tentatively) that the palaeolithic cave artists may have themselves been autistic!

The very existence of these autistic artists seems to provide the most compelling support for the existence of the sensory core, and for the idea that perspective art is, in effect, a transcript of that core. Yet what is the actual evidence? First of all, there is *no* evidence that autistic artists simply come to draw in their remarkable way without any practice; rather, we merely lack reliable information concerning the early development of their remarkable skills. Second, there is no evidence that these children fail to understand what they see. Indeed, they specialize to a remarkable degree in certain subjects, such as horses or buildings. They are often fascinated by picture books, and the style of such books is often reflected in their own work. Even the claim that an autistic artist such as Stephen Wiltshire 'draws exactly what he sees' (Casson, 1987, p. 5) does not bear close examination. The drawings mostly involve rounded forms which cannot be assessed for their perspectival accuracy, yet even when rectangular structures, such as buildings, are drawn, these often show striking inconsistencies in the use of perspective convergence (e.g. Selfe, 1985, p. 145, figure 7.6).

We also need to remember that the incidence of exceptional artistic ability among autistic children is rare. Autism does not automatically confer artistic ability. Recent studies comparing autistic children in general with appropriate control groups reveal no overall differences in artistic ability (Atlas, 1985; Charman and Baron-Cohen, 1993). On the other hand, absence of conceptual deficit does not preclude the precocious development of exceptional artistic ability. As my own research is beginning to reveal, many cases exist of remarkable artistic ability among young children who show no impairments in their linguistic or conceptual abilities.

Drawing the wrong conclusions

Over the last 20 years or so, a tradition of experimental research on children's drawings has been established, especially in Britain. These studies have rightly been praised for their ingenuity. In the standard task, the experimenter presents an object, such as a cup, for the child to draw, but perversely turns the object away from the child to hide its most interesting or salient feature, such as the cup's handle. Typically, a child of up to 8 years or so will nevertheless include the hidden feature in the drawing, and hence be deemed to be an intellectual realist.

What the new research has shown is that children can be induced to exclude the hidden feature under appropriate conditions, and hence become a visual realist. If, for example, children are not allowed to inspect the cup before they begin to draw it, or the experimenter does not explicitly name the object but simply asks the child to draw 'this object', virtually all of the children will omit the handle (Bremner and Moore, 1984).

Such studies have been celebrated not merely for their ingenuity but also for their methodological rigour and theoretical significance. These studies are supposed to *show* that children can easily be induced to be visual realists, and hence *prove* that the old stage theories are wrong. Let's examine these points in turn.

The first problem with the modern experimental research is that it is almost entirely based on the task of drawing from a model, something children rarely attempt in their own spontaneous drawing! It is hardly surprising, therefore, that the child proves so sensitive to subtle changes in instructions, and is grateful for any attempts by the experimenter to impose some 'human sense' on an unusual task. Although seldom mentioned in the reports of these studies, it is fairly common for the child to declare 'I don't do cups', and then – to the dismay of the busy experimenter – spend 15 minutes or more covering the paper with an infinitely more interesting creation. And it is not as though the more cooperative children just get on with the task, simply producing a visually or intellectually realist drawing according to the experimental conditions. There is a good deal of attempted negotiation ranging from the child pulling a puzzled face and making tentative pleas for clarification, to protesting at the experimenter's awkwardness: 'Can't you turn the doll round so I can see its face!' Certainly, such studies provide impressive evidence of the importance of 'context effects' *in* experimental research. But what are they telling us about the *normal contexts* in which children engage in drawing as a spontaneous and playful activity? That 'communication factors' have come to loom so large in the current understanding of how children choose to draw (e.g. Morss, 1990, p. 202) may be an artefact of the experiments themselves.

A further problem is that there may well have been serious overinterpretation of the actual results of these experiments. In the recent research, the distinction between intellectual and visual realism has, in effect, been 'operationalized' as the inclusion or omission in the child's drawing of the salient hidden feature. The term 'visual realism' is rather slippery, however. It could mean any one of the following:

1. The drawing happens to exclude a certain occluded detail.
2. The drawing consistently excludes all hidden surfaces and features.
3. The drawing is in 'informal perspective', i.e. there is some use of perspective convergence, but the picture is not projectively consistent, e.g. there is no consistent use of vanishing points.
4. The drawing is in *consistent* linear perspective, i.e. there is consistent use of vanishing points, but the projection does not conform to the actual station point of the artist.

5. The drawing is in *accurate* linear perspective, i.e. the projection is both consistent and appropriate to the artist's station point.

The fact that the young child can be shown to be a visual realist in the first very limited sense of the term does *not*, in itself, imply any of the other four senses. Yet it is now common practice in the recent literature to claim that the new research shows that young children can be induced to draw in 'perspective'. It does no such thing. Indeed, it is not unusual to obtain drawings from such experiments which satisfy the misleading, operational definition of visual realism yet are not 'in perspective' even in the second, very lenient, sense of the term. One can obtain drawings of cups which omit the handle yet are in 'plan view' while the model itself was in profile, and drawings of a doll (presented with its face away from the child) which look simply like a front view with the features of the face omitted.

However, it is not merely that the modern researchers have wrongly rejected the old repression theories on the basis of questionable evidence. They have actually given a new lease of life to the essential logic of the theories they claim to have undermined. When explicit reference is made to perceptual theory, it is not difficult to detect the repetition of the logic of repression theory even in the guise of modern theory – something 'holds children back' (Freeman, 1987, p. 147) from drawing in perspective:

> The information at the retina is in the forms of *projections* of objects. . . . According to Marr (1982) the *initial stages* in visual processing do indeed involve a viewer-centred specification of the projective appearance of the scene, but this *automatically* becomes reworked into an object-centred structural description. It requires a *very* complex set of operations to decompose that into a viewer-centred representation again, and this involves actively curbing normal perceptual habits . . . . (Freeman, 1987, p. 147)

In Freeman's revival of repression theory, there is little to suggest that access to the sensory core (the 'viewer-centred specification') could be readily achieved by the child. Most researchers, however, seldom make any serious explicit appeals to perceptual theory, and, in fact, come to a quite different conclusion:

> The weight of evidence suggests that even quite young children have the capacity for view-specific drawing, but that for one reason or another they do not often choose this mode of portrayal. So instead of attempting to establish a simple developmental sequence running from intellectual realism to visual realism, our current task is to identify the factors that *sway* the child towards one type of drawing or another. (Bremner and Moore, 1984, p. 372; emphasis added; see also Morss, 1990, p. 202)

This account of drawing development anticipates a more general trend in modern developmental psychology, in which there is a de-emphasis, if not outright denial, of the development of basic skills and abilities, and a redefinition of development as the resourceful deployment of pre-existing abilities. The child's *resourcefulness* is supposed to develop, rather than his or her *resources*. Thus neither intellectual nor visual realism develops in any interesting sense. They are simply there from the outset, their appearance being 'governed by secondary and contingent factors' (Morss, 1990, p. 202).

This, then, is how modern researchers have reinstated the basic commitments of the schema of the sensory core. Once again, an ability to draw in perspective is supposed to be lurking within the child, waiting to be released under the appropriate conditions. And once again, if implicitly, the available data have simply been assimilated to the structure of a persistent scientific myth. There is no evidence, however, that young children, whether they are autistic or not, can simply come to draw in perspective by accessing the sensory core. Indeed, there is no serious evidence, despite years of scientific rumour, that the sensory core exists.

Beyond linear perspective

Scientific theories become myths in the absence of alternative stories to expose and challenge their fundamental assumptions. It is curious, therefore, that research on children's drawings remains so insulated from radical developments which have occurred throughout the twentieth century in both the visual arts and perceptual theory challenging the priority of linear perspective. In the remainder of this chapter, I shall consider one alternative account, an 'ecological' approach to vision and pictures deriving from the work of the psychologist James Gibson (1907–79).

The fact that visual perception occurs over time – and on the move – was central to the later work of James Gibson. Indeed, Gibson's main objection to the traditional theory of vision was that it was image-based, or, in other words, a 'picture theory of vision' (see Costall, 1990). One of his primary contributions to visual theory was to stress that the world itself is highly structured or 'constrained' so that the information available to the perceiver, far from being highly ambiguous, is specific to the layout and properties of the environment:

> [The] perception of an object does not depend on a series of . . . perceptions of its forms or perspectives, but depends instead on the invariant features of the forms or perspectives *over time*. Object-perception does not depend on form-perception but on invariant-detection. And these invariants are 'formless', that is to say, they are not themselves forms. (Gibson, 1973, p. 43; emphasis added; see also Gibson, 1979, pp. 247 and 249)

Having distanced the problems of normal vision from those of picture perception and production, one might suppose that Gibson would have had little to say directly about pictures. Yet he kept returning to the problem of pictures over many years.

The concept of the 'visual field' in Gibson's early work seemed to correspond to the traditional notion of the sensory core, since it was supposed to be restricted to a perspective-like experience of things (Gibson, 1950). Yet even so, Gibson did not regard it as providing the basis for normal vision. Rather, he presented a social constructivist account, suggesting that an ability to see things 'in perspective' derived from the social practice of picture-making (e.g. Gibson, 1966, pp. 236–7). In his final book, however, Gibson realized he had still conceded too much to the traditional scheme of the sensory core:

> The notion of a patchwork of colors comes from the art of painting, not from any unbiased description of visual experience. What one becomes aware of by holding still, closing one eye, and observing a frozen scene are not visual sensations but only *the surfaces of the world that are viewed now from here*. They are not flat or depthless but simply unhidden. (Gibson, 1979, p. 286)

In this way, Gibson challenged the idea that an innocent eye, or even a sophisticated one, might access an internal, perspectival image which could then be copied onto a piece of paper to produce a perspective picture. The *production* of perspectival pictures requires a positive developmental explanation (see Costall, 1985). However, Gibson's work also has implications for how we should understand the *perception* of both perspective pictures, and other kinds of pictures.

In his theory of formless invariants, Gibson (1973; 1979) reconsidered the relation between vision and pictorial representation. After all, not only photographs but also line drawings and even caricatures can be highly effective perceptually, and the fact of their effectiveness must be telling us something fundamental about vision. Gibson came to realize that the relevant structures underlying even perspective pictures were not the perspectival shapes projected onto the picture plane – shapes that are indeed specific to a particular station point – but structures common to (invariant across) various locations, and hence available within any of those specific views. To take a simple example, the optical continuity corresponding to adjacent edges in a scene is preserved across a whole range of viewing positions (Sedgwick, 1980). Here are Gibson's brief suggestions about what these formless invariants might include:

> The information-bearing features are things like the following: alignment or straightness (being 'in line' but not necessarily a line as such) as against bentness or curvature; perpendicularity or rectangularity; parallelity as against convergence; intersections; closures and symmetries. These features are present in an unchanging array but they are best revealed in a changing array, one kind of change being transformation. (Gibson, 1973, p. 45)

There are some striking links between Gibson's rather sketchy proposals and recent work in computer vision based on the idea of 'nonaccidental properties', i.e. powerful informative structures which are not tied to a particular perspective and hence are generally unaffected by slight variations in viewpoint (Binford, 1981; Lowe, 1985; Biederman, 1987; see Costall, 1993).

The basic implication of Gibson's theory of formless invariants is that neither vision nor pictorial representation is based on linear perspective. Vision is not a unitary process of 'inverse perspective', but rather a resourceful exploitation of a whole diversity of more general, informative structures. Even though a perspective picture can incorporate some of these structures, the structures themselves are not inherently 'perspectival' – they are not tied to any one 'view'. It follows that perceptually based art is not confined to linear perspective, nor even to a wider set of 'projection systems' based upon natural perspective (cf. Hagen, 1986). There is a whole realm of pictures beyond perspective, ranging from children's drawings to expert caricatures, which skilfully deploy optical information. The traditional contrast between perceptual and conceptual art can no longer be sustained.

An ecological approach to children's drawings

As long as children's drawings are measured against the ideal of linear perspective they will (as Sully conceded) necessarily be regarded as 'defective' (Sully, 1895, p. 396). Once, however, the traditional assumptions underlying the familiar contrast between visual and intellectual realism are challenged, we can begin to evaluate children's drawings on their own terms.

According to the early student of children's drawings, Georges-Henri Luquet, what is needed in the first instance is a kind of 'natural history' of child art based on direct but non-intrusive observations of children while they are drawing:

> The investigator needs to be able to observe the child without interruption, and share the same environment, whilst ensuring that the observations remain unnoticed by the subject. The investigator needs to become part of the furniture, as it were, in order not to distort the child's spontaneous activity. This demands direct observation of the same child throughout the course of his or her various drawing activities. (Luquet, 1922, p. 211)

Luquet himself provided a fine example of the value of such an approach in his intensive study of his own daughter, Simonne (Luquet, 1913). Luquet was prepared to take his daughter and her drawings seriously. Unlike Piaget, Luquet was not engaged in a study of childish 'mistakes' (G. Matthews, 1980), but in a celebration of his daughter's often ingenious attempts *to make sense* by drawing (Luquet, 1913). Luquet's own remarkable work, and that of a few recent investigators, should be sufficient to make us very wary of the paradigm of children's drawings presupposed by the recent experimental studies. Not only do young children seldom draw from models, but, more fundamentally, 'drawing' may, at least for the young child, have little to do with the final 'product'. The actual drawing (i.e. the traces left on the paper) may be incidental to the *act* of drawing, a highly charged representational activity often involving a great deal of gesture and talk (e.g. Luquet, 1924; J. Matthews, 1984).

Although Luquet coined the terms visual and intellectual realism[1] (Luquet, 1927/1977), he was among the first students of children's drawings to question, if tentatively, the primacy of linear perspective. 'Visual realism', he argued, 'is no

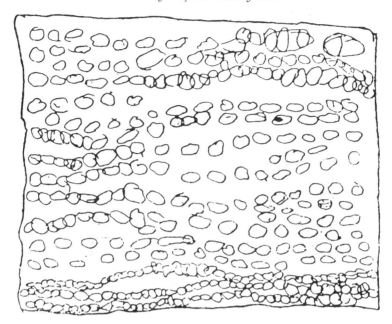

Figure 2.1 A field of potatoes (after Luquet, 1927/1977)

less a convention than is intellectual realism' (Luquet, 1927/1977, p. 191; see also Luquet, 1913, p. 248). When Luquet adopted the term intellectual realism, he placed the emphasis very much on *realism*. Intellectual realism as much as visual realism is, he insisted, an honest attempt to *represent* the object, not merely *symbolize* it. For Luquet, it was a serious option, and not just for children. Apparently unaware of the contemporary Cubist manifestos, he concluded that intellectual realism should be taken up by skilled artists: 'Who knows, but we might be faced with a completely different art yet one capable of producing equivalent effects by quite different means' (Luquet, 1913, p. 248).

The reason why Luquet coined the term *intellectual* realism is clear. He thought that such pictures were based not on vision, but rather on an internal mental model of the object depicted. It is not so obvious, however, why he adopted the term *visual* realism, given his misgivings about the perceptual status of linear perspective. What needs to be questioned is the very contrast itself. *All* realistic pictures are based on optical invariants. They are all, therefore, 'visual'. The true contrast is not between visual and intellectual realism, but rather between perspectival and non-perspectival realism.

Let us now consider an actual drawing (Figure 2.1), one which seems to be the epitome of intellectual realism, a 7-year-old's drawing of a field of potatoes, the 'abstract elements of which exist only within the mind of the artist' (Luquet, 1927/1977, p. 128).

Herbert Read, an early critic of the 'conceptual fallacy' (i.e. the false antithesis of perceiving and knowing) protested that Luquet had seriously misunderstood this particular picture:

> it does not imply, as Luquet supposes, that the child ignores the evidence of its senses, the green plants above the ground, in favour of an intellectual conception of the invisible tubers in the ground: it means rather that for the child the primary association of the potato is the tactual one, or merely the visual one – the potato in the kitchen ... (Read, 1956, p. 136)

Earlier still, William James had also challenged the supposed contrast between knowing and seeing. As he insisted, seeing is *one* way we come to know about things (James, 1879/1983, p. 47). Both James and Read were committed, however, to a traditional notion of sensation as the basis of perception, sensations being discrete and essentially perspectival. Gibson's point, however, is different. We can 'grasp' the object from any perspective precisely because the relevant information is not tied to that perspective. The humble potato is, in this respect, an ideal case, being rounded, like a potato, whichever way you look at it. But so too, Gibson argued, does the cattiness of a cat remain whichever way you look at it. Its furriness, litheness and elegance are not confined to any one view.

In this chapter, I have been arguing that research on children's drawings has been constrained and distorted by the concept of 'the sensory core', a conceptual scheme which underpins the modern contrast between perceptual and conceptual art, and the notion that perspectival art is the 'natural' form of representation. Once the myth of the sensory core is dispelled, the old puzzle of why there are so many pictures 'out of perspective' simply disappears. But a challenging new problem comes to take its place. How did we ever come to find linear perspective so natural?

Notes

1. Initially, Luquet had used the term 'logical realism' rather than 'intellectual realism' (Luquet, 1913).

Chapter 3

An information-processing approach to drawing development

John Willats *University of Birmingham*

The idea of an information-processing approach to children's drawings is taken from Marr's account of visual perception (Marr, 1982). Central to Marr's account are the different levels at which an information-processing device (such as the human visual system) can be understood.

The first level defines the 'computational theory' of the device: what the system is doing at the most abstract level. The second level describes how this theory is carried out: the rules that map the input to the system into the output. And the third level describes the actual physical mechanisms which give effect to this process. Marr also emphasized that we need to ask not only *what* the system is doing, but *why* it is doing it, and he illustrated this by an analogy with what happens at the check-out in a supermarket.

What both a cash register does and what a check-out assistant would do if the cash register had broken down is add things up. *Why* they perform the process of addition and not, for example, multiplication, is because adding up the cost of individual items is the operation which is required to arrive at the final bill. However, the algorithms which a cash register and a person would use in order to carry out this operation, and the physical means which each would use to support the operation, are obviously quite different in the two cases.

Cameras and computers are both devices that produce pictures, and the ways in which they do this can be analyzed in terms of these three levels. At the first level of analysis a camera takes in the information available in the optic array – the geometry and intensity of light as it falls on the lens – and maps it directly on to the surface of the film. In Marr's terms the input to the system takes the form of a *viewer-centred description*, or view, and the output (a photograph) also takes the form of a viewer-centred description. At the second level we might want to say something about the way the optic array is collected and inverted by the lens system, and at the third level something about physical properties of the lens and the chemistry of the film.

In the case of the computer the input usually consists of what Marr called an *object-centred description*: typically, a list of coordinates that describes the three-dimensional shape of an object independently of any particular point of view. This list can then be used to produce a picture, using rules which transform a three-dimensional object-centred description into a two-dimensional viewer-centred description: for example, a picture in perspective, or some other system based on projective geometry. At the second level, we would want to describe the algebraic equations which give effect to these rules; and at the third level we would want to talk about the physical construction of the computer in terms of wiring, silicon chips, and so on.

Thus at the first and most abstract level cameras are devices whose input is a viewer-centred description and output a viewer-centred description; whereas computers are devices that are capable of transforming an object-centred description into a viewer-centred description.

In order to understand drawing development we can think of children as information-processing devices for producing pictures, and then restate the various theories of drawing in terms of these three levels (Willats, 1987). In Luquet's theory of intellectual realism (Luquet, 1927/1977) the input to the drawing process during the period of intellectual realism is an internal description derived from a 'conceptual structure': the 'internal model' which 'takes precedence over direct perceptual experience' (Freeman, 1972, p. 129). Luquet's internal model at this stage seems to have many features in common with Marr's 'object-centred description', and is now often interpreted in this sense (Crook, 1985; Light, 1985). During visual realism the child is also drawing from the internal model, but this model includes information about the appearance of objects from a particular point of view, and corresponds more closely to a viewer-centred internal description.

Piaget and Inhelder (1956) endorsed Luquet's account of drawing development, but they also attempted to say *why* the change from intellectual realism to visual realism took place. This was, they thought, because the child's 'mental image' of an object, which is similar to Luquet's 'internal model', changes as children become consciously aware of their own viewpoint:

> To see an object with a given perspective is to view it from a particular viewpoint, but it is not necessary to be consciously aware of this viewpoint in order to perceive the object accurately. On the other hand, to represent this object in perspective by means of a mental image or a drawing necessitates a conscious awareness of the percipient's viewpoint, together with the transformations induced in the perceptual object by this viewpoint. (Piaget and Inhelder, 1956, p. 178)

Nicholls and Kennedy (1992) identified two well-defined stages in children's drawing of a cube. In the first, 'one-square' stage children base their drawings on similarity of features: 'parts of the object being geometrically similar to arrangements of lines on the drawing surface'. In the second, 'square-with-obliques' stage their drawings are based on 'matching directions from a vantage point' (Nicholls and Kennedy, 1992, p. 240). Thus, according to Nicholls and Kennedy, children base their drawings on object-centred descriptions in the first stage and viewer-centred descriptions in the second stage.

In contrast, according to the theory of depiction proposed by Margaret Hagen (1985; 1986), both the input and the output take the form of *views*, whatever the child's age. In so far as children's drawings differ, they do so only to the extent that they provide views taken from different vantage points, so that pictures in perspective provide a view in which the spectator is relatively close to the scene, whereas pictures in orthogonal projection, oblique projection and the other parallel systems provide views taken from 'optical infinity', that is, a considerable distance away. In this account drawings of a cube in orthogonal projection – Nicholls and Kennedy's 'one-square' drawings – as well as drawings in oblique projection – their 'square with obliques' – are both derived directly from *views* of a cube.

In all these accounts the rules mapping the input into the output are left more or less unspecified, presumably because they are assumed to be relatively trivial.

I have introduced the idea of treating children as information-processing devices by analogy to the camera and the computer in order to illustrate the different accounts which these theories give of children's competence in picture production. Of course, these analogies only hold true at the first or computational level. The actual mental processes by which transformations are effected by children, and the physical mechanisms which serve these processes, are obviously quite different. Nevertheless, they can be helpful as somewhat crude models, and I want to use them to highlight the contribution made to the course of development. Changes in drawing *rules* play a similar role in picture production by children and in mapping or transformation rules in a computer program. Most theories of drawing concentrate on the nature of the input to the system: in Hagen's theory this always takes the form of view, so that no significant developmental changes take place. In theories such as Luquet's the input takes the form of a conceptual structure for the young child and a view for the older child, so for these theories the major change which takes place during development is the change from one kind of input to another. I think that some such change probably does take place, but that the course of drawing development is determined as much or more by changes in the mapping or transformation rules as by changes in the nature of the input to the drawing process.

Drawing rules: projection systems

In an account I gave earlier (Willats, 1977a,b) of an experiment in which children were asked to draw a table with various objects on it from a fixed vantage point, the resulting drawings were classified in terms of five different projection systems. These projection systems can be defined in terms of the different views obtained by a spectator at different station points (Dubery and Willats, 1972; 1983; Hagen, 1986); but they can also be defined in terms of drawing rules mapping directions in an object-centred description into corresponding directions on the picture surface. Which of these definitions is more appropriate in this case? In order to explain the results of this experiment, I suggested that the changes which took place in the early stages came about as a result of changes in drawing rules applied to what I would now call object-centred descriptions, whereas in the later stages some of the older children appeared to be basing their drawings directly on views.[1]

To begin with, the youngest children were unable to represent coherent relationships between the various objects. Then, in the next stage, the children mapped up-and-down directions in an object-centred description of the scene into up-and-down directions in the picture, and side-to-side directions in the scene into side-to-side directions in the picture; but they ignored directions in the third dimension because they had no way of representing them. This resulted in drawings in orthogonal projection (Figure 3.1b). In the next stage the children used vertical directions on the picture surface as a way of representing edges in the third dimension, and this resulted in pictures in vertical oblique projection (Figure 3.1c). However, drawings in this system tend to be ambiguous because one direction on the picture surface is used to represent two different directions (side-to-side and front-to-back) in the scene. In the next stage this problem was resolved by using oblique directions on the picture surface to represent edges in the third dimension, resulting in pictures in oblique projection (Figure 3.1d). The two final stages seemed to be derived from two alternative kinds of mapping. Drawings in naive perspective could be explained in terms of a more complex rule applied to the same object-centred description: 'use oblique lines converging upwards to represent edges in the third dimension' (Figure 3.1e). Drawings in *true* perspective, however, appeared to be derived from *views*: the directions of the lines representing the side edges of the table corresponded to the directions of these edges as they appeared in the visual field (Figure 3.1f). Had these terms been available at the time, I would have said that the younger children were basing their drawings on internal object-centred descriptions, but that as they got older they adopted increasingly complex and effective drawing rules. Then, in the final stages, some of the children switched to basing their drawings on viewer-centred descriptions.

Limitations of the 'projection systems' approach

I still feel that this account is substantially correct, but it has a number of limitations. In a replication using a much larger number of subjects, Lee and

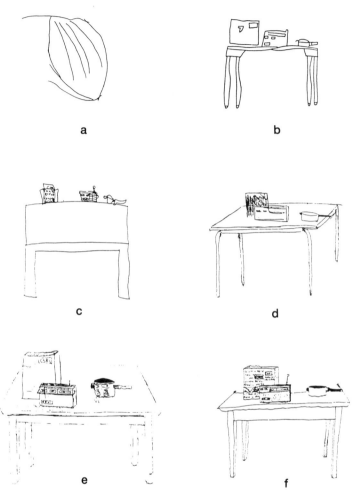

Figure 3.1 Children's drawings of a table (a) by a blind child (taken from Kennedy, 1983); (b) orthogonal projection, mean age 9.7 years; (c) vertical oblique projection, mean age 11.9 years; (d) oblique projection, mean age 13.6 years; (e) naive perspective, mean age 14.3 years; (f) perspective, mean age 13.7 years (taken from Willats, 1977a; 1977b).

Bremner (1987) were unable to find any clear-cut distinction between naive perspective and true perspective. This highlights a fundamental problem: it is usually impossible to decide, simply on the evidence of finished drawings, whether pictures which *provide* possible views have been derived from viewer-centred descriptions, or obtained by applying transformation rules to object-centred descriptions. If it were not for the fact that all the children in this experiment were drawing the scene from the same fixed viewpoint it could be argued, quite plausibly, that since all the drawings shown in Figures 3.1b–f provide possible views, they might all have been *derived* from views. This problem is a very general one: Nicholls and Kennedy, for example, assumed that their 'square-with-obliques' drawings of a cube – that is, drawings in oblique projection – had been derived directly from views because they look like views. This assumption is not necessarily justified, however: these drawings – or at least some of them – might equally well have been derived from object-centred descriptions by using a rule like 'draw the front face as a square, and add oblique lines representing the side edges'.

Another serious limitation of the projection systems approach is that definitions of these systems given in terms of the directions of lines representing straight edges cannot be applied to pictures of smooth objects like people. Costall pointed out that this limitation 'is highly restrictive. It means that the different drawing systems *can only be differentiated by reference to the orientation of a very particular kind of thing – a tidy, rectangular object*' (1993, p. 337; emphasis in the original). Consider, for example, the four figure drawings shown in Figure 3.2 produced by children of different ages and taken from the Florence Goodenough collection. They obviously represent some kind of developmental sequence; but this is not a sequence which can be described in terms of different projection systems.

Yet another limitation of the 'projection systems' approach is that it is unable to account for pictures which cannot be described in terms of one or other of the projection systems, and which do not, therefore, approximate to possible views. These include pictures like the drawing of a table by a blind subject illustrated by Kennedy (1983) (Figure 3.1a), which appears to represent topological rather than projective relations, and the very common fold-out drawings of rectangular objects, like the drawing of a box which stands on the table top in Figure 3.1c.

These limitations suggest that in order to give a full account of children's drawings, we need to provide a much richer account of the nature of the representations for the input and output to the system, and the rules that map the input into the output.

According to Marr, all shape descriptions can be described in terms of two design features: their coordinate systems, which can be either object-centred or viewer-centred, and their primitives,[2] which can be zero-, one-, two- or three-dimensional. Marr was, of course, concerned only with internal representations, but his terminology can also be used to provide a comprehensive scheme describing the possible mapping between internal representations of object and scenes, and external representations in the form of pictures.

Denotation systems

The projection systems approach I have described above takes edges as scene primitives and lines as picture primitives. Another possible mapping, however,

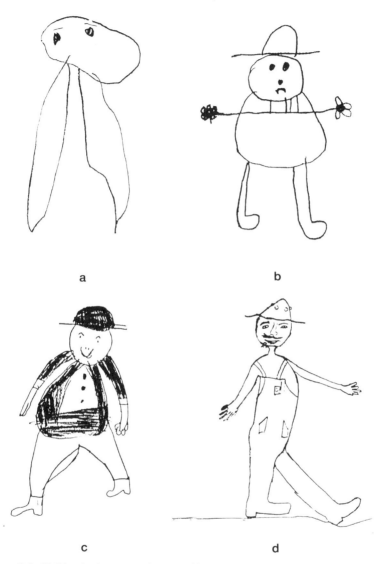

a

b

c

d

Figure 3.2 Children's drawings of a man (a) girl aged 4 years 4 months; (b) girl aged 5 years 7 months; (c) girl aged 8 years 6 months; (d) boy aged 9 years 5 months (Florence Goodenough collection, Pennsylvania State University)

takes faces as two-dimensional scene primitives and regions as two-dimensional picture primitives (regions are the areas enclosed by lines). This may well account for the drawing of the box shown in Figure 3.1c, which is similar to the characteristic 'fold-out' drawings of a cube described by Nicholls and Kennedy

(1992). In these drawings regions in the picture are used to represent the true shapes of the faces of a box or a cube: that is, regions as picture primitives are being used to stand for, or *denote*, faces as picture primitives.

Probably many of Nicholls and Kennedy's 'one-square' drawings of a cube were also based on a denotation system in which regions denote faces. As they suggest, some of these drawings probably represent a single face of a cube; but not necessarily all of them. As Mitchelmore (1978) has pointed out, such drawings may either represent one face of an object or an outline of the object *as a whole*. Again, it is not normally possible to decide on the basis of a single finished drawing which mapping has been used. However, the remarkable 'striped' squares representing a cube with a different colour on each face found by Vanessa Moore (Moore, 1986a; Willats, 1992a) and the drawings of a die showing *all* the dots within a single square (Willats, 1987; 1992a) seem to show that for children below the age of 5 or 6 years a single square is more likely to be intended to show the volume of a cube as a whole rather than a single face. We can say that in these drawings a square region, or two-dimensional picture primitive, is being used to denote a volumetric scene primitive.

Finally, pictures like photographs and pointillist pictures can be defined in terms of one-dimensional or point primitives: dots or blobs of paint or pigment in the picture denote point intensities in the optic array. Children do not normally use a denotation system of this kind, however.

Topological relations, extendedness and shape modifiers

In order to capture the full range of pictorial structures we thus need to give an account of a number of different *denotation* systems; but we also need to extend the range of *drawing systems* to include systems other than the projection systems. Piaget suggested that the spatial relations between parts of objects in children's early drawings are based on topological geometry rather than projective geometry, and this is probably correct.

In addition, we also need a formal way of describing the three-dimensional shapes of individual parts of objects, and this can be done by using what Denny (1978) called the 'extendedness principle'. Extendedness refers to the shape properties of longness, flatness and roundness – that is, saliency of extension in one, two or three dimensions. Drawing systems based on the extendedness principle map the extendedness of scene primitives into the extendedness of corresponding picture primitives: in tadpole figures, for example, like the drawing shown in Figure 3.2a, a round region is used to represent round volumes like the head or head/body, and a line or a long region is used to represent long volumes like the arms or legs.

It is important to realize that extendedness is not just a way of classifying smooth regular objects. A round object like a ball can be classed as a lump (a three-dimensional shape which is extended in all three dimensions), but so can rectangular objects such as houses, or irregular objects like stones, clouds or fruit (Denny, 1979a; 1979b). In their first drawings the *only* property children represent is extendedness, so that they will use a round region to represent a cube or a square, as well as a circle or a ball: in the drawing of a table by a blind child shown in Figure 3.1a, a round region has been used to represent a rectangular table top.

At a slightly later stage children add what I have called 'shape modifiers' (Willats, 1992c) to represent additional shape properties like 'being bent', 'being pointed', 'having flat faces', and so on. For example, Piaget and Inhelder (1956) noted that children will occasionally add 'ticks', intended to represent the property 'having corners', to a round region representing a square (Hayes, 1978). Similarly, the round regions in children's early drawings which represent a cube or a house may later be replaced by square regions. The straight lines which form the outlines of these regions cannot be identified with particular edges, however, but represent the more general property 'having flat faces'.

As children learn to incorporate more of these properties in their drawings their representations of the human figure become more differentiated (Arnheim, 1954). In the figure drawing shown in Figure 3.2b, for example, the extendedness of the various body parts is still being represented by the extendedness of the lines or regions used to represent them – lines for the arms, long regions for the legs and round regions for the head and body – and the relations between these parts are still represented by topological relations like touching and enclosure rather than by projective relations. In addition, however, the line representing the mouth and the regions representing the legs have been modified by the shape modifier 'being bent'. Drawings by older children, on the other hand, are probably based primarily on viewer-centred descriptions: in the drawing shown in Figure 3.2d, the convexities and concavities of the outline represent the shapes of contours in the visual field (Marr, 1982). The drawing shown in Figure 3.2c probably illustrates an intermediate stage, based in part on the representation of the extendedness of three-dimensional shapes in an object-centred description, and in part on the shapes of regions in the visual field.

Properties like 'being straight' and 'being bent' are sometimes referred to as 'nonaccidental':

> The central organizational principle is that certain properties of edges in a two-dimensional array are taken by the visual system as strong evidence that the edges in the three-dimensional world contain these same properties. For example, if there is a straight line in the image (*collinearity*), the visual system infers that the edge producing that line in the three-dimensional world is also straight. The visual system ignores the possibility that the property in the image might be the result of a (highly unlikely) accidental alignment of eye and curved edge. Smoothly curved elements in the image (*curvilinearity*) are similarly inferred to arise from smoothly

curved features in the three-dimensional world. These properties, and the others described later, have been termed *nonaccidental* (Witkin and Tennenbaum, 1983) in that they would only be rarely produced by accidental alignments of viewpoint and object features and consequently are generally unaffected by slight variations in viewpoint. (Biederman, 1987, p. 119; emphasis in the original)

Extendedness appears to be a nonaccidental property in this sense. Round volumes or lumps will always project round regions at the retina from whatever direction they are viewed, so in this case the extendedness of the three-dimensional shape will always be reflected in a view. Similarly, the most likely view of a long volume or stick will be a long region, although in this case there are in addition two possible unlikely views: if a stick is viewed end-on the projection to the retina will be a small round region (Willats, 1992c). Thus children who base their drawings on the nonaccidental properties of three-dimensional shapes are, in many cases, likely to produce possible views. In the drawing shown in Figure 3.2b, for example, I have suggested that the regions standing for the legs are intended to represent the two three-dimensional shape properties 'being extended in one dimension' and 'being bent'; but because these are both nonaccidental properties the resulting regions actually look rather like *views* of legs.

From the point of view of drawing development this is something of an advantage, and I have suggested in an earlier paper (Willats, 1984) that nonaccidental resemblance provides the mechanism which drives the developmental process. To begin with, children appear to base their drawings on object-centred descriptions, but at some stage during drawing development they notice that their drawings are beginning to resemble possible views and begin to judge them in these terms. Eventually, this leads them on to draw directly *from* views. In general, it seems intuitively true that pictures that provide possible views are better as representations than pictures that merely represent topological relations like touching, enclosure, and so on. (By a 'good representation' I mean a picture in which it is possible to see the orientation and three-dimensional shape of the object which the picture is intended to represent (Willats, 1992b).) For example, the way the hats are represented in Figures 3.2c and 3.2d, which provide plausible views of 'a hat on a head', are better as representations than the drawing in Figure 3.2b, which does not show a possible view, but correctly shows the topological relation of 'touching' between the brim of the hat and the head.

However, nonaccidental resemblance does make it difficult to determine, on the basis of finished drawings, whether individual children are basing their drawings on views or deriving them from object-centred descriptions. In fact, it could be argued that all the drawings shown in Figure 3.2 are derived directly from views, and that the apparent anomalies they contain (like the hat touching the head in Figure 3.2b) are simply the result of production problems: poor motor control, planning problems, lapses of memory, and so on. This is the same problem we have already encountered in analyzing children's drawings of tables, and it brings us back to just the same kind of questions. Is it only older children who 'draw what they see', as Luquet's theory of intellectual and visual realism would suggest, or are all children's drawings derived from views, as Hagen argues? Or are some older children still basing their drawings on transformations from object-centred descriptions but using them to produce plausible views?

The representation of foreshortening

Piaget and Inhelder (1956) attempted to test Luquet's theory by asking children of various ages to draw a stick (such as a pencil) presented to them both side-on and end-on: that is, in foreshortened and nonforeshortened positions. They argued that if children always draw views they should have no more difficulty in representing the stick in a foreshortened position than in a nonforeshortened position: a round region is no more difficult to draw than a line or a long region. In the event, however, Piaget and Inhelder found that the younger children (below the age of about 7 or 8 years) used a line or a long region to represent the stick whatever its orientation, whereas the older children were able to represent the foreshortening of the stick by a change of shape: a pencil pointing directly towards the child was represented by a dot or a small circle. These results, Piaget and Inhelder concluded, demonstrated the truth of Luquet's theory.

The experiment described below (Willats, 1992b) is somewhat similar to that described by Piaget and Inhelder in that it was designed to test children's ability to represent foreshortening by a change of shape, although it also provided an opportunity for testing children's ability to use different denotation systems. In addition, the results also throw some light on the question of *why* children's drawings change. Do children's drawings change because older children see things differently in some sense: either because their 'conception of space' changes, or because they become consciously aware of their own viewpoints, as Piaget and Inhelder suggested? Or do children's drawings change because they are actively seeking solutions to specific drawing problems – in this case, the problems involved in producing good representations of sticks and discs in foreshortened positions?

Figures 3.3, 3.4 and 3.5 show typical examples of the drawings obtained in an experiment (Willats, 1992b) in which children aged 4 to 12 years were asked to draw sticks (the arms of a wooden figure) and discs (a plate held in the arms) presented to them in both foreshortened and nonforeshortened positions. Each child was asked to draw each feature in both conditions, so that each child produced two drawings, showing between them the arms and the plate in both foreshortened and nonforeshortened positions. In Figures. 3.3, 3.4 and 3.5 the drawings which the children produced for the foreshortened condition are shown highlighted.

The drawing systems used by the children were assessed in terms of the representation of extendedness. Each drawing produced in the foreshortened

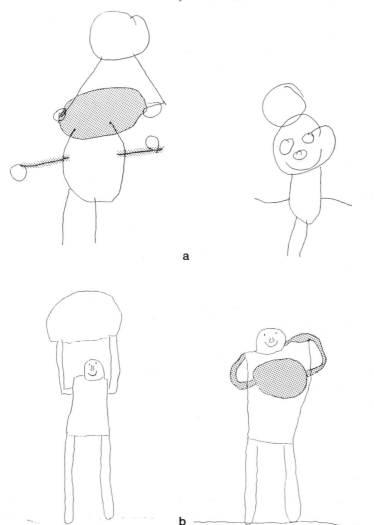

Figure 3.3 (a) girl aged 4 years 6 months. Arms: *no* change of shape, *single lines*. Plate: *partial* change of shape, *single region*; (b) boy aged 7 years 5 months. Arms: *no* change of shape, *single regions*. Plate: *no* change of shape, *single region* (from Willats, 1992b)

condition was assigned to one of three classes: *no* change of shape, a *partial* change of shape and a *full* change of shape. The results showed that very few of the 4-year-olds changed their drawings of either the arms or the plate in order to represent foreshortening. This is in agreement with the results obtained by Piaget and Inhelder, and suggests that at this age children are basing their drawings on

Figure 3.4 (a) girl aged 7 years 6 months. Arms: *partial* change of shape, *single regions*. Plate: *full* change of shape, *region with interior lines*; (b) girl aged 7 years 7 months. Arms: *full* change of shape, *single regions*. Plate: *full* change of shape, *single region*. After finishing the drawing the girl said, 'Those are his arms!' and pointed to the small circles (from Willats, 1992b)

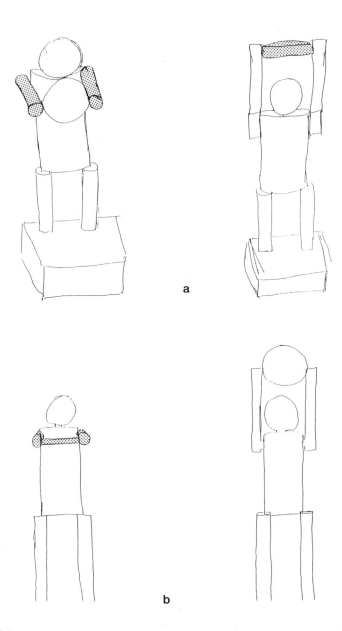

Figure 3.5 (a) boy aged 11 years 10 months. Arms: *partial* change of shape, *regions with interior lines*. Plate: *full* change of shape, *regions with interior lines*; (b) boy aged 12 years 1 month. Arms: *full* change of shape, *regions with interior lines*. Plate: *full* change of shape, *single region* (from Willats, 1992b)

object-centred descriptions. In contrast, about two-thirds of the 7-year-olds and nearly all the 12-year-olds changed their drawings *in one way or another* to take account of foreshortening. This suggests that these children were basing their drawings, at least in part, on viewer-centred descriptions. To this extent, these results support Luquet's and Piaget's contention that young children draw what they know and older children draw what they see.

There was, however, a further finding. Whereas most of the 7- and 12-year-olds represented the foreshortening of the plate by a *full* change of shape (Figures 3.4 and 3.5), they represented the foreshortening of the arms by a *partial* change of shape: that is, by a long region partially reduced in length rather than a round region (Figures 3.4a and 3.5a).

There seems no reason to suppose that these children 'saw' the arms partially foreshortened but the plate fully foreshortened. Presumably this solution was adopted as a compromise solution to the formal problem of representing foreshortened sticks. A round region would have provided a true view of an arm in a foreshortened position, but would not have provided an acceptable representation of an arm. A minority of the 7-year-olds did use a single round region to represent the arms in the foreshortened condition, but some of these children were clearly dissatisfied with this solution. One girl, whose drawing is shown in Figure 3.4b, looked up at me, pointed to the circles, and said 'Those are his arms!' On the other hand, a long region would have provided an acceptable view of an arm, but would not have shown the foreshortening. A partial reduction in length provided a possible compromise solution.

The same problem does not, however, arise with foreshortened discs. A long region does not look very much like a foreshortened disc (that is, a disc seen edge-on), but then neither does a round region look very much like a disc seen face-on. In fact, there is no satisfactory way of representing discs *at all*, using regions as picture primitives (Willats, 1992c). Consequently, children who were able to represent the disc in a foreshortened position represented this foreshortening by a full change of shape.

The results also showed that the different age groups used different denotation systems. Most of the 4-year-olds used single lines to represent the arms and a round region to represent the plate, and very few of these children changed their drawings to represent foreshortening (Figure 3.3a). This suggests that these children were using lines or regions to stand for the volumes of the arms and the plate in an object-centred description.

About a third of the 7-year-olds were probably using a similar system, but using single regions rather than lines to represent the arms (Figure 3.3b). Most of the remaining 7-year-olds changed their drawings in order to represent foreshortening, but used single regions to represent the arms and the plate. This suggests that these children were basing their drawings on a denotation system in which single regions are used to represent corresponding regions in the visual field (Figure 3.4b).

Finally, a majority of the 12-year-olds used lines to stand for the contours and edges of the arms and the plate. Both of these are primitives in a viewer-centred description, and nearly all these children changed their drawings in order to represent foreshortening. This is in fact the only denotation system within which foreshortening, especially the foreshortening of a stick, can be represented effectively (Figure 3.5b).

Again, this developmental sequence cannot be adequately explained by saying that older children 'draw what they see': there seems to be no reason to suppose that 12-year-olds 'see' edges and contours any more clearly than 7-year-olds. Instead, the 12-year-olds in this experiment had learned to use lines rather than regions as scene primitives, and this enabled them to solve the problem of representing foreshortening in an effective way.

Conclusions

Marr's account of information-processing devices is valuable because it prompts us to ask the right questions about drawing development, and to ask level one questions *first*. These questions are: What are children doing when they are learning to draw? And why are they doing it? I have tried to answer these questions by saying that children learn to draw by acquiring increasingly complex drawing rules, and that they acquire these rules because they want to produce pictures which are better as representations.

I began by raising the very general question of whether all children base their drawings directly on views, as Hagen (1985; 1986) suggests. The difficulty of deciding this question arises from the fact that most drawings, even those by very young children, can be interpreted as views; but there is often no way of deciding on the evidence of single finished drawings, whether or not they have been *derived* from views. The existence of anomalous drawings such as the 'striped' drawings of a coloured cube described by Moore, and the results of the experiment described above in which children were required to change their drawings in order to represent foreshortening, suggest that not all children's drawings are derived directly from views, but that younger children base their drawings on object-centred descriptions.

However, drawing does not just depend on the nature of the input to the drawing process; it also depends on using the appropriate drawing rules. In an earlier paper I described how children of different ages used different projection systems, based on progressively more complex rules mapping the directions of edges in three-dimensional space into lines on the picture surface. This 'projection systems' approach is, however, too limited to give an account of the whole of drawing development. A more general approach involves defining denotation systems as well as drawing systems, and extending the range of drawing systems to include the representation of topological relations, extendedness and other nonaccidental shape properties.

Drawing development is thus extremely complex. No doubt children have to become aware of views, consciously or unconsciously, in order to be able to draw them, but seeing a view correctly is not all that is needed in order to produce a good representation. Learning to draw depends on learning the appropriate drawing rules, and children do this by actively seeking solutions to specific drawing problems.

Notes

1. This description of drawing development is probably much too simple. I suspect that there is an interplay during the course of the drawing process between the child's perception of the object to be drawn, the application of drawing rules to both object-centred and viewer-centred internal descriptions, and the child's judgement of the emerging drawing; and that this interplay takes place at virtually all stages of development. In this respect, the nature of the actual drawing process is quite unlike that of either running a computer program or taking a photograph.
2. The primitives of a system are the smallest available units of information. In many cases, however, it may be difficult to decide just what the smallest units of information are. In the case of fold-out drawings, for example, lines are physically present in the drawing, but individual lines cannot be associated with particular edges, and I have argued that it is only the regions enclosed by these lines which carry shape information. It is thus crucial to make a distinction between the *marks* in a picture, and the more abstract concept of *picture primitives*. This distinction is similar to that made in natural language between sounds and phonemes (Willats, 1992b).

Acknowledgements

I am most grateful to Alan Costall of the University of Southampton, Claire Golomb of the University of Massachusetts, Sergio Morra of the University of Cagliari and Emiel Reith of the University of Geneva for their very helpful comments on an earlier version of this chapter.

Chapter 4

Observational, experimental and neuropsychological studies of drawing

Peter van Sommers *University of Technology, Sydney*

There are several ways of exploring how our minds operate as we draw. The most obvious one, reflection and reporting, is not as productive as one might expect. We generally pay little attention to the details of how we make drawings, just as we scarcely notice how we form words and sentences.

If you find this claim a little unbelievable, you can try it out for yourself at a very primitive level by drawing a stylized flower – a disc surrounded by six petals. Do it reasonably quickly, as you normally would. Then ask yourself which way and in what order you constructed its elements. If you are a right-handed drawer, you would almost invariably have started with the disc, begun near its top and drawn counter-clockwise. You probably proceeded then to the petal near one o'clock, started low down on the left where it attaches to the disc and drew it *clockwise*. All the petals on the right are normally drawn in that direction; those on the left the other way around.

Of course, if you do the drawing slowly and pay attention, you can discover these things for yourself, but even then, unless you are a particularly thoughtful and analytical person, you still won't understand *why* you did it that way. The reasons are largely associated with ergonomics; that is, economy of effort and a kind of subconscious planning. Details of the research uncovering this can be found in van Sommers (1984, chapters 1–4). The basic method of establishing the logic of graphic action throughout this work included videotaping and analyzing stroke by stroke how a group of artistically untrained adults and children did common graphic tasks.

It also documents what happens when the same drawing is repeated many times over substantial periods of time. What this experiment reveals, among other things, is that there are several consistent constraints that operate at the level of action and planning for action when we draw, but that when we develop our own idiosyncratic ways of portraying things, we base our developing skill on a visual record of our idiosyncrasies, rather than a record of our practical actions. In other words if you draw a stairway or a bicycle in your own characteristic way, we will be able to analyze your performance in two parts:

(1) Those principles of action that you share with most other people. These affect which way you draw lines, where you start, how you anchor lines to one another, how you rotate around circles, how you build by accretion from the 'core' of a drawing (see Figure 4.1).

(2) You may have your own characteristic ways of drawing a stairway or a bicycle, or for that matter a crocodile, a telephone, a fork, a shoe, and so on. In the case of a common object like a face or a tree, you might have two or three standard ways of portraying it, and you can easily develop more. The point I made earlier, however, is that although in producing these stock portrayals, virtually everybody follows a mechanical logic in basic stroke-making, etc., they carry forward their idiosyncratic habits of portrayal by automatically retaining some record of the visual elements and visual organization of their earlier efforts.

There is a very strong tendency for people (and we have studied this particularly in children) to repeat old, established visual formulas. We have termed this effect 'graphic conservatism' (Jones, 1972; Stanton, 1973; van Sommers, 1983; 1984, ch. 8). Once a drawing strategy has been developed, indeed even if the person has simply *thought* about how to portray an object, further development most commonly takes the form of adding detail and embroidering the drawing rather than revising its fundamental form. This type of deep graphic inertia goes a long way towards explaining why most ordinary drawing remains so ordinary, even when children (and adults) develop quite sophisticated knowledge about the structure of the items they are portraying. What this suggests is that our graphic education might well cultivate a kind of deep flexibility and a sense of graphic innovation at a primary organizational level.

I turn now to a second method of uncovering drawing strategies, one that is common to all kinds of psychological analysis, namely examining the *pattern of errors*. By looking at the *nature* of an error we can infer something about the way the drawer's mind worked, and by seeing how the erroneous version is reproduced in later drawings, we can trace how drawers utilize their largely unconscious visual records of the various anomalies and 'patch-ups' in their drawings.

In spite of what I said initially about the disappointing yields from self-analysis, it is none the less productive to ask people to talk their way through their drawing processes. For example, in order to explore the relationship between what people know about an object and what they draw, I have asked them (van Sommers, 1989, pp. 137–41) to keep repeating a drawing of a bicycle and to talk about their struggles to retrieve information about the object as they did so.

Objects like bicycles are notoriously badly drawn. It is not uncommon for intelligent adults to depict them with the chain joining the front and rear wheels.

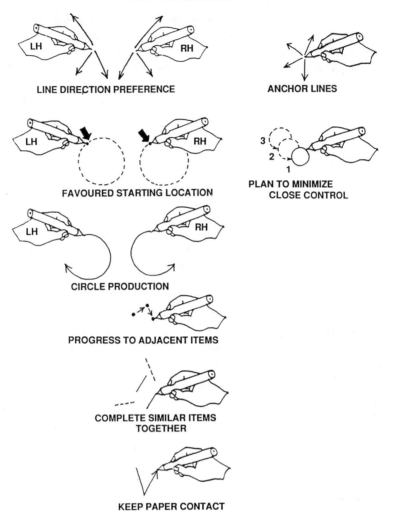

LINE DIRECTION PREFERENCE

ANCHOR LINES

FAVOURED STARTING LOCATION

PLAN TO MINIMIZE
CLOSE CONTROL

CIRCLE PRODUCTION

PROGRESS TO ADJACENT ITEMS

COMPLETE SIMILAR ITEMS
TOGETHER

KEEP PAPER CONTACT

Figure 4.1 Eight principles of action involved in drawing and writing. They arise from kinesiological, economic and planning considerations (from van Sommers, 1991, with permission of Academic Press)

Even the Apple Computer logo has this feature. At first it seems that we are surprisingly ignorant about the structure of common objects. This is to some extent true. But when you discuss the relationships between the various parts of a bicycle with someone, or ask people to point out those areas of their drawings where they feel something might be defective, it becomes clear that many of the problems they have in drawing complex objects are not so much knowledge problems as problems of *formatting*. Unless we draw from life regularly, we do not necessarily store information about objects in our memory in a way that is optimally useful for drawing.

In a sense, the illustrator's or photographer's way of 'freezing' objects in the world in certain instantaneous poses is an unnatural activity. In everyday life we often know objects more by how we use them than by how we look at them. For example, one of my normal adult informants could explain the way the two pedal cranks of a bicycle were joined to a horizontal axle, but could not mobilize that information visually to produce a drawing. If we are not in the habit of viewing objects with graphic portrayal in mind, we have to know how to 'interrogate' our own knowledge systems. A good deal of the time we do not even know what we know. We shall encounter this issue again in this chapter when I discuss the question of visual imagery and its use in drawing.

Drawing and even copying commonly involve a type of visual problem-solving, and some problems are harder than others. I do not mean just that some objects are intrinsically more difficult, although of course that is true; but each individual object can be looked at in different ways, some of which will create more graphic difficulties than others. I found that when accomplished drawers are copying difficult items, they may succeed equally well no matter how they interpret an object; but there is a second range of competence that depends on a judicious initial choice of visual structure. Poor drawers are relatively indiscriminant about how they attend to an item and frequently start from a perceptual analysis that is attended by all sorts of traps (van Sommers, 1984, pp. 135–60).

I would like to report that this problem can easily be overcome by a little basic education in visual analysis, but in a study that remains unpublished (because its results were so consistently negative) I found that simply showing people how a set of designs can be interpreted and then reinterpreted in different ways and inviting them to analyze carefully a second set very like them before they drew was completely without effect. If basic visual re-education of this sort is to succeed at all, it will obviously have to be more thorough and persistent than a simple, one-off lesson.

To the three methods I have so far mentioned – (1) taping people's drawing performances on video and conducting experiments to clarify why they proceed as they do; (2) analyzing their errors; and (3) encouraging drawers to 'talk through' the road-blocks and identify areas of ambiguity – we can add a fourth: analyzing graphic performance of graphically competent people who have suffered brain impairment. In the following sections I shall deal with evidence from this source.

The neuropsychology of drawing

There is a good reason why I have concentrated on brain impairment effects in people who were known to have been graphically competent. To put the matter bluntly, if you find a brain-impaired person's speech is defective, you can generally assume that the brain impairment caused it. But if you find their drawings are poor, you cannot make any such assumption. The unevenness of adult graphic competence has been alluded to by John Willats in an earlier chapter: 'the level of ability in most adults is no higher than it is in children'. In my experience this is broadly true, although it might be fairer to say that competence usually reaches a plateau when people leave any educational institution that requires or encourages drawing.

What is the main outcome of studies with brain-impaired artists or drawers? The central insight is fairly obvious when you stop to consider it, namely that there is no one unitary drawing faculty or drawing processing ability that fails to one degree or another, but that we are dealing with a complex system, which can be damaged at a variety of points. (My views about this system are elaborated in two papers: van Sommers, 1989; and Franklin, van Sommers and Howard, 1992.)

This is basically a modular information-processing account. One tenet of this approach is that studies of drawing processes have above all to be *analytical*. The older tradition in educational psychology of studying groups of drawers with broad-spectrum tests may be of restricted usefulness. To illustrate this point, I shall describe a series of phenomena from my own case-studies and a few from other workers. I shall work backwards in an informal way from motor output to imagery problems, memory problems, perceptual deficits, and conclude with a comment on aesthetics.

Motor output

One of the best documented cases of a profound loss of drawing ability in an artist was that of a French political cartoonist, Claude Sabadel (Lorant and van Eeckhout, 1980). While on holiday in the west of France, Sabadel contracted an infection in a major artery in his neck, which radically restricted blood flow to the left side of his brain. By the time the source of the problem was identified, he had lost both his speech and the use of his right (drawing) hand. His rehabilitation was minimal until one of his physiotherapists, van Eeckhout, persuaded him, against some resistance, to persist with drawing with his left hand. His initial drawing was of his home village (Figure 4.2). It seems tremulous and crude, but careful inspection shows that it is quite well-organized three-dimensionally, and is far from the equivalent of an infant's scribble. Sabadel eventually progressed to reach a high level of competence. Not only did he re-establish himself as a professional cartoonist, but he made sophisticated drawings which portrayed the distortions in perception he experienced during his period of recovery.

A careful inspection of drawings done before and after his illness reveal a subtle but significant stylistic shift. What remains ambiguous about his case, however, is how much central graphic relearning was involved, as opposed to improvement in dexterity, since the problems with one necessarily masked the other.

Figure 4.2 Claude Sabadel's early left-handed drawing of his native village following loss of the use of his right hand in adulthood (from Lorant and van Eeckhout, 1980, with permission of Sandoz)

There is less ambiguity in the case of KBS, an English electrician who suffered a left-sided stroke in his late fifties. Although KBS was not a full-time artist or draughtsman, he was a skilled amateur who, before his illness, produced elaborate scraper-board illustrations. He could do nothing at all with his right hand when I studied him and had entirely given up attempts to draw, with three notable exceptions, which I shall describe. In the meantime, however, he trained himself to use his left hand for all normal, everyday activities, so that by the time he finally *did* try to draw, the motor skills of his left hand were excellent, and two drawings and a copy that he produced without prior rehearsal were very competent (Figure 4.3), showing that his left-sided stroke had not in fact impaired his graphic competence to any substantial degree.

A third case appears more intriguing. This is an Australian male, AC, who suffered various language difficulties following a left-sided stroke. His drawings were always rather tremulous and ataxic but sometimes they also appeared quite disorganized. The four marks reproduced in Figure 4.4 represent his attempt to draw a simple side-elevation of a bed: mattress, legs and bed-head.

This disorganization does not look like an 'output' problem, but in fact it is.

Figure 4.3 First drawings with his left hand by KBS, a competent adult artist who developed good dexterity in his left hand before attempting to draw

Figure 4.4 Drawing of a bed by AC, a stroke patient whose sensorimotor coordination was defective, resulting in a systematic error in pen placement on the page

Almost by chance I discovered that when this patient aimed the point of his pencil at a spot on a page, it regularly touched down about 1 cm to the right of its goal. This perceptual-motor dysfunction meant that each successive component of his drawing spread out to the right. What such a seemingly trivial perceptual-motor aberration could produce serves to illustrate my earlier point very clearly, namely that what helps in this area of study is a sensitivity to particularities and an interpretation of their possible significance rather than a global view of graphic competence.

Imagery

It is reasonable to assume that imagery ('forming pictures in the mind') can play a significant part in drawing. But there are several aspects to imagery, two of which I want to contrast, namely the process of *forming* imagery as opposed to *utilizing* it.

Cases of loss of visual imagery have not been common in the literature, but some have been recorded. One of the most famous was an Italian male, MG, studied by Basso, Bisiach and Luzatti (1980). MG lost not only his ability to visualize the city in which he lived (Milan) and his apartment, but also odour, taste and sound imagery. He also reported that he no longer had any recollection of dreaming. Two things are worth mentioning about him: first, that his inability to create images of places did not mean that he did not 'remember' them, because he could still get about quite well, both in the city and around his home. The critical question from our point of view is, of course, whether he could still draw from memory, and the answer is yes, at least to a limited degree – he produced sketchy but recognizable pictures of various objects, one of which was a pheasant (Figure 4.5). Yet he could neither form an image of this creature nor describe it.

The other case is just the converse: a person who could form imagery, but had difficulty drawing from it. When I examined him in 1985, CT was an out-patient at the Salpetrière Hospital in Paris (Derousne and Beauvois, 1985). He had been an extremely competent draughtsman, but for ten years had been unable to work in his profession. He could copy simple drawings and his way of copying was not mechanical, for he was sensitive to his knowledge of what the drawing represented. (The method for establishing this is set out briefly in van Sommers, 1989, pp. 144–9, where this case is described in more detail.)

CT could form visual images, but could not 'read out' this imagery in the form of an adequate drawing. The task I developed to investigate his ability to form three-dimensional images included the following item: 'What solid three-dimensional form would the capital letter "B" form if it were rotated in space around its vertical "backbone"?' After some thought CT drew two concentric circles (Figure 4.6a). When asked to interpret these he said, with a hint of triumph, that they were the plan version of two balls, one on top of the other. This was technically correct but was a rather unconventional way to depict the object, so he was asked to draw it from the side. After considerable effort he produced the picture shown in Figure 4.6b. This process was repeated with other items. He knew that a rotated Y made an object like a glass, but he had great trouble formatting it graphically, and combined its circularity with a standard elevation in odd ways (Figure 4.6c).

CT had abandoned his profession, but he was a good-natured and obstinate

Figure 4.5 Drawings of a clock, man, house, daisy and pheasant by MG, a man who suffered profound loss of visual imagery

trier, and he could pick up a drawing strategy once it was explained to him and incorporate it into his repertoire of *particular* graphic skills. He was pleased with his two concentric circles because he had circumvented his usual problems with drawing from imagination by adopting a technique that he had often practised while trying to re-establish himself as an architectural draughtsman, namely producing simple plan and elevation. Since he saw difficulties in doing a three-

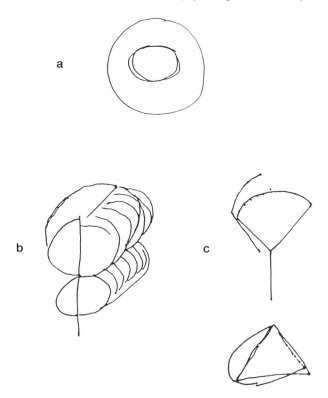

Figure 4.6 (a) First attempt by CT to portray the rotation of the capital letter B in space. It represents a plan version of two spheres, one on top of the other; (b) CT's subsequent attempt to draw the two spheres in three dimensions; (c) CT's attempts to portray a capital Y rotated in space, a form that he had identified as a glass

dimensional version and knew that an elevation would not fit the situation (that would simply yield two Bs back to back), he drew a plan.

I produced the three-dimensional imagery test based on rotating numbers and letters as a supplement to a two-dimensional test which I had constructed earlier. Respondents had to manipulate two-dimensional items, triangles, squares, circles, numbers, etc., in their heads. The mental manipulations included such manoeuvres as adding, overlapping, rotating and deleting part or all of the components. The goal was to produce a simplified version of a common object. Hence a simple ladder with one side removed might look like a comb, or a square with other squares added will make a cross, and with certain lines deleted, a frame for a noughts and crosses game.

This two-dimensional imagery test is a better predictor of drawing skill than the standard paper and pencil tests of spatial abilities. During its development and since, I have noticed a phenomenon in 'normal' people (that is intact, uninjured university students, etc.) that is quite different from the 'read-out' problem experienced by the Parisian draughtsman. Often, these subjects fail items on this test, not because they could not hold the items in their memory or manipulate them, but because they could not recognize what they represented until they had actually drawn them. So somebody would assemble what would seem like an unambiguous diagrammatic representation of a church, an open umbrella or an ice-cream cone, but be unable to identify it as an object until after they had drawn it. Here we have normal subjects with information in their heads that allows them to draw, but which in a sense they cannot 'see' with their mind's eye, or which they cannot bring into contact with their stored knowledge of real objects.

I suspect that the problem here is that in order to make the step from diagrammatic image to object, the image may need to be whole – or at least it helps if it is. Although all the solutions to these test items are simple, they may well be near the upper limit of the capacity of the imagery 'scratch-pad'. I do not believe that there are many people who can conjure up and hold a highly complex visual 'picture' in their mind's eye. We tend to assume we can, but in fact our imagery processing tends to be sequential rather than simultaneous, and fragmentary rather than cohesive.

Take the task studied by Brooks (1968), for example, of forming an image of a block capital letter and counting its corners. Even those informants who do this easily and competently say that as they move round the letter piece by piece, they never see the whole letter in 'clear', but inspect it in sections as though through a hole, while the remainder of the letter is only sensed in a vague way.

As I have discussed elsewhere (van Sommers, 1989, pp. 150–4), I have severe doubts about whether our limited capacity imagery buffer can be expanded in its capacity. This is not, of course, fatal to its usefulness in drawing. It is rather that we have to abandon the idea of an elaborate, simultaneously present image in the mind as a basis for drawing and should think rather of a sequential and heterogeneous assemblage of material – some iconic, some abstract, some static, some procedural – and a read-out process that is iterative. In other words, as we draw we 'fly by the seats of our pants', working back and forth between source, strategy and developing product. Just because we come up with a single product in the end, we should not be deceived into thinking that that product had its origins in a single intact image, or even a single concept.

Memory

The Parisian who could not easily draw his own images also had trouble with short-term visual memory. He could look at a design like the clover symbol on the computer keyboard six times and still be unable to reproduce more than one feature of it at a time. A more systematic account of this sort of inadequacy is

Figure 4.7 Attempts by MH to reproduce simple geometric forms from immediate memory. She progressed left to right across the forms and systematically omitted the final strokes of each (adapted from Franklin, van Sommers and Howard, 1992, with permission of Basil Blackwell Ltd)

found in the case of MH (Franklin, van Sommers and Howard, 1992). MH was a commercial artist, who even at the age of 77 and after some deterioration in her language and other cognitive functions, retained remarkable graphic competence in certain areas. However, when she was shown the simple geometric forms on the left of Figure 4.7, could only reproduce them correctly when she could store the item as a name and when that name happened to yield a replica of the original form. (In one or two cases she seems to have given a name to the figure, drawn from the name, but missed the true configuration.)

At first sight, MH's drawing from immediate memory looked haphazard, but when we referred back to the analysis of how people typically compile simple drawings, that is the typical progression of their drawing actions (van Sommers, 1984, ch. 6), we found that most of the failures were in fact incomplete drawings;

in other words, she could store information momentarily, but either the passage of time or the process of laying down the first parts of the figure eradicated or interfered with its completion.

Certain puzzles remain about MH's uneven performances – some were of startling good quality, many quite inadequate. Certainly she performed best when she had a model to work from and then could incorporate material into her drawings derived from past experience. Some of her clumsy performances when she was copying may have resulted from overconfidence. In other words, when the model was complex she knew she had to refer back to it constantly. When it was simple she may have felt she did not need to check on it and fell victim to her poor short-term visual memory. When we deal with the perceptual aspects of drawing we shall return briefly to this case, because of MH's resistance to the visual overload that affects some others.

Meaning

Another feature of MH's drawing introduces us to the issue of meaning in graphics. It is obvious that if a person is unable to understand a language, she can hardly be expected to draw what she is told to draw. Failure to understand language may be the result of brain damage, as well as lack of learning, and such a failure may be partial, so that a person may draw one item but fail another, or draw an object other than that specified. None of these things strictly speaking is graphic impairment, although occurring by themselves they would certainly provide a puzzle for a student of drawing.

There is another problem that is closer to the heart of the drawing system, namely agnosia, a failure to recognize objects – whether real objects, pictures of objects or sketches. Since we can copy a meaningless design or draw a nonsensical object, we can clearly copy or draw a meaningful one even when we fail to identify what it is or what it is used for. But our copies or drawings are likely to show anomalies when we operate like this. In 1932, F. C. Bartlett published some drawings of an owl that turned into a cat as it was copied successively by people who either did not know what it represented or misidentified it.

When this failure to identify an object occurs as a result of brain impairment, we get effects like those displayed by JR, an agnosic artist studied by Wapner, Judd and Gardner (1978), shown on the right in Figure 4.8. Items that should be unified are disjointed; outlines are followed that make no practical sense. The interpretation of these anomalies, many of which are minor features of the drawings, represents another case of the graphic detective work to which I have been referring. What seems at first to be simply an awkward drawing turns out on close inspection to be systematically anomalous.

The technique of concentrating on form and de-emphasizing meaning has

Figure 4.8 Copying errors made by JR, an agnosic artist, studied by Wapner, Judd and Gardner (1978)

been recommended as a useful graphic technique by very successful writers on drawing like Nicolaides (1941) or Edwards (1979). The logic underlying the techniques of Nicolaides and Edwards of drawing upside down or with the left hand or without looking at the page, is in part to evade the tyranny of those personal stylizations that govern so much vernacular drawing. But it is strongly to be doubted if these processes reduce the world to a meaningless array of colour, light and dark. One only has to see the trouble that computer-driven pattern recognition programs have run into in trying to make sense of photographs of landscapes without a knowledge of the form of the various items within them to recognize that these drawing techniques are only 'meaning-free' in a limited sense. People using these techniques do not draw apples as half-moons just because the rear edge of the object is close in colour or darkness to the background. The techniques make us highly attentive to form, but not agnosic.

Before I leave the problem of meaning and the loss of access to meaning, it might be well to refer the reader to an extended case-study (Humphreys and Riddoch, 1987) of a visually agnosic patient and the drawings he produced. This case-study extends the logic of fractionation or differentiation that I have been pursuing as it describes at least five different sorts of processes that are subsumed under the general title of agnosia.

Perception

I will provide just one example to illustrate the contribution that perception can make to drawing competence. It is not difficult to find examples in the literature on neuropsychology of people whose visual fields are incomplete or whose perception of the world seems to be shot full of tiny holes, or cases where the whole of one half of the world is missing from their attention. (Sabadel, whom I mentioned earlier, drew pictures of this experience.)

I mentioned earlier the case of a woman, MH, who seemed to benefit from rich visual detail in pictures or objects in working in her professional graphic register. I worked with another artist who found visual detail overwhelming. EM was a 60-year-old teacher of drawing and painting. It was not clear what had happened to her neurologically, but while she could recognize when her pictures or those of her students were unsatisfactory, she could not isolate why. I asked her to produce a picture of a country homestead like one on the wall of her studio which she had produced before her illness. Many artists are coy about their dependence on reference material, which can make attempts at 'before-and-after' investigations hazardous, so I was careful to tell EM to use the same sorts of aids she had used previously. She proceeded to work from a photograph on which she imposed a grid in the classic manner. But the mass of lines thus produced were her undoing, for she was unable to track the graphic logic of the web of boundaries and construction lines. This may well have been exacerbated by another perceptual difficulty she suffered. Although her depth perception in the three-dimensional world was usually adequate and she could see depth in a stereoscope, she had a particular deficit in extracting depth from a single picture. For example, she could not 'see' the depth in a Necker cube – a picture of a cube that shows all edges and is usually drawn without perspective. It is possible that this lack of perceptual depth robbed the picture she was trying to reproduce of one of the important organizing principles that allows the normal person to make sense of the pattern of edges and boundaries.

I found subsequently that this difficulty in reading two-dimensional images as three-dimensional, which in EB's case was acquired, is by no means rare in the ordinary adult population. A sample of 12 normal Cambridge adults were asked to interpret 25 drawings like those in Figure 4.9 as three-dimensional objects such as folded screens and to indicate where the missing lines should be placed. Two of the subjects could not get a single item correct, and another four had as many wrong as right. A few of their incorrect responses are shown on the right.

This is another area that merits further attention in the case of children. It always seemed so self-evident to me that everyone could 'read' 2½ D pictures, that is pictures of three-dimensional objects. But the experience described above made me reflect that since the visual appearance of things is normally highly redundant, no special geometric analysis is necessary to 'see' them in depth. A dog is a dog and a carrot is a carrot, and we know both to be three-dimensional.

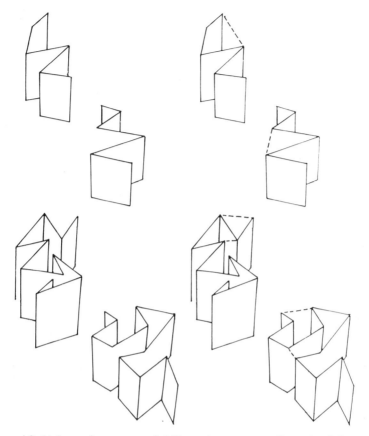

Figure 4.9 (a) Items from a test of ability to interpret two-dimensional forms as three-dimensional; (b) Some unsuccessful attempts by normal adults to add missing lines to the forms

The deficiency, if there is one, shows up when we have to establish the depth and substance of an image, not from common knowledge, but from the abstract geometry of the drawing or picture.

Visual aesthetics

The topic of aesthetics is vast, controversial and surprisingly unfashionable. To guide us in the analysis of case material we should, I suppose, have a breakdown of the major concepts people are using when they refer to visual aesthetics. I have a personal bias towards what I term 'decorative aesthetics' as a core topic, which includes all the questions of visual composition – shape, balance, symmetry, proportion, colour, texture, and so on – but others differ about priorities. Over the past half-century, two opposing things have happened: the image has taken over more and more from the word in society in general, and the word has taken over from the image in intellectual circles as the critics have imposed a strong conceptual emphasis on visual aesthetics. Meaning and metaphor and political correctness have dominated the analysis for several decades.

It is interesting, therefore, to ask what the neuropsychologists reached for when they encountered patients who reported that they had lost their sense of visual quality: the Golden Section, Mondrian paintings and the curves of classical calligraphy, or images that express the Angst of our modern predicaments? The neuropsychologists apparently spurned both, and showed their credentials as aesthetic populists. They offered pictures of women and attractive pastoral scenes.

So as a beginning, we have at least four cases (Bauer, 1982; 1984; Davidoff, Matthews and Newcombe, 1986; Habib, 1986; Lopera and Ardila, 1992) where adults recognized that their appreciation of visual material had changed. We know that most of these cases are vision-specific, because patients still responded as they previously did to nonvisual material, and we also know that it was not simply a perceptual or interpretative breakdown. Habib's (1986) patient had been a watercolour artist. She spoke about flowers: 'Their charm doesn't enter my mind any more. Looking at the landscape through the window, I see hills, the trees, the colours, but all those things cannot convey their beauty to me. Everything looks ordinary . . .' Yet she responded emotionally as she normally would to sounds and she talked to herself about the visual environment to gain access to her feelings for it. One of the patients had been a town planner, and he could still read plans and understand what was intended; he simply could not evaluate them in terms of their attractiveness. Here we have a surprisingly consistent and to my mind rather fantastic phenomenon, and one with important potential. Evidently, there has not yet been time to develop the theory and the testing materials needed for a full-scale analytic attack on the structure of this system, although the short report by Habib in particular makes a strong move towards that fractionation and teasing apart of elements that is the peculiar strength of this type of research.

Conclusion

The study of brain-impaired artists helps us to construct a model of how the mind processes graphic work. Some of the deficits they show are unlikely to be found in the work of normal drawers, others are quite relevant. But it is my view that the strategy of investigation carries an important lesson for those interested in normal graphic competence and performance. There is not a lot to be gained in any context from treating drawing skill as a unitary faculty rather than the complex process that it is. The global approach is implicit in any investigation that depends on general quantitative 'scores' assigned to performances or 'stages' assigned to general graphic development. We do better to adopt the role of detective or diagnostician and analyze in detail where problems arise. I have never felt handicapped by too much evidence. In much of my research, the microhistory of how each drawing was compiled line by line has been extremely valuable, if not essential.

Next, it is helpful to have a practical mind and a draughtperson's mentality. When it comes to practical drawing education, the best teacher is the one who understands intimately what a drawer is doing, and has the confidence to examine the detail of drawings and drawing production. The same applies to the researcher. Conducting standard group research is one thing, but watching the individual performance and the individual product with an informed eye, and recognizing when and how to probe and experiment on the spot, is often the path to deeper understanding.

Chapter 5

From line to outline

John M. Kennedy *University of Toronto*
Andrea Nicholls *New York College of Optometry*
Mary Desrochers *University of Toronto*

Lines in outline drawings can stand for the same referents in drawings by young children, guided by vision (Lange-Küttner and Reith, this volume) and drawings by the blind, guided by touch (Kennedy, 1993). To explain this, we give a theory of a perceptual process in vision and touch that turns a line into what we call an axis.

Outline, surfaces and the blind

Figure 5.1 contains a drawing by Ole, a blind man aged 32, using a raised-line drawing kit. Ole was born blind with some sensitivity to light but no form perception. He reports using raised-line drawings as maps and he recalls having had a few raised-line pictures in biology. The kit he used to make the drawing is a rubberized stiff board, covered by a thin plastic sheet. A raised line appears on the sheet when a ballpoint pen is drawn across it, with modest pressure. Ole was given the task of drawing a flat foreground square overlapping an irregular flat shape.

In Ole's drawing, the lines marking the edges of the square show what is called 'figure-ground'. That is, they show a complete foreground figure, against an occluded background surface, and the lines of the figure are the edges of the foreground but not the background surface. The foreground square figure does not dovetail into the background irregular figure. That would entail two foreground figures or 'figure-figure', where the edges of two foreground surfaces abut, and neither surface overlaps the other. Ole's drawing has two T-junctions. In each T-junction, the crossbar of the T shows the edge of the foreground

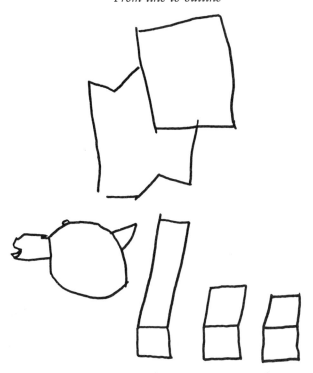

Figure 5.1 Drawings by blind adults: a foreground square overlapping an irregular figure; a dog's head; three blocks of various lengths

square figure and the stem of the T shows the edge of the irregular rear surface which is overlapped by the square. Gibson (1979) describes overlap as one surface 'partially occluding' another.

Figure 5.1 also shows a dog's head, with a muzzle, an eye and an ear. The head was drawn by a blind woman, Kathy, who lost her sight when she was between 2 and 3 years of age. The lines showing the head stand for the occluding boundaries of rounded surfaces. Alongside are three other drawings she made. She was asked to draw three blocks of different lengths, with square front faces. Kathy's three drawings include lines standing for corners where two faces meet, namely the front square faces and the top rectangular faces. The lines indicate a change of slant since the two surfaces are at different orientations to the observer. The corner is a convex corner, unlike an interior corner of a room, which is a concave corner.

Evidently, lines can show flat and curved surfaces in outline drawings, change of depth at edges from foreground to background, and change of slant at corners. The result is very useful. Virtually all perception depends on perceiving surfaces (Gibson, 1979), and surfaces can only be flat or curved. It is extremely rare to be

Figure 5.2 A profile drawn with a thin line appears as two profiles when the line is thick

in a scene with no occluding boundaries, e.g. the panorama provided by the interior of a smooth sphere.

A line has two contours, not just one (Figure 5.2). When the distance between the line's two contours is small, the line shows a single profile. It is easy to see the two contours (e.g. one white–black, and one black–white, reading from left to right). But it is very difficult to see the shapes of the two contours independently. As the line thickens, it becomes easier to see two profiles, i.e. the shapes of the two contours can be perceived independently. The curious fact we wish to emphasize is that when a line has two contours close together, the two contours can be perceived, but the shape of the line shows a single profile, not two. The sensory core, as Costall (this volume) might put it, of an outline drawing is this function of lines. The double contour is a 'representational concept' for a single referent – an edge or corner.

Figure 5.3 shows thick and thin lines, black and white. The contours of the thin lines and thick lines look parallel, in what Rubin (1915) called an equal-

 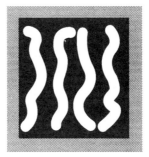

Figure 5.3 Apparent parallels result from contours of different shape

breadth phenomenon. The lines look like ribbons or wires. Curiously, the apparent parallelism is a result of two contours that are of different shapes. The difference between them is easiest to see when the contours take tight turns. Then one contour is a C-shaped curve, and the other is V-shaped. In point of fact, only straight sections of the line have truly congruent contours.

Apparent parallelism involves two contours acting as one unit (Rasmussen and Vejleskov, 1986) defining one axis of orientation, as Figure 5.4 shows. Here, two rectangles are defined. The larger rectangle contains the smaller one. When the smaller one's contours are parallel to the outer one's, the pair of contours define the two sides of a single frame. The pair of contours seem to be a single unit. As the interior rectangle tilts away from the outer rectangle, the impression of a single unit is lost.

In Figure 5.5 there are two blocks. In each, the contours of a thick line contain a convex corner of the block. The convex corner is not located perceptually at either contour of the line; nor is it midway between the contours. Rather, it is found in an asymmetrical location in each of the thick lines.

Young children's use of outline

Evidently, a line and its contours can indicate a feature of surface layout in several different ways, though outline drawings most often use lines to define single features, such as edges, corners and wires. To test implications from our account of outline we have asked young children what their line drawings mean. We anticipate that children's line drawings are guided by the use of lines we have described.

When children draw a cube, two of the earliest responses are a circle and a square (Willats, 1981; Cox, 1986; Nicholls and Kennedy, 1992). The circle is likely developmentally earlier. Do children who respond in this early fashion to the task of drawing a cube show any skills with outline in their drawings? We

Figure 5.4 The parallel contours are seen as one unit and as the contours tilt they come to shape two independent units

tested children at the Ontario Science Centre in a series of studies. We showed the children a cube of 3 cm^3, and asked them to draw it. We selected children

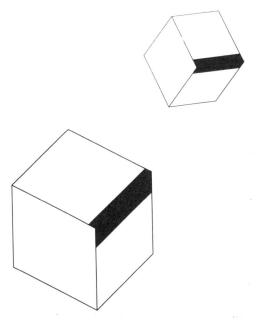

Figure 5.5 The convex corner is not located in the centre of the thick lines

who drew a circle for further study. We showed them two pipe cleaners, arranged in various ways. Other tasks were added after these two tasks in later studies, e.g. drawing a square and a crescent (which we called a moon).

In the first study, eight children (six aged 4 and two aged 3) who drew a cube as a circle were asked to draw what was called 'a straight snake' and 'a wiggly snake'. The pipe cleaners were placed on the table in pairs. One was straight, with a small circle made at the end of the pipe cleaner to represent the snake's head. The other was bent in a sine curve (with three bends). Again, one end of the pipe cleaner was formed into a small circle to represent the snake's head. The pipe cleaners were first oriented single-file in a line transverse to the subject; then, once the child had completed the drawing, the pipe cleaners were placed in parallel, close to the child's median plane, at right angles to their previous orientation with the heads oriented as though the snakes were crawling directly away from the child.

All eight children drew the snakes using lines. All drew the wiggly snake with a line that was more curved than the line for the straight snake, whether the snakes were transverse or median ($p < 0.01$, binomial, for both transverse and median cases).

In a second study, 'snakes' were arranged at right angles to one another, in a T formation, with the 'tail' of one snake close to the middle of the other. Eighteen children who drew a cube as a circle were tested (ten aged 3, eight aged 4). The first task was to draw two straight snakes, and the second was to draw two wiggly snakes. All 18 drew a T formation in the first task. Fifteen of the 18 children drew the wiggly snakes using more curved lines than when drawing the straight snakes ($p < 0.01$ binomial).

In the third study, seven children (five aged 3, one aged 4 and one aged 5) who drew a cube as a circle were asked to draw two straight snakes shown 'crawling over each other' in an X formation. Six of the seven children drew an X. One 3-year-old drew two parallel lines. We also showed these children a square piece of paper and asked them to draw it. Six drew a circle. We then showed them a crescent-shaped piece of paper and asked them to draw that. Five drew a C shape. The results suggest the children use a circle for some shapes (cube and square) and for Xs and Cs use shapes similar to Xs and Cs. A single line suffices for a crescent, it seems. The children may be noting the central axis of the crescent, or an occluding edge, since both are C-shaped.

Evidently, children who use circles to stand for cubes can use line in an outline fashion to show the shapes of wire figures. In development, shortly after drawing cubes as circles, children draw cubes as squares. (Since many children draw both cubes and squares as circles, they may be intending to draw square facets of the cube when they draw cubes as circles.) In our fourth study we tested children who drew cubes as squares. Our interest lay in what the lines forming the squares meant (see Willats, this volume). Do the lines stand for convex corners of the cube in the outline style?

Ten children (three aged 4, six aged 5 and one aged 6) who drew a cube (3 cm^3) as a square were asked to show what part of the cube each line stood for. The children were asked to make 'their best drawing' of the cube. When they had finished they were given the cube and asked to 'put the cube on the table, sitting the way your drawing shows it'. Then the child was asked to 'put your finger on this line', as the experimenter pointed at a line in the drawing. Then the child was asked to 'put your finger on the part of the cube this line shows'. Three alternatives were scored: if the fingerpad on the pointing finger touched a convex corner of the cube, that was taken to be the referent. If the fingerpad touched a vertex of the cube (where three faces met) the vertex was taken to be the referent. If a face of the cube was touched but no corner or vertex, then the referent was taken to be the face. Occasionally, a child put the length of a finger along a convex corner of the cube. Then the corner was taken to be the referent. If the child put the fingerpad touching the table and the side of the cube, the referent was taken to be the convex corner of the base of the cube.

To be consistent with the outline style of drawing, the lines in the child's square should depict the convex corners of the cube. Eight of the ten children ($p < 0.01$, binomial test, with three alternatives) indicated three or four of their four lines stood for corners, which is consistent with outline style. Five of the eight indicated that all their lines stood for corners (four of these indicating the four convex corners of the top of the cube, and one indicating the four convex corners of the base of the cube).

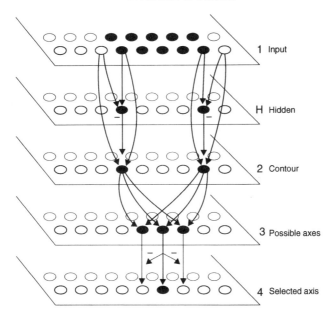

Figure 5.6 An axis-extraction system of cell layers. H is a 'hidden' layer. Negative signs show inhibition

We repeated this study with nine older children (four aged 6, four aged 7 and one aged 8) who drew a cube as a square. In eight cases, the child indicated that the majority of the lines stood for convex corners of the cube. In one case, two of the lines indicated convex corners and two of the lines indicated faces of the cube (to the side, not the top or front). In eight of the nine drawings, the child indicated the square stood for the front face of the cube.

These studies indicate that at the developmental level where cubes are drawn as circles, children can draw wire-like shapes as lines, and produce shapes similar to the shapes of the referents. When children draw cubes as squares, the referent they usually intend for the line is a convex corner, in keeping with outline style.

Axis extraction

The use of outline depicting edges, corners and wires often involves two distinct contours being treated in perception as showing a single feature. Let us call the location of the feature indicated by the line the 'axis' of the line. What perceptual process may be responsible for the extraction of an axis of a line? Figure 5.6 is a hypothetical cell network which contains some of the key properties. The cell network could be present in vision or touch, but we shall describe it in vision first, for simplicity's sake. It is an 'axis extraction' network.

First, we shall describe the connections from layer 1, and then their effects. Layer 1 is the input layer. It is a layer of cells that can be 'off' (black) or 'on' (white). The black cells represent a cross-section 5 cells wide of a line which might be, say, 300 or 400 cells in length. Layer H (for hidden) is below layer 1, and layer 2 is one step further. Layer 1 cells are connected directly to layer H cells and layer 2 cells. If any of the layer 1 cells is active, then it can fire a cell in layer 2. However, one layer 1 cell is insufficient to fire an H cell. A layer H cell will only fire if it receives activation from two input layer cells. Then it sends inhibition (shown by a negative sign) to a layer 2 cell.

The effect of this wiring is that layer 2 cells fire to contours, but not to continuous fields without contours. Notice that if all the input layer cells were 'on' (white), they would send activation to the hidden layer and layer 2. The hidden layer would then send inhibition to layer 2. Therefore, a layer 2 cell would be in receipt of inhibition and excitation, which would cancel each other. Now consider the effect of a contour. There is a border in the input, shown by a white cell and a black cell adjoining. The white cell sends activation to the layer 2 cell. It also sends activation to the hidden layer, but it alone cannot trigger the hidden cell, which requires inputs from two layer 1 cells to fire. Therefore, no inhibition is sent to layer 2, and its cells fire, activated by layer 1 cells. This arrangement of layers is called an XOR network, or 'exclusive-or' system. Layer 2 fires when there is input to one layer 1 input cell, or its neighbour, but not when there is input to both.

Notice that layer 2 cells fire equally well to black lines and white lines. For a white line, the five central cells in Figure 5.6 should be changed to white, and the outer cells should be black. The effect on the contour-detecting cells in layer 2 is identical.

An outline requires more than contour extraction: it requires the line's two contours to interact. Hence layers 3 and 4. In layer 3, cells are activated by cells, or pairs of cells, in layer 2. That is, a layer 3 cell can fire to input from a single cell from layer 2, or to a pair of cells, or to both. This allows a single axis to be fired by a single contour (e.g. a contour showing a profile) or by a pair of contours (e.g. a line showing the same profile). However, as Figure 5.5 indicates, the location of the axis can be at any of several locations within the flanking contours of the line. To accommodate the results of Figure 5.5 there are several possible axes being activated at layer 3. Extracting the relevant axis – a single axis – requires more influences to be brought to bear. Layer 4 in Figure 5.6 shows the central axis being selected, which may be the default option. That is, when a thin line is drawn with no particular recognizable referent the common reaction may be to perceive it with a central axis. This is shown by the central option cancelling the other options at layer 4. But influences from the overall configuration or schemata (Thomas, this volume; Morra, this volume), showing blocks or parallel frames, for example, may provide important influences to layer 4 so that the axis that is chosen can be placed asymmetrically rather than centrally.

The axis-extraction network could be tactile, or visual, or both. The input could be a raised line, not just a black or white line. Tactile lines have two flanks, albeit they are ridges. The tactile line's flank resembles a tiny cliff, providing extra pressure on the fingerpad on the raised side of the cliff. Figure 5.6 can be taken as showing a cross-section through the input from a raised line. The white cells show low pressure; the black cells show high pressure. The contour extraction system is activated by a difference in pressure in the input. All the cell layers operate as before to extract the flanking cliffs (tactile contours) and axes.

An important feature of the visual network is that it operates with black lines or white lines. Similarly, the tactile network would operate equally well with raised lines (ridges) and recessed lines (cracks). In either case, tactile contours and axes would be extracted. The axes are abstractions corresponding to locations, rather than purely visual or tactile phenomena. That is, they are not brightness, colour or pressure percepts. In a word, they are amodal – matters that are not inherently in one modality or another.

We suppose that the machinery for abstracting axes is present in both vision and touch from early on in life. How early we are uncertain. But we anticipate that the cell networks are mature in infancy, being part of the infant's perceptual equipment rather than acquired like some aspects of depiction via influences from society (Lange-Küttner and Edelstein, this volume).

Outline and shape-from-shadow

Axes are abstractions. They indicate locations, not the polarities of borders (e.g. which side is bright and which is dark). Hence, outline should fail to activate perception that relies on knowing the polarity of a brightness border. Accordingly, let us consider the relationships between outlines, surfaces and shadows. Figure 5.7 contains three pictures based on a single shape, which is most recognizable in the left version as a man's face. The face is illuminated from above and the side so that the eyes, much of the forehead and half of the nose are in shadow. If this picture is a 'positive', the middle picture is a negative, where the illuminated region of the man's face is turned to a solid black field. The picture to the right is a line version, with a line replacing the solid contours of the negative and the subjective contours of the positive figure. When undergraduate subjects were shown these figures, we found the line picture is less recognizable than either the positive or the negative.

Figure 5.8 has another three versions of the face. The left picture is a subjective contour version with gratings on both sides of the contour to equalize luminance. This figure is slightly less recognizable than the line version in Figure 5.7. The next picture is a thick white subjective band. This is slightly more recognizable than the subjective contour figure. If the band is as thick as the black line version in Figure 5.7, it is about as recognizable as the line figure. As the white band is made wider it eventually becomes possible to see the man's face

Figure 5.7 A man's face in shadow, with the contour of the shadow shown in three versions – positive, negative and line. This figure and Figure 5.8 are based on a design by Mooney (1957), with permission

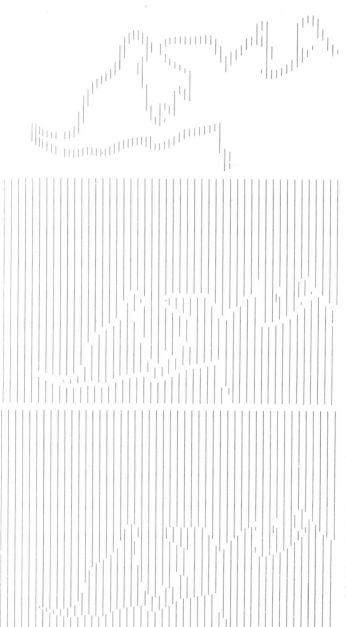

Figure 5.8 Figure 5.7's shape-in-shadow in three further versions

with illuminated regions and shadowed regions. Figure 5.8, right figure, is the reciprocal of the white subjective band. If the contour matching Figure 5.7 left version remains in place and the band is thickened by lengthening the lines, once again, eventually, it becomes possible to make out the illuminated and shadowed face.

The lesson from Figures 5.7 and 5.8 is this: vision cannot extract and use the 'positive' contour of a line when there is a negative contour close by, in parallel. As the line thickens, whether it is a black or white band with real contours or subjective contours, it becomes wide enough eventually for vision to use the positive contour without interference from its neighbour. The two contours stimulate axis perception. Once the axis of a line has been extracted it can only be used to represent corners and occluding edges. It cannot stimulate analyses of shapes in shadows, because once an axis has been extracted, it bears no information about the relative locations of brightness and darkness. It can only indicate the location of a change of depth or slant. These features of surface layout are tangible as well as visual.

In sum, outlines stand for features of surfaces in common to touch and vision. Outlines stimulate axis processing in young, sighted children, we conjecture, and the axes guide the use of line by preschool children. Similarly, we suggest, axes guide the use of raised line by the blind.

The transformation of figurative thought: implications of Piaget and Inhelder's developmental theory for children's drawings

Christiane Lange-Küttner *Free University Berlin*
Emiel Reith *University of Geneva*

This chapter considers the relevance of Piagetian theory for the study of the acquisition of graphic competence. We refer to Piaget, Inhelder and Szeminska's earlier work on the development of spatial cognition (Piaget and Inhelder, 1948/ 1956; Piaget, Inhelder and Szeminska, 1948/1960) and on Piaget and Inhelder's later work on mental imagery (Piaget and Inhelder, 1966/1971). First, we show that Piaget and Inhelder's theory of the development of children's space concept relates to the notion of a changing realism in drawings, as described by Luquet (1913; 1927/1977). Second, we describe Piaget, Inhelder and Szeminska's (1948/1960) distinction between the figurative, topological space concept of young children and the operative, Euclidean space concept of older children. We take up this distinction to show how the emergence of a spatial axes system coincides with an evaluation of objects that is qualitatively different from primary visual perception of objects. Third, we describe how Piaget and Inhelder explained the developmental change in the construction of graphic boundaries of forms by the Gestalt-like conservation of objects in the young child, and the later emerging ability to deconstruct and reconstruct the Gestalt, resulting in an operative conservation of the object. Finally, we suggest that graphic competence emerges with children's ability to establish a psychological distance in their interaction with the environment. We give some examples of how this distance-taking can be facilitated, and formulate some hypotheses about its origins in early childhood.

The notion of realism

In drawing, perception plays a role not only in controlling and monitoring the production of lines on the page, but also in judging the adequacy of the graphic construction – the graphic object – as a depiction of the real object. Luquet (1927/1977) claimed that children's representational intentions are realistic in the sense that they strive to portray the real objects they see in their environment, and that they want their drawings to resemble these objects. Failure to achieve this goal is the basic motive for devising better depiction methods and for obtaining advice from more sophisticated drawers. This view gains some support from the frequently cited study of Kosslyn, Heldmeyer and Locklear (1977). They asked children to select from a set of alternatives the best picture of a miniature house. They found that half of the kindergarten subjects (4 years) and all third-graders (8–9 years) preferred perspective drawings, although they did not produce such drawings themselves. Moore (1986b) tested children's preferences for realistic renditions, taking a *l'art pour l'art* point of view. Rather than asking subjects to choose the best depiction of a model, she asked them which was the best compared to drawings of younger and older children. In this situation, subjects of all age groups were more likely to favour representations which most closely resembled their own productions. This result has been replicated by Brooks, Glenn and Crozier (1988). Thus, it seems that although children do indeed strive to relate their graphic constructions to their visual experience of real objects (see also Cox, 1992, p. 107; Golomb, 1992, p. 113), they also possess criteria for judging the adequacy of drawings and for selecting the best drawing: their own. Although Piaget was aware of this self-sufficient satisfaction in children, he was more interested in the process of decentration from these idiosyncratic evaluations towards more objective judgements. Luquet's work on realism in drawing development (1913; 1927) provided him with a framework for discussing this issue (see also Piaget 1924/1928; 1926/1929).

Luquet (1927) distinguished three phases of realism in drawing. When children are in transition from one phase to the next, phenomena characteristic of both phases may coexist in a single drawing. During the phase of *failed realism* (age 3 to 4), the child does not construct explicit spatial relationships between the graphic objects on the page. During the phase of *intellectual realism* (age 5 to 8), the child explicitly depicts the spatial relationships between objects and parts of objects. However, the spatial relationships generally lack viewpoint coordination and remain incoherent. For instance, a cube may be drawn folded out, as a set of juxtaposed squares. Only during the phase of *visual realism* (beginning around age 9) does the child attempt to depict objects and their spatial layout as they might be seen from a given vantage point. The shape, proportion and layout of the graphic forms correspond more closely to our perception of the environment.

In the literature on children's drawing, Piaget is often referred to when spatial cognition is discussed. Yet, many authors contest his approach to drawing development. It is argued that one cannot use children's drawings as an index of spatial knowledge and perception because by doing so one neglects or severely underestimates the role of children's drawings skills (see, for example, Golomb, 1992; Willats, 1992b). Indeed, for many authors, in particular followers of

Arnheim and Gombrich, drawing is not a problem of seeing or knowing, it is a problem of drawing *per se*, that is, knowing the rules for translating knowledge and perceptual experience of real objects into forms on the page, or creating 'graphic equivalents' of real objects (Goodnow, 1977). Piaget was well aware that using spontaneous drawing as a means for investigating mental representations of space calls for caution. But since he is so often accused of ignoring the role of drawing skills, we quote him at length:

> Admittedly, to study the development of the child's idea of space on the basis of drawing alone would be an extremely hazardous venture. But assuming that this type of analysis is checked by other methods, and especially if one restricts oneself to the general features of drawing based on simple everyday shapes, there can be no doubt that drawing constitutes a certain type of representation. . . . A drawing is a representation, which means that it implies the construction of an image, which is something altogether different from perception itself, and there is no evidence that the spatial relationships of which this image is composed are on the same plane as those revealed by the corresponding perception. . . . From this last remark one might conclude that from the drawings by themselves we can learn nothing. On the contrary, they enable us to establish the spontaneous character of the structures inherent to representation, which can only later be submitted to detailed analysis by means of more or less artificial experiments. It is entirely from this point of view therefore that we intend to study the problem, and the development of drawing will provide a framework which we can fill in afterwards by means of more detailed analysis. (Piaget and Inhelder 1948/1956, pp. 46–8)

Piaget and Inhelder devised a series of copying tasks, which are described not only in their studies on the graphic space concept (1948/1956), but also in their publication with Szeminska on children's conceptions of geometry (1948/1960), as well as nearly 20 years later in their work on mental imagery (1966/1971). The earlier studies were based on children's verbal reports mainly; in the later studies on mental imagery, Piaget and Inhelder (1966/1971) also presented quantitative results, such as the frequency of types of responses per age group.

Luquet's model of drawing development did not only provide a framework for investigating space concepts, but also for studying the relations between perceptual and conceptual development. Luquet (1927/1977) pointed out that children's drawings are graphic *constructions*, not depictions of real scenes, and that children often draw perspectives which they have never seen. Luquet (ibid.) hypothesized that direct perception of reality plays only a minor role in graphic construction processes. Even at the stage of visual realism children refer to internal models, that is, mental description of objects, rather than to real, external models. Accordingly, Luquet (ibid.), and recently Chen and Cook (1984), found no differences in graphic performance when young children were asked to draw directly from a real model or to copy a drawing of it. These findings suggest that the degree of realism in drawings is less a function of direct perception than of mental conceptualizations of objects and their definition in terms of graphic forms. Again, we quote Piaget and Inhelder in full because they are frequently said to have claimed that young children draw what they know instead of what they see. Piaget and Inhelder's comments on children's efforts to depict a disc in perspective reveal their conviction that children always draw what they see, although not in the form they see it, and that perception and representation of an object are distinct cognitive processes, although the construction of a drawing involves both:

> To render a disc seen in profile by means of a half finished circle . . . is a clear proof that such children perceive the difference between a disc foreshortened and one seen full face. . . . Thus they draw, or choose from the model drawings, not the projective figure (a horizontal line) but a structure that expresses part of the outline without embodying perspective. In other words, some aspects of its properties considered in isolation. Thus, the viewpoint does not enter into the representation directly, but only by way of breaking up or mutilating the objects so that the child draws what he can see – but not exactly in the shape he sees it. (Piaget and Inhelder, 1948/1956, p. 178)

The developmental time-lag between perception and graphic representation was of major theoretical importance for Piaget. It is now a well-established fact that children at the age of failed realism rely strongly on their visual impressions (see, for example, Flavell, Green and Flavell, 1993). Before the emergence of reversible thought processes at about age 7, children's responses in various kinds of tasks show that they base themselves on perceptual information, or in Piagetian terms, figurative thought. Paradoxically, this dependence on perception does not, as we might expect, enhance visual realism in drawings. To resolve this paradox, it is necessary to turn to an aspect of Piagetian theory which has been overlooked so far in the literature on drawing development, that is, Piaget's extensive reference to Gestalt psychology – *la psychologie de la forme*. As early as 1936, in *La Naissance de l'Intelligence*, Piaget expressed his sympathy for Gestalt psychology. As we can see in the following quotation, Piaget relates his notion of the schema to the concept of the Gestalt:

> We . . . sympathize completely with the effort of Gestalt psychology to find the origins of intellectual structures in biological processes conceived as systems of relationships and not as the expression of substantial forces. We . . . show how the hypothesis of assimilation tries to surpass the theory of form and does not contradict it, and how the 'schema' is a 'Gestalt' made dynamic and not a concept destined to react against the progress of the Gestalt movement. . . . In the theory of form, intelligence ends by disappearing to the advantage of perception, and the latter, conceived as being determined by ready-made internal structures – that is to say, preformed from within – ends by becoming more and more confused with 'empirical' perception, conceived as preformed from without: in both cases, in effect, the activity disappears to the advantage of the elaborated whole. . . . In short, to criticize Gestalt psychology is not to reject it, but to make it more mobile and thus to replace its apriority with a genetic relativity. (Piaget, 1936/1952, p. 379)

Thus, Piaget acknowledged the importance of perception but did not consider it to be a major determinant in the development of cognitive structures.

According to Piaget (1971), young children perceive objects as *Gestalten*, that is, as meaningful and functional units, not as mere images. In this respect, Piaget's hypothesis anticipates recent research showing that infants respond to objects as bounded and unitary entities (Spelke, 1990). But central to Piaget's views is that the very act of perceiving is a dynamic process which becomes intimately related to and largely influenced by the emergence of conceptual thought. Of course, we can simply perceive an object and leave it as it is. But knowing an object means acting on it and transforming it (Piaget, 1971, p. 67). According to Piaget, transformation of an object can occur in two ways: by *modifying* its position, movements or features, and by *enriching* the object with new characteristics or relationships. These transformations can be performed physically or mentally through integration of the object into sensorimotor schemata, conceptual hierarchies or spatial axes systems. Thus, we claim that Piaget's notion of the changing *interrelation between perception and cognition* is crucial to explaining developmental change in drawing. The emerging of operatory thought which allows for the construction of spatial axes systems brings about an important change in the status of objects: they lose their Gestalt-like figurative integrity. This change has repercussions on children's abilities to modify graphic forms and to supplement them with new relationships.

The changing conceptualization of objects and space

Piaget and Inhelder (1948/1956; 1966/1971; Piaget, Inhelder and Szeminska, 1948/1960) showed that the conception of space in the preoperational child is dichotomous. Young children experience the world as composed of real objects – Gestalten – and empty space – a non-Gestalt. The Gestalt psychologist Jaensch (1911) called the empty space between objects the 'intermedium'. Young children tend to represent only what is visible: objects are visible and fill space, while the air is invisible and empty, and can thus be filled. For instance, preoperational children judge the distance between two objects, A and B, to be reduced if a third object C is placed between them. In their understanding, object C fills some of the space and so takes away a certain amount of that space, reducing the distance AB. Fabricius and Wellman (1993) called this phenomenon the *interposed object error*. But is it really an 'error'?

Perceiving the world as being composed of visible objects and emptiness is naturalistic in so far as it preserves the quasi-biological, ready-made, Gestalt-like identity of objects. Goodnow (1977) called this way of processing visual information 'respect for the psychological space of objects', Piaget and Inhelder (1966/1971) the 'pseudo-conservation of the gestalt of objects'. This way of apprehending space may explain early success in variations of the Piagetian three mountains task, in which, contrary to the traditional task, there is no overlapping of one object by another (Borke, 1975; Liben, 1978; Liben and Belknap, 1981; Light and Nix, 1983). Thus, it appears that preoperational children can construct other viewpoints when the *Gute Gestalt* of objects is preserved and not disturbed by overlap. An interpretation based on Piaget and Inhelder's theory of mental imagery (1966/1971), therefore, would explain the three mountains task not only as a problem of depth perception but also as a problem of the violation of the *Gute Gestalt* of objects. In 1948 Piaget and Inhelder conceptualized these processes as 'visual thinking', a term also used by Arnheim (1969), and only later in 1966 as 'figurative, gestalt-like thought'.

Topological space is constituted by whole figures or *Gestalten*, and involves the construction of qualitative relationships – such as proximity, separation, enclosure and continuity – between these figures. In many cases, topological space constitutes an efficient system of spatial representation in which objects can serve as landmarks for orientation. Nevertheless, since topological space implies the presence of figures or objects, it is also constrained by them: when there are no objects, there are no spatial relations either. Therefore, topological space has only a local and limited validity: as soon as objects serving as landmarks appear identical, the spatial array can no longer be structured and orientation fails. Thus, topological space is useful only when spatial arrays are relatively simple and the objects serving as landmarks are unique.

Contrary to the topological, figurative conception of space, Euclidean space is not constrained by the presence of objects. The *a priori* separation or independence of objects and space has dramatic implications for the status of both visible and empty space. Piaget traces the origin of the Euclidean space concept in children to major changes in figurative thought, which occur with the emergence of operational thought and the acquisition of reversibility. As mentioned earlier, mental operations transform objects and do not leave them as they are: objects lose their naturally perceived figural identity. Euclidean space implies a system of spatial coordinates and is by definition dimensional, infinite and independent of objects. Invisible space changes from being a finite, closed, room-like container, situated around or besides the object, to being a measurable expanse. Objects and space are integrated into a single homogeneous system and thereby become, in a sense, the same, possessing a common property. Objects are now merely states of matter and no longer meaningful 'things'. It makes sense that with the dissolution of the ready-made identity of objects – the end of the pseudoconservation of Gestalten – the need for a different kind of determination now emerges. According to Piaget and Inhelder (1966/1971), spatial objects become conserved operatively. Operative conservation differs from figurative pseudoconservation in two ways. First, it involves an exact rather than a global, intuitive determination and measurement of objects. Second, operative conservation implies a greater degree of freedom in modifying the Gestalt of objects. The *Gute Gestalt* can now be broken down into elements, as well as supplemented with relationships between elements. In other words, the Gestalt can be deconstructed and reconstructed.

The 'boundary taboo': conservation of the Gute Gestalt of the graphic objects

What are the implications of pseudo- and operative conservation for the depiction of objects? Although preoperational children can combine graphic elements – picture primitives – into graphic configurations, generally they do not produce true-to-life depictions. Reith (1987; 1988; 1990) and Metzger (1956) have shown that the young child can use two distinct procedures for graphic construction of a model object (see Figure 6.1). In the first, children aggregate lines and simple geometric forms that stand for the various parts and features of the model. This results in schematic constructions which portray the components of the model but do not conserve its visual appearance. In the second procedure, children follow the global visual outline of the model but without differentiating the features within the contour. This results in a silhouette drawing.

In both drawing procedures children avoid disrupting or violating the natural boundaries of objects. In the first procedure they conserve the Gestalt of each part, in the second they conserve the Gestalt of the whole. Using a rather mythological expression, Piaget and Inhelder (1966/1971) referred to this effect of the Gestalt-like pseudoconservation of forms as the *boundary taboo*. In one experiment they asked 4- to 7-year-old children to draw a model composed of two juxtaposed cut-out squares of equal size. The length of the common boundary was reduced by moving the upper square to the right in front of the child. The types of errors obtained in this task are illustrated in Figure 6.2. They can be divided into two main categories according to the way the subject transforms the model. In the first (errors A–D), the squares are separated: the Gestalt of each square is preserved but not the contour of the model as a whole. In the second (errors E1–G), the Gestalt of one or both squares is deformed in an attempt to conserve certain aspects of their relative position (top, bottom) as well as their global outline. Thus, the displacement of one square with respect to the other is represented either by a *false separation* or by a *deformation*. In this experiment the models were cardboard shapes – that is, geometrical objects. However, Reith (1987) obtained similar errors when children were required to copy line drawings depicting natural scenes. Overlapping or juxtaposed figures in the scene were separated or distorted.

Figure 6.1 The development of use of contour lines in children's drawings of figurative and nonfigurative three-dimensional models (from Reith, 1988)

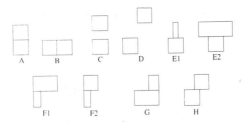

Figure 6.2 Drawing after Piaget and Inhelder (1966/1971)

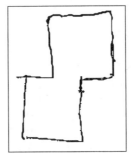

Figure 6.3 Translation of one square relative to another. Spontaneous circumscribing (tracing) of the new perceptual configuration with a pen (see text)

Piaget and Inhelder's experiment was replicated in a case-study with a boy aged 4 years and 4 months. This child found a third solution for representing the displacement (Lange-Küttner, 1994). He circumscribed the new configuration with a pen (see Figure 6.3). Then, in accordance with the instruction, he made a free-hand sketch of this new configuration (see Figure 6.4). The result was an essentially correct depiction of the model's outline, with the horizontals slightly overestimated. This example clearly shows that the child was unable to construct common boundaries. However, he produced a *false fusion* between the two forms, rather than a *false separation*, thereby creating a new Gestalt. During the following days the boy felt unhappy with his solution. In subsequent attempts he decomposed the graphic configuration again by interrupting the global outline and using different colours for the two sides (see Figure 6.5). Another solution was to alter the meaning of the configuration, interpreting it as a dog or a castle (see Figure 6.6).

In Figure 6.7 we have plotted the frequencies of the different types of error in

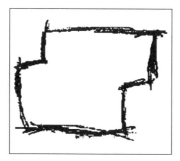

Figure 6.4 Free-hand sketch of the translation of one square relative to another (see text)

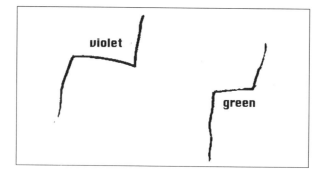

Figure 6.5 Subsequent reinterpretation of the translation of one square relative to another. Interruption of the global outline (see text)

the square-drawing task according to age, as reported by Piaget and Inhelder (1966/1971, p. 54). False separation is most frequent at age 4 and deformation at age 6. Both types of errors are equally frequent in 5-year-olds. These findings are consistent with more recent research. In a study by Ingram and Butterworth (1989) on depiction of a small and a big model cube combined in various spatial arrangements, solutions involving the production of separated graphic forms were more frequent in children below 6 years than in older subjects. In two other studies, one on children's abilities intentionally to modify their habitual ways of drawing houses and human figures (Karmiloff-Smith, 1990; 1992) and one on children's depictions of cylinders (Caron-Pargue, 1992), it was found that the first step in the successful integration of the whole and the constituent parts of an

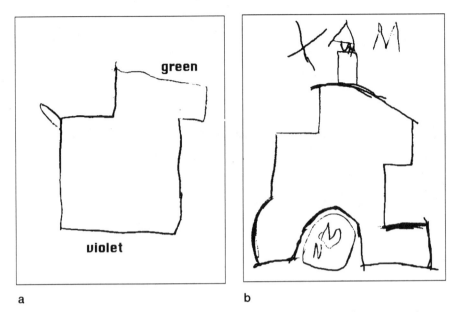

a   b

Figure 6.6 Further attempt to draw the translation of one square relative to another. Interpretation of the configuration as a dog or a castle (see text)

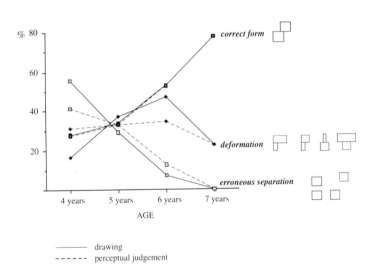

Figure 6.7 Translation of one square relative to another. Frequencies of the different types of response at different ages on drawing and picture selection tasks (from Piaget and Inhelder, 1966/1971)

object is to distort either the Gestalt of an element or the shape of the whole. The psychological resistance to distorting graphic forms sometimes leads to more radical solutions. In Karmiloff-Smith's study (1990), for instance, young children frequently blacked out parts or omitted them completely. These solutions are comparable to the *false separation* in their disruptive effect on the object's spatial relationships.

The emergence of measurement by supplementation of axes systems

Since the emergence of operatory thought causes objects to lose their quasi-biological, ready-made identity, new modes of determining visible objects and invisible space are needed. The solution is measurement. The discovery of measurement is illustrated very nicely in a study by Piaget, Inhelder and Szeminska (1948/1960), in which they asked children to reproduce the exact location of a point situated in the upper right corner of a rectangle. Subjects were provided with various measuring tools, such as a ruler, a stick, strips of paper and pieces of string. The authors found that young children performed the task exclusively by eye, and that they generally disregarded suggestions to use the materials provided for measurement. Subjects' visual estimations of the location of the point were fairly accurate, except that they tended to confuse left and right, or top and bottom of the rectangle. When they did use the materials provided, they measured only the model and not their reproduction of it. Thus, they used the materials only as aids for making perceptual estimations, not as tools for constructing the copy. Older children focused on the interval between the point and the corner of the rectangle. They positioned the ruler on the model to connect the point to the corner, and then tried to preserve the orientation of the ruler as they moved it over onto the rectangle in which the point was to be reproduced. These children had thus objectivized the invisible interval between the point and the corner, and tried to reproduce it by means of a sensorimotor action. The oldest subjects located the point exactly by measuring its distance from both the horizontal and vertical sides of the rectangle, and acknowledged the need to perform measurements to solve the task accurately. It is important to note that the projection lines between the point and the sides of the rectangle are not actually visible; they are a construction of the child. They do not exist in the object, but have to be supplemented mentally or projected onto the object.

Two aspects of this experiment – the fact that young children are able to determine an object intuitively and their reluctance to use any tools other than their eyes – have been observed in more recent studies. In a task requiring children to balance different types of blocks, some filled with lead at one end, Karmiloff-Smith (1988) found that 4- and 5-year-olds successfully use propriocep-tive feedback to perform the task. However, they do not use information obtained from balancing one block for balancing the next one. They treat each block as a new problem, as a different perceptual Gestalt. On the other hand, 6- and 7-year-olds construct theories about the procedures for balancing the blocks and apply these theories rigidly across blocks and situations. They tend to fail more often than their younger peers because they ignore the positive and negative proprioceptive feedback from the object to improve their theories. Finally, the 8- and 9-year-olds are able to coordinate theories and proprioceptive feedback, and show the same level of success as the youngest subjects.

There are some interesting analogies between the changes in behaviour in the block-balancing task and those in the construction of drawings. The 4- and 5-year-olds' success in balancing blocks, based on using feedback from the physical Gestalt, closely resembles their accommodation to the Gestalt when they draw the outer visual contour of a model object. The 6-year-olds' rigid application of theories reminds us of the deformations and active decomposition of the Gestalt into separate parts, as in intellectually realistic cube drawings. Both in block-balancing and in drawing, these intellectual exaggerations seem to prepare the way for success in older children. Eight- and 9-year-olds' drawing methods, which include the construction of embedded contours and bifunctional boundaries, are evidence of the ability to coordinate knowledge of the physical, three-dimensional structure of an object and perceptual information about its viewpoint-specific appearance (Reith, 1988). This coordination of physical and visual dimensions of objects shows that older children have retreated from dealing directly with the physical Gestalt-like aspects of objects.

Children's reluctance to use measurement and explicit spatial axes systems, which implies the dissolution of the unity and individuality of objects, has also been brought out by Bryant (1982). He found that providing information that measurements improve the solution of a task did not convince young children that they should use measuring tools. Only in tasks where perceptual intuitions and measurement lead to the same result do children actually begin to make use of the tools.

The developmental change from Gestalt-like figurative thought to operational thought has specific consequences for the graphic depiction of three-dimensional space and human figures. For instance, Simó Teufel and Lange-Küttner (1993) showed that the emergence of spatial axes systems in drawings no longer allows for idiosyncratic depiction of the size of human figures. Reduction and a greater uniformity in size become necessary to group the figures in relation to an explicit axes system.

Figures 6.8 and 6.9 specify the graphic processes that emerge with the transformation of figurative thought. The tolerance for modifications of Gestalten, as well as the supplementation, differentiation and bending of explicit spatial axes systems enable children to simulate depth on a two-dimensional plane. They can now construct overlapping shapes to depict one object behind another, and vary the relative size of figures to indicate distance. They can also produce visually realistic, dynamic renditions of the human figure in their natural shape by

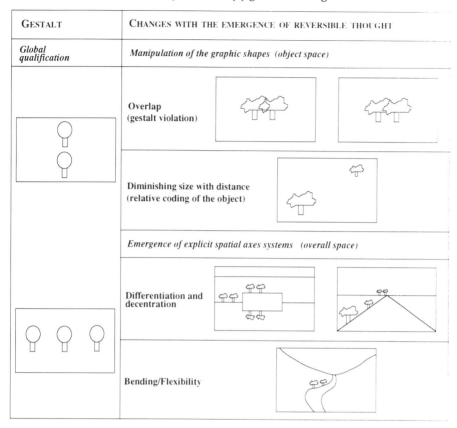

GESTALT	CHANGES WITH THE EMERGENCE OF REVERSIBLE THOUGHT
Global qualification	*Manipulation of the graphic shapes (object space)*

Figure 6.8 Figurative thought and operativity in the development of the graphic space concept

transforming primary geometric shapes into irregular forms, and by decentring and bending the invisible body axes.

To summarize, we have shown that visual realism in drawing does not emerge until age 8 or 9 because the graphic construction of the appearance and the correct geometric properties of objects requires a transformation of figurative thought. The emergence of operations allows the subject to deconstruct and reconstruct, to structure and measure both real objects and graphic forms. We have also given some examples of 4- and 5-year-olds' abilities to deal with complex visual configurations on a sensorimotor and perceptual level. This developmental unevenness, or *décalage*, between visual perception and the production of visually realistic depictions is the result of young children's tendency to conserve good visual forms and spontaneously to 'repair' them when they are perceived to be damaged (Metzger, 1936/1975).

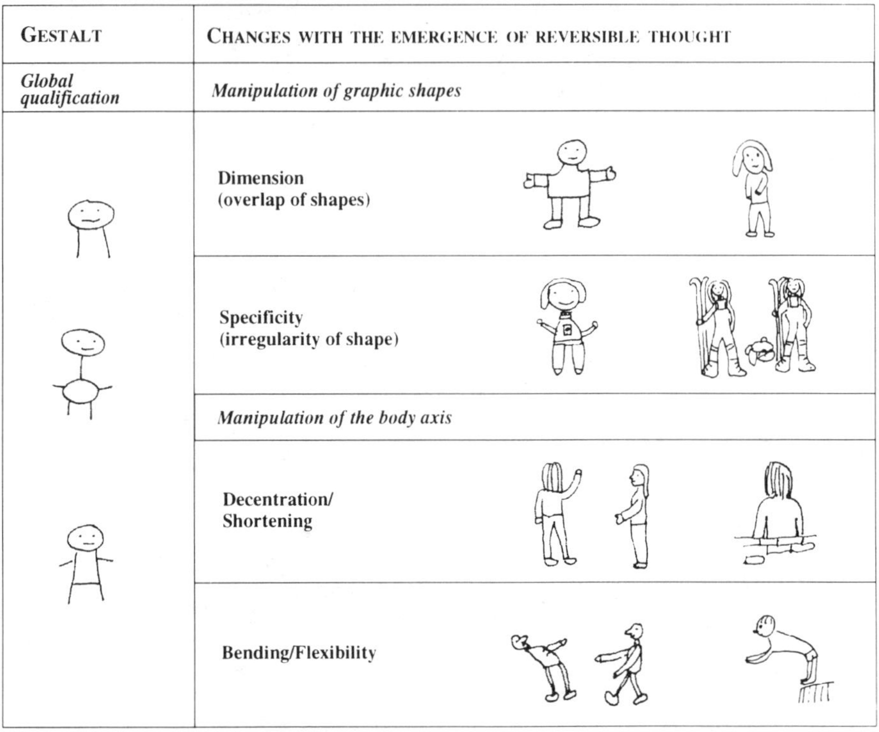

GESTALT	CHANGES WITH THE EMERGENCE OF REVERSIBLE THOUGHT
Global qualification	*Manipulation of graphic shapes*
	Dimension (overlap of shapes)
	Specificity (irregularity of shape)
	Manipulation of the body axis
	Decentration/ Shortening
	Bending/Flexibility

Figure 6.9 Figurative thought and operativity in the development of human figure drawing

Psychological distancing from natural perception: its facilitation and origins

The transformation of a visually given world by its assimilation into conceptual hierarchies and reference systems amounts to the creation of a psychological distance between subject and object. In other words, the subject's interaction with the world becomes mediated by an ever-growing number of conceptual structures. Must we then conclude that mediation by high-level conceptual processes is always necessary for successful performance in complex tasks, such as the production of drawings that render the visual appearance of objects and space?

Since the Italian Renaissance it has been known that accurate depiction of the visual projection of objects and scenes, or perspective drawing, can be facilitated by the use of various technical devices such as a da Vinci window (Dubery and Willats, 1983; Cox, 1992). A da Vinci window consists of sheet of glass placed in the fronto-parallel plane between the drawer and the model. While keeping a

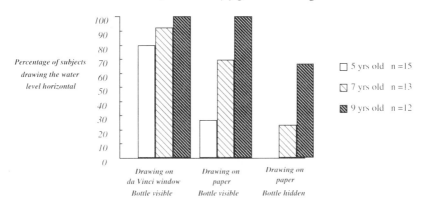

Figure 6.10 Percentages of subjects in each age group responding correctly to the water-level task in each experimental condition

fixed viewpoint by looking through a peep-hole, the drawer traces the outlines of the model directly onto the glass. This device facilitates the work of drawing in several ways. It allows one to 'extract' the two-dimensional visual image of a model and to act on it in an immediate manner. The image becomes tangible in the sense that one can place lines directly 'on top of' the contours and edges of the model. Moreover, there is no need to generate a mental description of the object to execute the drawing: one simply traces it, just as one might trace the figures in a photograph using transparent paper.

Reith, Steffen and Gillèrion (in press) studied the facilitating effect of this device in 5-, 7- and 9-year-old children. The model was a tilted jar containing coloured liquid. They chose this model because Piaget and Inhelder (1948/1956) have shown that below the age of 8 or 9, most children do not draw the water level horizontal: young children draw it as a scribble or a blob in the centre of the bottle; older subjects draw a line parallel to the bottom of the bottle even when the bottle is tilted instead of parallel to the ground (or to the table top on which the bottle rests). In the present study, subjects drew the bottle under three viewing conditions. In the first condition subjects drew it directly onto a da Vinci window, then on paper from memory, and finally again on paper but with the model in plain view. It was found that the number of correct depictions of the horizontal water level varied according to the viewing condition (Figure 6.10).

When tracing on the da Vinci window, almost all subjects, even 5-year-olds, drew the water level horizontal. In the free viewing and hidden model conditions, on the other hand, performance followed the same age trends as those reported by Piaget and Inhelder (1948/1956) and in replication studies (Beilin, Kagan and Rabinowitz, 1966; Perner, Kohlmann and Wimmer, 1984; Ackermann-Valladao, 1987).

Several conclusions can be drawn from this study. First, it shows that children draw the water level perpendicular to the sides of the bottle not because they actually see the water level perpendicular rather than horizontal, but because they refer an internal model which preserves the canonical orientation of the water. Second, it shows that young children are able to deal with the objective spatial properties of projective shape on a sensorimotor level. When tracing on the window, they can reproduce complex visual forms successfully, coordinating the outer and inner boundaries of objects: there is no false separation or deformation of the graphic forms denoting the bottle and the water. We believe this occurs because the da Vinci window situation allows the subject to treat the model as tangible. Third, the study demonstrates the effect of emerging conceptual structures on drawing performance. Nine-year-olds can reproduce the horizontal water level correctly without the help of the window because they are able to objectivize and measure the model by constructing a spatial reference frame of horizontal and vertical axes, and thereby transform a functional object into a metric extension. In other words, as children grow older they become able to distance themselves from the natural mode of perception in which objects are treated as bounded and functional.

The fact that especially young children seem to benefit from direct, physical contact with objects has been demonstrated in other studies. Cox (1986) showed that the frequency of visually realistic depictions of a model cube – drawings that show only the sides of the cube that are actually visible from the given vantage point – was significantly increased when children were first asked to place their finger on the visible sides of the cube. With this procedure, even 7-year-olds could be induced to use oblique lines to represent the receding sides of the cube. Bremner and Moore (1984) also found that the allowance of prior visual and tactile exploration of a model favoured the production of more advanced graphic constructions. Young children frequently included features of an object (the handle of a cup) which were more often omitted under the ordinary viewing condition.

We can conclude that the development of graphic competence seems to be essentially a function of the ability to override fixation on a perceived, visible, ready-made world, that is, to forgo exclusive dependence on figurative thought. Paradoxically, the ability to draw an object realistically improves as the psychological distance to the visual identity of the object increases. Whereas young children produce global qualifications of ready-made unitary Gestalten, older children depict objects as states of matter. They draw cognitive constructions reconciled with visually given entities. Thus, we come to the conclusion that visual realism is in fact a sophisticated form of intellectual realism. To modify the notion that intellectual realism is drawing what one knows while visual realism is drawing what one sees, we would suggest that visual realism is knowing what to change and what to ignore in visual information.

What are the origins of psychological distance-taking in early childhood? Are there early forms of distance-taking in infancy? Recent research indicates that *the discovery of the invisible* seems to be a significant factor for the dynamics of development from very early on. In studies on referential communication in mother–child interaction, Butterworth and Grover (1988) studied the development of the ability to attend to invisible objects. They showed that 6-month-old infants attend to objects their mother is looking at only when these objects are also in their own visual field. Thus, there is an early mechanism of joint visual attention. At one year of age, this ability becomes robust to distracting items. Only later do children turn away from their own visual field to find out about the objects behind them, which their mother is looking at. Butterworth and Jarrett (1991) point out that this sensorimotor process, which they term the geometric mechanism, is not a turning around but a turning away. Butterworth and Grover (1988) discuss the fact that the joint attention mechanism implies the ability to draw invisible lines between the mother and the referent of her gaze, that is, to construct spatial axes between figures. The turning away from the mother is believed to signal the child's discovery, on a sensorimotor level, of space as a container of all objects (Butterworth and Jarrett, 1991). It is a first generalization in which persons and objects are considered to be things in a common space.

The turning away might also be interpreted as a sensorimotor precursor to *visual reversibility* or mental rotation (Just and Carpenter, 1985), since it is a movement away from visible objects where they are to invisible objects wherever they might be. Reversibility is the property of a system that enables return to the point of departure. The toddler might anticipate a sequence that involves relinquishing the immediate sight of the mother, tolerating her invisibility, focusing on a third object which was previously invisible, and finally returning to the point of departure. Thus, we might say that it is not *looking per se* but on the contrary *looking away* that leads to the discovery of the invisible. This interpretation is in accordance with recent theories which consider cognitive development to be dependent on the ability *not to pay attention to* irrelevant and interfering stimuli (Dempster, 1992), or which consider the weighting of perceptual cues to be a crucial dimension in development (Friederici and Levelt; 1986; 1990). We believe that these phenomena – tolerance of the invisibility of the mother, interest in invisible objects, selective attention and the weighting of perceptual cues – might constitute precursors to psychological distance-taking.

We do not use the term precursor as literally as does Karmiloff-Smith (1992) when she argues that sensorimotor abilities cannot explain the acquisition of specific competencies such as language. Of course, to study domain-specific knowledge we need to take into account the particular problems within each domain. However, certain domain-specific processes may be facilitated by early changes in the subject's ways of relating to objects. For instance, the modification of simple geometric forms into irregular complex shapes, or the supplementation of human figures with spatial axes systems, imply the ability to maintain a psychological distance to objects, an ability that may also be a prerequisite in domains other than drawing. In other words, we believe it is necessary to specify and account for the changing styles of subject–object interaction.

To conclude, the development from global to articulated depiction is not due to a simple process of extraction of visual information from the world. It is the ability to establish a psychological distance from the immediate, natural experience of the world of objects that enables children to deconstruct and reconstruct their primary Gestalt-like apprehension of objects as meaningful functional units. This distancing process may be important in domains other than drawing, and may play an important role in conceptual development in general. To end, we quote Piaget:

> While a concept obviously obtains indispensable information from the corresponding perception, the concept is not, however, extracted from perception by simple abstractions and generalizations, as Aristotle believed, and as contemporary positivists still think. If this were the case, the concept, while more general, would be poorer than the corresponding perceptions because it would only have abstracted some of the perceptual aspects and neglected others. Actually, a concept such as that of perspective or that of a system of references or coordinates is a good deal richer than the projective perceptions or the perceptual coordinates, because it always entails a system of operations or transformations (classifications, seriations, correspondences, measurements, etc.). This operative aspect of concept is not reducible to the perceptual structures, it derives from sensorimotor structures or from structures of action in general. (Piaget, 1977, 22f)

Acknowledgements

Work on this chapter was supported in part by a research grant from the Jean Piaget Foundation for Psychological and Epistemological Research to the second author and by a habilitation grant from the Committee for the Advancement of Junior Scientists, Free University Berlin, to the first author. We thank Edith Ackermann at MIT for her insightful remarks on an earlier version of this chapter.

Chapter 7

A neo-Piagetian approach to children's drawings

Sergio Morra *University of Cagliari*

A brief introduction to neo-Piagetian theories

Neo-Piagetian theories flourished in the 1970s and 1980s, aiming to reconcile Piaget's findings with the new findings of information-processing psychologists and the criticisms raised by them to Piagetian theory. All neo-Piagetian theories posit a major role for *information load*; they suggest that the Piagetian tasks that define more advanced stages place a greater information load on subjects, and that increases in information-processing capacity with age enable progress through Piagetian stages (Pascual-Leone, 1970; Pascual-Leone and Goodman, 1979; Fischer, 1980; Halford, 1982; Case, 1985). Some neo-Piagetian theories also posit a major role for *cognitive conflict*, i.e. the need to overcome salient misleading information or overlearned habits in order to acquire Piagetian operational structures (see Pascual-Leone, 1987; 1989; Juckes, 1991).

Neo-Piagetian theories aim to account for a wider range of phenomena than classical Piagetian tasks only. Pascual-Leone's and Case's theories are presented here, because in the field of drawing they provide a framework for some theoretical modelling and experimental research.

The Theory of Constructive Operators (TCO: Pascual-Leone, 1987) posits a two-level architecture of mind. At the first level there are *schemes*, broadly divided after Piaget between *figurative* and *operative*[1] and regarded as the basic units of cognition. A scheme has a specific information content, and individual subjects' repertoires of schemes can be widely different; thus, schemes are also called 'subjective operators'. An important property of schemes is hierarchical organization: a scheme is a meaningful unit, and more complex schemes have simpler schemes as constituents. This seems particularly relevant in the analysis of children's drawings.

At the second level there are *general-purpose mechanisms*, without a specific information content, also called 'metasubjective' or 'silent operators'. Their functions are *increasing or decreasing scheme activation*, and allowing *formation of new schemes*. In formal notation they are designated with different letters. In this chapter, we consider learning mechanisms (C, LC and LM operators); a central attentional mechanism, whose limited capacity increases with age (M operator); a central inhibitory mechanism (I operator); a mechanism (F operator) that brings about field and s–r compatibility effects. On some occasions, different meta-subjective operators activate different, incompatible schemes; this can be described (and eventually experienced) as a cognitive conflict.

Learning mechanisms, according to Pascual-Leone (1976), allow (1) differen-tiation of old schemes by including more components in them, as in Piaget's accommodation (the *C operator*), or (2) a slow, experience-driven coordination of co-activated schemes into higher-order integrated units (*LC operator*); or (3) fast coordination in one or few trials of schemes co-activated by the M operator (see below) into superordinated structures (*LM operator*). When a component of an LC- or LM-acquired structure is activated, the other components tend to be activated as well. These structures often are at higher levels of abstraction than their constituent schemes.

The *M operator* is conceived as a mechanism, endowed with limited attentional resources, which activates a limited number of task-relevant schemes. Its capacity increases with age. Very young children can activate only a few sensorimotor schemes at a time (Pascual-Leone and Johnson, 1991; Alp, 1994), but representational schemes, emerging in the second and third year of life, would heavily tax the limited capacity of this operator. According to Pascual-Leone (1970), an average 3-year-old child has enough M capacity (i.e. capacity of the M operator) to activate a simple executive (e.g. a goal) plus one representational scheme, either figurative or operative. At the age of 5 years, the average M capacity would allow the activation of an executive plus two representational schemes and continue increasing in an approximately linear way, until the capacity of simultaneously activating seven schemes is reached during adolescence. The increasing size of M capacity is indicated as $e+1$, $e+2$, ... $e+7$, where e stands for *executive*. Several tests were proposed for measuring M capacity (Pascual-Leone, 1970; Case, 1985; Morra, 1994).

The *I operator* is complementary to M, in that it inhibits task-irrelevant schemes. It is called for when a situation tends to activate overlearned but misleading or interfering schemes, or whenever currently active information becomes irrelevant and must be suppressed. For a recent review, see Dempster (1992).

The term *F operator* refers to cognitive mechanisms producing as simple representations as possible. The organization phenomena described by Gestalt psychologists (Kanizsa, 1979), and those of stimulus–response compatibility (for a cognitive model, see Kornblum, Hasbroucq and Osman, 1990) would be accounted for by this sort of mechanism. A cognitive style such as field dependence/independence is explained by Pascual-Leone (1989) in terms of relative strength of the field and learning operators, on one side, and the central activation and inhibition operators on the other side.

Case (1985; 1992) modified the TCO in two main aspects. One goes beyond the scope of this chapter and concerns explanation of M capacity growth. The other concerns cycles in development. While Pascual-Leone proposed only one major qualitative shift in cognition with the emergence of representational schemes, Case (1985; 1992) suggested three changes, starting at the ages of 1, 3 and 9 years, with acquisition of schemes called *relational, dimensional* and *vectorial*. M capacity (called short-term storage space in Case's model) is measured in different ways for each cycle, corresponding to successive levels of cognitive schemes.

One can fairly say that Pascual-Leone's and Case's theories (except for minor differences in task-analysis procedures) yield the same predictions in the age range from 4 to 10 years (studied in most neo-Piagetian research on drawing). Outside this range, however, the two theories can make different predictions. Case's theory may prove of special interest in studying early stages of drawing development.

Figurative schemes in drawing

A figurative scheme is a unitary mental representation of an object or a state of affairs. By 'object' here we also understand an animate object, a class of objects or a specific part of an object. Figurative schemes often have a hierarchical organization including features, parts and functional properties of the unitary represented item.

It has long been thought, following Luquet (1927/1977), that children 'draw what they know' (as opposed to what they see), and that their drawings reflect their 'internal models' of objects. I believe that this position is no longer tenable and thus shall try to clarify the nature of figural schemes involved in children's drawings.

Freeman (1972) noted some problematic aspects of Luquet's account. For instance, Luquet reported *duplicité de types* in drawings, but one would not assume that a child that draws an object in two different ways has two different models of it. Kosslyn, Heldmeyer and Locklear (1977) showed that one cannot directly infer children's representations from their drawings, because these are different from what they select as good pictures of the represented objects. Golomb (1973) demonstrated that children spontaneously draw less than they know, but in proper conditions their knowledge is represented in drawings. Furthermore, drawing is sensitive to instructions (Barrett and Bridson, 1983) and communicative purpose (Light and Simmons, 1983). For these reasons, one can hardly speak of 'internal models' or figurative schemes *of the objects* as determinants of children's drawings.

Van Sommers (1984) studied the sources of individual stereotypes in drawing. A longitudinal study, in which subjects drew the same objects many times while being videotaped, showed that children conserve a drawing's visual appearance over repeated performance, while they change the order of drawing of parts and the direction of strokes. Also, embellishments and occasional changes, introduced in a drawing, are often preserved in later drawings of the same object. Furthermore, when children were induced to draw a given object in a particular way under experimental conditions, they tended to preserve some of the experimental drawing's peculiar features in their next drawings under standard conditions.[2]

Van Sommers (1984) concluded that drawing is a problem-solving activity, and what children store in memory is the *visual appearance of a previous satisfactory solution* (rather than, for example, a motor routine). When a child has found a satisfactory way of depicting, say, a bicycle, the visual aspect of the solution is remembered and reproduced as needed, until some new problem in bicycle representation is eventually encountered. Let us assume, then, that the repertoire of graphic figurative schemes used in drawing consists of mental representations of the visual appearance of previous solutions to pictorial problems. Creation of such schemes is considered later (see pp. 98–9).

A scheme is assumed to function as *a unit* and at the same time, is assumed to have *a hierarchical organization*. There is evidence for this view, for example, in studies on geometrical solids or knots (Caron-Pargue, 1985a; 1985b; 1987; 1992). Every drawing, even those by young children, is a meaningful unit and, with age, they become more articulated and differentiated. But the point of interest here is that early representational units, even though holistic and undifferentiated, do not disappear in development; they are still used as parts or components of subsequent, more articulated drawings.

Another line of research relevant to hierarchical organization of figurative schemes is Willats' (1985; 1987; this volume) analysis of denotation systems, or how objects and their features are mapped to picture primitives (i.e. elementary units of shape). Increasing mastery of denotation systems yields a more articulated hierarchy of parts in object depiction. Willats (1987) also notes that a child can intentionally distort regions (e.g. use obliques to represent the third dimension, turning a square into a diamond) only when regions are no longer picture primitives, because lines have taken this role. This account seems to agree with and complement Caron-Pargue's remarks on 'disintegration of shape'.

The studies reviewed in this section were not undertaken from a neo-Piagetian perspective; most of them take a classical information-processing framework. However, they are compatible with neo-Piagetian views, and indeed, help to clarify the nature of the figurative schemes that we assume in a child's repertoire. They are hierarchically organized analogous representations of the visual appearance of previous solutions to pictorial problems and become more complex with increasing age.

Operative schemes in drawing

An operative scheme is a mental representation of a transformation or the blueprint for an action that transforms (in a physical or symbolic way) objects or states of affairs. Operatives are assumed to be cognitive units, just like figurative schemes.

The simplest operatives are motor schemes. These are important in drawing, but not examined here (see Matthews, 1984; and van Sommers, 1984; 1989 for relevant studies). I assume that, when a child has acquired a graphic figurative scheme, the motor aspects of its translation on paper are fairly automatized, so that the subject must only monitor that all main components of that scheme are actually drawn. On particularly demanding occasions, however, children and adults can place the motor aspects of drawing performance under attentional control.

Another important class of operative schemes are those for representing spatial relations. For instance, a young child who strives to draw a face may think of placing a mouth under the eyes, and plan where to draw a round shape for the mouth. In this case, the mental representation of a round shape is a figurative scheme, and the mental action of planning its position is called an operative scheme. Operative schemes are also used for spatial relations between items; for example, it was often reported that 'above' on paper may stand for 'behind' in real world. In this case, the perceptual (figurative) scheme for 'behind' activates and releases the operative scheme for 'above'. As another example, consider a child who plans to draw a cat chasing a rat. Not only must the cat and the rat be drawn in appropriate orientation so that one can chase the other, but also be in appropriate positions so that it does not appear that the rat is chasing a cat. We consider the child's decisions on orientation and location of these items as activation of operative spatial placement schemes.

Strategies and drawing devices, such as hidden line elimination for representing a partially occluded object (Freeman, Eiser and Sayers, 1977), and other systems of drawing rules that mentally represent procedures to *modify* a figurative scheme (see, for example, Willats, 1977a; 1985) are also considered operative schemes.

It should be noted, however, that we regard a mental representation of a transforming procedure as an operative scheme, i.e. a functional cognitive *unit* only once it has been acquired in a subject's repertoire. For instance, a child can decide to place the mouth under the eyes only after learning how to draw one item under another, or use oblique projection as a scheme only after experiencing such a device. Until an operation has been learned or discovered, it is not represented as a scheme and can only emerge as an outcome of ongoing processes in problem-solving or drawing activity (see pp. 102–5).

Metasubjective operators in drawing

The role of learning in drawing is widely recognized (see Thomas, this volume), although few studies have attempted to distinguish it from other factors (but see Phillips, Hobbs and Pratt, 1978; van Sommers, 1984). We assume that different learning operators have specific roles. For instance, *inventing and acquiring a new scheme* involves LM learning (see p. 94). *Differentiating and enriching an existing scheme* may involve either the C or the LM operator, according to the availability or lack of facilitating cues in the environment. *Cultural influence*, such as familiarity with styles and cultural stereotypes, could take place through LC learning.

Consider how a *new* figurative scheme is acquired. Discovery may sometimes be accidental (*fortuitous realism*: Luquet, 1927/1977), or eventually a child is taught how to draw an item, in which case LM and C operators would be involved. But if *usually* a scheme is a mental representation of a previous solution's visual appearance, then how does one achieve that solution?

One possibility is modifying an existing scheme. A child who lacks a scheme for a goat may activate by default a dog's figural scheme, then consider the goat concept and its salient features, such as horns and beard; co-activation by the M operator of figurative schemes for the dog, the horns and the beard would result in planning to draw a 'horned and bearded dog', i.e. a goat, and in Lm learning of this scheme.

Another way is by relying on other representations than graphic figurative schemes, such as conceptual and perceptual figurative schemes. Children may attend to perceptual features of a model and try to imitate them in drawing strokes (Lurçat, 1985; Reith, 1988). Lacking both a model and a graphic scheme, however, only conceptual information can be available. Neuropsychological evidence shows that a drawing can be generated from even poor conceptual knowledge. Trojano and Grossi (1992) describe a visual agnosic patient who can accurately copy and operate on mental images, but is severely impaired in drawing from memory because he cannot recall the objects' perceptual features. However, he recalls the objects' functional properties and thus produces some kind of drawing. His drawings though, are poor and distorted, often containing errors; some resemble those drawings of young children called 'pre-schematic' by Lowenfeld and Brittain (1975). We may suppose that young children also try to represent symbolically the information that they can recall and say aloud to themselves. Normal children, of course, have the advantage of also being able to recall perceptual features, but usually they represent in drawings only a part of the information available to them (see Golomb, 1973). In this case, M capacity would first activate conceptual knowledge and then allow activation of graphic symbols for the most salient features in activated knowledge (eventually resorting to shapes learned in scribbling). The LM and C operators allow, at this point, learning of the newly generated scheme.

The counterpart of the foregoing argument is that some aspects of drawing are hardly acquired by learning alone. Drawing involves novel performance and problem-solving; explaining these by previous learning leads to a *learning paradox* (Pascual-Leone, 1980; 1987; Juckes, 1991). In short, if a cognitive structure explains a truly novel performance, and if one claims that it was learned, then one should admit that learning occurred without mental activity or overt behaviour. To solve the paradox, factors other than learning must be considered. In general, the TCO assumes that ongoing behaviour or cognitive processing depends on the currently most activated set of schemes, and that activation of schemes depends on numerous factors, of which learning is only one.

In planning and problem-solving, which often occur in drawing, the M operator would activate relevant schemes; if a figural scheme is well learned, an M capacity of $e+1$ suffices to retrieve it and monitor its motor and graphic rendition. Otherwise, the complexity of solutions would depend on the capacity simultaneously to activate several schemes; thus, a child's M capacity would set *an upper limit* to her or his performance.

Also well-learned but inappropriate schemes could be activated in problem-solving, or misleading information could be salient. These eventualities call for active inhibition of information that interferes with the solving of a problem. The theoretical prediction is that subjects with an effective I operator perform better in those drawing tasks in which misleading information tends to be activated.

However, creativity in drawing and art involves an ability *not* to inhibit information that appears irrelevant, but rather, to incorporate it in ongoing performance. Pascual-Leone (1983; 1984) speaks of Interrupt/Disinterrupt control processes, referring to the ability either to inhibit or abandon inhibition of irrelevant, misleading or incongruent information. According to Pascual-Leone, fluency tests may operationalize this ability. Thus, we expect fluency to be related to drawing creativity and graphic problem-solving.

The F operator tends to favour a simple solution compatible with the largest set of activated schemes; thus, it may have an ambiguous function in drawing and art. Sometimes it helps a balanced solution or a good Gestalt to emerge; but at other times it may encourage a biased compromise solution or a simple and inappropriate Gestalt. For instance, completion of a drawing is likely to be a compromise between intended meaning and available cues, which may induce response biases (see, for example, Freeman, 1980; for an analysis of such biases and compromises in Piaget's water level drawing task, see Pascual-Leone and Morra, 1991).

Detailed discussion of the role of the F operator in drawing goes beyond the scope of this chapter. Suffice it to say, on the grounds of Pascual-Leone's (1989) discussion of field dependence, that high-quality picture composition (see, for example, Golomb, 1992) may demand some characteristics of field dependence, such as a strong F operator that facilitates production of good Gestalten, and some of field independence, such as the ability to include several elements in a plan and disregard obvious solutions (i.e. strong M and I operators). These characteristics are probably found in subjects with an intermediate degree of field dependence and a flexible cognitive style.

Research on the M operator and planning of drawings

In earlier sections, I have considered how the various operators can be involved in drawing, and how the TCO yields testable predictions; emphasis was placed on the role of M capacity in solving drawing problems. Evidence on spatial problem-solving is reviewed here.

Dennis (1992) hypothesized that a capacity of 1 unit allows a child to plan drawings of unrelated objects; 2 units enables her to draw a foreground scene, depicting the relation between an object and its setting. In order to include a foreground and a background scene, 3 units are required, because a 'pointer' to a part of the scene must be stored while actually focusing on the other part; and 4 units allow spatially integrated drawings, with a middle ground that connects the fore- and the background.

To test these predictions, Dennis (1992) studied the performance of 4- to 10-year-old children, on tests of M capacity and on five drawing tasks: (1) Draw a man; (2) Draw a girl standing in a park next to a tree; (3) Draw two boys shaking hands in a park, with a fence just behind them; (4) Draw a man and a woman holding hands in a park, a baby in front of them and a tree far away behind them; (5) Draw a mother looking out of the window to see her son playing; she only sees her son's face, because he is peeking out from behind a tree. Tasks (1)–(5) were so designed as to embody the spatial relationships described above, and task (5) even more complex relations.

The results showed an increase with age in the ability to depict spatial relations, *which paralleled the increase in M capacity*. There was a correlation of 0.80 between M capacity and drawing score; with age partialled out (a strict test, because much true variance of M capacity is developmental, rather than due to individual differences) it dropped to 0.34, which was still highly significant.

While Dennis (1992) considered the overall spatial organization of a drawing, Morra *et al.* (1988) studied the planning of specific positions for different items before a drawing was made. We gave children, aged 6 to 11 years, M capacity tests and a drawing planning task with two conditions, free and constrained respectively. In the free condition, subjects were required to think of an interesting scene to draw and describe it verbally; they were then asked to point, on a sheet of white paper, to the positions where they would draw each item. Finally, they were allowed to make the drawing, which was scored for correspondence between the actual and the planned positions. (For a full account of the scoring rules see Morra *et al.*, 1988.) The constrained condition differed from the free condition in that in the first condition subjects were asked to include a number of specified items in their drawings.

We assumed that cognitive processing includes the following stages: deciding to represent a certain scene; activating the relevant figurative schemes; applying operative schemes onto figurative ones, in order to construct a spatial mental model of graphic space; and drawing, which in turn may suggest changes in the initial plan. When a child sets out to draw, M capacity limitations would create a bottleneck. A subject could remember the position of an 'anchor' element of the scene, placed in a salient position (e.g. in the middle of the sheet), and *no more other independent items than available units of M capacity*, in places encoded in relation to the anchor position.

We hypothesized different relationships between M capacity and planning scores in the two conditions. In the free condition, we expected an upper limit of $k+1$ positions in the plan of a subject with an M capacity of $e+k$, with a probabilistic model accounting for how many of these k units would actually be used. By contrast in the constrained condition, we expected that subjects with an M capacity of $e+k$ could include on average $k+1$ positions in their plans. A set of 12 quantitative predictions was derived from this model and was clearly supported by the data.

Other research studied the relation between M capacity and construction of spatial mental models according to verbal descriptions (Morra *et al.*, 1991), and planning maze routes in logo computer graphics (Arnold and Johnson, 1991; Johnson and Kane, 1992). In summary, although research on the role of the M operator in spatial planning is not extensive, all available evidence is in agreement with the neo-Piagetian predictions. Other theories would perhaps make less specific predictions, but might agree that the ability to hold a large amount of information is somehow related to planning. In the next sections, then, evidence for a more general validity of the M operator is presented. In the tasks reviewed below, however, performance is assumed to be multidetermined, M capacity being just one of the relevant factors.

Research on modification of figurative schemes

Consider how the M operator is involved in modifying a figurative scheme. One can remember the tenet that a scheme has a hierarchical organization. A methodological consequence follows, that according to research requirements, one can either focus on the global scheme or consider a set of its components. Two research lines are mentioned here. In one, on representing human movement, specific features are analyzed. In the other, on depiction of emotions, it seemed appropriate to keep evaluation at a global level, to compare diverse topics as humans, ships and trees.

Much available research, of course, considered children's ability to modify their drawings. The examples reported here, however, are specifically neo-Piagetian, because M capacity is considered, together with other relevant factors.

Morra and Perchinenna (1993) followed up Goodnow's study on drawing a person picking up a ball. Goodnow (1978) provided excellent descriptions of devices children used, but not a model of the cognitive and developmental processes involved. In a pilot study we produced a list of features that a child might alter in the human figure to show this movement. The list included elongated arms; both arms on the same body side as the ball; lower arm–trunk insertion; profile; height lowered at least by one third; body axis bent or inclined; bent knees; etc., for a total of 15 features. We also considered that children's drawings could be affected by the presence of a model or by the presence of contrasts that alert them to the relevant changes (see Davis, 1985; Cox, 1986).

We suggest that children with a larger M capacity can better attend to the relevant features and plan the intended changes; that a model facilitates the task by activating via perceptual input the human figure features (for which, however, a child must still find appropriate denotations in drawing); and that a contrast may alert children to the demand of showing what is peculiar to this representation of the human figure, i.e. activate task-appropriate executive schemes.

We gave children aged 5 to 8 years M capacity tests (see Morra, 1994) and two drawing tasks in which they had to depict a person standing upright and one who is picking up a ball. In some experimental conditions, two photographs were used as models; they represented a young woman, standing upright in one case and picking up a ball in the other. There were three conditions for contrast: (1) sequential, in which subjects were first asked to draw a person upright and then one picking up a ball, implicitly suggesting that the second drawing should differ from the first; (2) simultaneous, in which both photographs were placed together in front of the child, and the order of tasks was the same as above; (3) control, in which the person picking up a ball was drawn first, so that no contrast was elicited. Subjects were scored for the number of features in which the two drawings were differentiated.

The scores were significantly affected by age, model and contrast.[3] There was no significant interaction, suggesting that these factors affected independent psychological mechanisms. When M capacity was taken as the covariate, the effect of age became nonsignificant, suggesting that the effect of age on drawings was significant because M capacity increases with age, and that no other age-related change was important in this experiment. A correlation of 0.38 between M capacity and drawing scores was found; this dropped to 0.33 and remained highly significant with age partialled out. M capacity was particularly related to changes in features, such as bent body axis, curved line for the back and bent knees, which do not lend themselves to be added as on-the-spot solutions, but seem to require planning beforehand.

These results can be interpreted as showing separate effects of (1) activation of the schemes, which represent features of the human figure, by perceptual input; (2) activation of executive schemes by means of a contrast, implicit in the instructions; (3) M capacity, the ability to plan changes in the figurative scheme for a person before drawing it.

Representing an emotion is another possible reason for modifying a graphic figurative scheme. Even 4-year-olds have some ability to alter human face drawings to depict emotions (Zagòrska, 1988). By contrast, Carothers and Gardner (1979) showed that depicting a tree or a flower so that it shows happiness or sadness is a very difficult task for 7-year-olds. Our research (Morra, Caloni and D'Amico, 1994) focused on deliberate depiction of emotions.

We thought that finding a way to modify graphic schemes according to emotions is a problem-solving activity, at least if the topic is not a human or an animal, to which emotions can properly be ascribed. Thus, M capacity should be relevant to this scheme modification task. In addition, considering many different possible solutions may be an advantage; thus, we also considered subjects' fluency.

In a sample of children aged 6 to 11 years we found a clear relationship between M capacity and the drawing scores for a tree or a ship, but the correlation between M capacity and the drawing score for a person was nonsignificant. M capacity seemed to set an upper limit on drawing scores, but only for the topics that require metaphoric representation of emotions (ship and tree). These results suggest that M capacity is relevant to emotion depiction problems in which novel representations must be invented, while in the case of the human figure, in which knowledge of overt emotion manifestation is available, it is probably not needed to coordinate various cognitive units to invent a novel solution. Learning, rather than M capacity, may thus account for performance with human figure.

The correlations between verbal fluency and the drawing scores were significant and similar for all topics. Clearly, fluency is a different variable from M capacity, and one can suggest that Interrupt and Disinterrupt control processes are relevant to finding high-level, creative solutions to the pictorial problem, irrespective of whether a topic requires the invention of novel solutions, or fluency in retrieving relevant acquired information from long-term memory.

Research on cognitive conflict in drawing

The tasks described above may involve a conflict between a *habitual scheme* for persons or ships and *the demand to alter it for an unusual goal*. Thus, executive schemes and the M operator seem to work against learning effects. The conflict may be weak, however; and in a task that is probably facilitated by learning (drawing a person who shows an emotion) there was no conflict and the capacity of the M operator was almost irrelevant.

There are situations in which *misleading cues are very strong*, so that executive schemes and the M and I operators act *in opposition to* the operators F and LC

(Pascual-Leone, 1989; Pascual-Leone and Morra, 1991). In such cases, effects of both M capacity and field independence should be clearly manifest.

Drawing a partial occlusion may be a task of this kind, at least when the model consists of two similar shapes, one of which conceals a part of the other from view. Cox (1985; 1986) reported that partial occlusion drawing is not so difficult, even for preschoolers, when different objects make a pattern of something emerging from behind something else, but it is most difficult when the two objects are equal. Various reasons may account for this. First, similar objects can be encoded as a group, according to the Gestalt principle of similarity. Second, the simplest and most compatible response to 'a group of x' is repeating several times the graphic scheme for x; the F operator may induce drawing two complete and equal shapes. Furthermore, drawing a complete graphic scheme of x for the object in full view reinforces the habit of drawing an x in that way (LC operator), so that this habit is strongest at the point of drawing the partially occluded object. In fact, it is very common for children to draw two complete, equal, separate shapes.

In research with Angi and Tomat, we hypothesized two possible strategies by which a child can draw partial occlusion. One of them is an explication in neo-Piagetian terms of 'hidden line elimination' (Freeman *et al.*, 1977): a child must co-activate (1) a graphic figurative scheme for the occluded object, (2) a figurative scheme representing the hidden part, and (3) an operative scheme for mental deletion of a part from a graphic scheme.[4] This strategy has an M capacity demand of $e+3$.

Another possible strategy has a demand of only $e+2$, but also requires a quite analytical perceptual attitude. The involved schemes are: (1) a figurative scheme for the *visible part* of the partially occluded object, and (2) a spatial operative one for correct placement of (1) in the drawing.[5]

This analysis yields three predictions. First, field-independent subjects draw more partial occlusions, because any of the described strategies must compete with the tendency to draw complete shapes, i.e. the operators M and I must overcome F and LC; in addition, the latter strategy demands an analytical style. Second, subjects with an M capacity of $e+3$, who could follow any of the described strategies, draw more partial occlusions than subjects with a capacity of $e+2$, who can only follow the latter. Third, the effects of field independence and M capacity appear only if the model elicits a cognitive conflict. If a model is such that one object appears to 'pop out' from behind a quite different one, no such effect is expected, because the F operator might even facilitate the encoding of the scene as a partial occlusion, and *no misleading habit is reinforced*.

To test these predictions, we tested a sample of first-graders for M capacity and field independence, and presented them with four drawing tasks. The first two tasks involved simple shapes: a ball partially occluding another ball, a cube partially occluding a cone. The two other tasks involved toys with complex shapes: a car partially occluding another car, two singers whose heads emerged from behind a piggy bank. Each partial occlusion drawing scored one point.

The partial occlusion scores were submitted to analysis of variance; significant effects were found both for field independence and M capacity. Separate chi-square tests for each model showed an effect of M capacity or field independence only with the balls and the cars models.

More research is needed on cognitive conflict in drawing, but these results are promising evidence of predictive power of the TCO. They also agree with Pascual-Leone and Morra's (1991) discussion of the water line drawing, which poses a similar conflict for children. Just as in the research on emotion depiction the nonconflictual task (drawing a person with an emotion) yielded different results from the others, in the case of partial occlusion, too, only the drawing of models that elicit a cognitive conflict is affected by subjects' M capacity and field independence.

Perspectives and implications

Neo-Piagetian research on drawing is not yet extensive; however, I hope that the concepts and research summarized in this chapter will persuade the reader that there is something in it to justify further study. General psychological theories are often criticized on the grounds that they are too general. Neo-Piagetian theories are clearly general. But, contrary to theories shaped, say, as theories of perception, learning or logical thinking, which only were extended as 'general' psychological theories in time, the TCO (as well as the neo-Piagetian theories suggested after it) was shaped as a general theory from the start, based on invariances found in different areas of psychology. For this reason, it may have some undesirable complexity in posited concepts and interplay among them. On the other hand, it offers a chance to generate new questions, research paradigms and testable predictions.

In general, one should first identify the cognitive units (schemes) that are likely to be involved in a task by means of qualitative analysis of task demands and children's different types of performance. Then, hypotheses should be made on the kind of processes required: for example, problem-solving, cognitive conflict, knowledge retrieval, strategies or control processes. On these grounds, and taking into account the general theoretical propositions, one can make task-specific predictions.

An open problem is how to extend neo-Piagetian methodology to children's first steps in representational drawing. Golomb (1992) convincingly argues that children invent graphic symbols, a notion in line with Piagetian and neo-Piagetian views of early symbolic processes (see, for example, Piaget, 1946; Pascual-Leone, Johnson and Benson, 1989). The problem, however, is that (as noted in the first section) Case and Pascual-Leone suggest different accounts of schemes, and hence, of the action of the M operator between 1 and 4 years of age. Research in this area is possible, but only at the cost of struggling with more general theoretical problems.

Applied research is still called for. If much learning in drawing occurs through problem-solving, educational research may consider problem posing, i.e. the effects of confronting groups of pupils with representational and pictorial problems. Some techniques used in experimental research could lend themselves to applied use. For instance, Morra *et al.* (1988) found that older children, with greater M capacity, can plan more complex drawings, and noted that this seems to conflict with the often observed decline of interest in drawing. Perhaps, training methods that involve (among other exercises) our drawing planning task may help older children to improve their composition skills and thus maintain an interest in creative drawing. More generally, as far as psychological theory can capture artistic creativity, educators may wish to train some of the control processes involved in it (see, for example, Case, 1978; Pascual-Leone *et al.*, 1978).

In sum, neo-Piagetian theories seem to have a broad range of implications, both in research and applied issues, and they can generate articulated and testable predictions. For these reasons, one can hope that they will stimulate extensive activity in our field.

Notes

1. Executive schemes (see below) are regarded as a subclass of operatives.
2. There is evidence that in brain-damaged patients too there may be a strong tendency to apply overlearned graphic schemes, e.g. a rabbit may be drawn with a human face (van Sommers, 1989).
3. There was no significant difference between sequential and simultaneous condition.
4. This analysis of the required schemes was based on qualitative analysis of children's errors. For instance, a child who makes a transparency drawing would either lack scheme (3), or have insufficient M capacity to coordinate it with schemes (1) and (2); thus, the drawing shows which part is occluded, but it does not show that it is not visible.
5. In this case, if scheme (2) is missing, the visible part would be drawn as a separate entity, almost floating in the air: an unusual error, but one that is sometimes reported.

Chapter 8

The role of drawing strategies and skills

Glyn V. Thomas *University of Birmingham*

There is a naive tendency, to which we can all fall victim, to regard children's drawings as if they were direct translations of mental states and images onto paper. On further reflection, however, it should be obvious that drawing is not an easy skill to acquire and that young children generally become more skilful in their drawing as they grow older and more practised. In these very general terms then, we might expect that something of the developmental changes in children's drawing products can be attributed to their acquisition of drawing skills. In this chapter, I shall suggest that drawing development is largely accounted for by children's discovery or invention of pictorial schemata and of procedures for creating these schemata on paper. Evidence can be drawn from two areas: (1) topics that children themselves choose to draw and for which they can develop well-practised strategies; and (2) topics that are unfamiliar and thus pose new challenges.

Historical background

For many years, interest in children's drawing has been confined to the finished pictures that they make and not to the processes involved in making them. Many lay people still associate the study of children's drawing solely with clinical or educational uses of children's drawings for psychological assessment. The Goodenough–Harris 'draw-a-man' test, for example, is the product of a long tradition of using children's drawings of a human figure as a test of intelligence. The test is conceptually very simple. The child is asked to draw a man or a woman, and points are credited for each detail included, and for good alignment and proportions among the parts of the drawing. For our present purpose it is important to note simply that the test concerns only the appearance of the finished drawing.

A similar preoccupation with only the surface structure of the drawing is also characteristic of the various psychodynamically based systems of personality assessment using children's drawings. The classic text by Karen Machover (1949) on personality assessment via drawings of the human figure exemplifies this tradition. Features of the finished drawing are interpreted as though they were simple products of mental states. Thus, for example, a drawing which emphasized the mouth would be taken as indicative of concerns related to oral gratification and denial. It is not our concern to discuss here the use of these tests, although we can note in passing that their reliability and validity are open to question (see, for example, Thomas and Silk, 1990; Cox, 1993). The important point about these still popular assessments is that they concern only the final product of drawing and neglect the process of drawing itself.

Even within mainstream developmental psychology, the notion that children's drawings could be taken as a faithful reflection of mental contents was surprisingly influential until relatively recently. Piaget's account of children's drawing, for example, incorporated Luquet's earlier theory of drawing development (Luquet, 1927/1977; Piaget and Inhelder, 1956; 1969). These developmental accounts, like the traditional drawing tests, were almost totally concerned with the product of drawing and scarcely at all with the process.

In the last 20 years, however, it has been increasingly recognized by developmental psychologists that an account of drawing which considers only the product of drawing is at best incomplete (see Freeman, 1972). Since then, the importance of considering the drawing process has become widely accepted, largely because of the evidence and analysis presented by Freeman (1980). The importance of this development is considerable: not only is the drawing process of interest in its own right, but, as Freeman systematically documented, it can play a crucial role in determining the final product.

The importance of the drawing process

The traditional notion that drawing could ever be a straightforward translation of an internal representation or visual impression onto paper is easily dispelled by asking otherwise well-educated and accomplished adults to make a picture. To illustrate this point, I have sometimes asked classes of university students to make drawings of an animal such as a bull. Most of the resulting pictures contain gross inaccuracies of detail and proportion. Very often, for example, the relative positions of ears and horns on the bull's head are incorrect (see Gombrich, 1965). Van Sommers (1989) has reported corresponding problems and inaccuracies when undergraduate students are asked to draw a bicycle. I am sure that nearly all concerned would *recognize* the inadequacies of the drawings; so it is not strictly visual knowledge that is faulty (for further discussion, see Gombrich, 1965).

So why is drawing a picture often so difficult? The short answer is that successful picture-making depends on much more than simple knowledge of the appearance and structure of the subjects to be depicted, and requires practical skills that are specialized and quite unique to picture-making.

What is a picture?

It is easier to consider what special skills might be required to construct a picture if we have some conception of what a picture is. Defining what a picture is turns out to be a more complicated matter than you might think at first (see Gibson, 1979).

Some pictures, especially traditional Western oil paintings, are easy to think of as copies of the scenes they represent. This 'copy' theory, however, is clearly wrong in relation to children's drawing. The human figure drawings in Figure 8.3 below, for example, are easily recognizable, but depart radically from the appearances of real people.

A more defensible position is that pictures, although quite different from real scenes, *suggest* somewhat similar perceptual interpretations. The theory of perception underlying this view is that we construct perceptual interpretations from the light entering the eye.

The undoubted strength of this constructivist position is that it provides a framework for understanding the subjective component of much perception. The difficulty with this view is that it offers no clear criteria for judging one perceptual or pictorial interpretation against possible alternatives. I shall take the line that this constructivist approach gives us a useful starting point for understanding pictures, but that the account is incomplete.

Specifically, we need in addition to consider what it is that allows each of us to construct apparently similar perceptual or pictorial interpretations of a set of marks on a flat surface. No special learning seems necessary for people to be able to recognize the topics of many pictures. Hochberg and Brooks (1962) found that a young child without prior experience of identifying objects from their pictures was able to recognize correctly line drawings of a number of familiar objects. There have been similar findings from cross-cultural studies of people without prior experience of pictures. It seems likely, therefore, that our perceptual systems are so constructed as to dispose us to perceive lines in drawings as contours (see Kennedy, 1983; Kennedy, Nicholls and Desrochers, this volume).

This view of perception and picture perception casts pictures as props which help us create the impression – or even the pretence – that we are seeing the topic depicted (see also Walton, 1990). If pictures are essentially devices which stimulate perceptual interpretations, then children's drawing development can be seen as the discovery or invention of a variety of drawing devices which work as pictures. This constructivist approach to pictures seems particularly appropriate to children's early drawing, which is characterized by a marked lack of visual realism and allows for considerable subjectivity in interpretation.

The role of the schema in picture-making

What are the sources for the patterns and devices that children come to use to make their pictures? A popular answer is that the children develop pictorial skills on the basis of observation and knowledge of the world. Willats (this volume and 1981; 1985; 1987) has argued that there is a fundamental regularity in the translation from the structure of three-dimensional solids in the world to the two-dimensional denotation devices children use to represent them on paper. The occurrence of some regularity of this kind, however, does not necessarily mean that children draw pictures 'from life'. On the contrary, direct observation of children suggests that most, if not all of their spontaneous drawing is from memory or copied immediately from other pictures.

It is also a mistake to think that you can easily draw a scene on paper. The development of naturalistic styles of art came relatively late in the history of Western art, as did devices such as Dürer's perspective grid and sighting post to assist in drawing from life. The continuing employment of such devices is a further indication of just how difficult it can be to use reality as a basis for a picture.

If not drawn from life, how then can pictures be made? Gombrich (1960; 1977) has proposed that artists learn formulae for making pictures either by trial and error or by copying other pictures. He used the term 'schemata' for the formulae: they consist simply of patterns and marks which trigger pictorial responses in a viewer. A good but crude example of such a schema is the flattened 'm' shape which many children learn to use to signify a flying bird, another is the stacking of two circles to create an impression of a cat (see Figure 8.1).

If we turn to the history of art, we find considerable evidence for the importance of schemata and the production strategies for creating pictures out of them. Gombrich (1960; 1977) has argued that even the most accomplished professional artists are heavily dependent on a relatively limited range of drawing schemata. Because there is no easy route to the discovery of effective pictorial schemata it should be no surprise to find that many artists learn to make pictures simply by copying other pictures.

In the past, pictorial schemata were often taught explicitly; for example, the pattern books for medieval apprentices to copy and to learn from. Once mastered, these schemata could be varied and recombined to produce 'original' works.

The role of such schemata can be seen in even the most accomplished and visually realistic pictures (Gombrich, 1960; 1977). On close examination the

Figure 8.1 Flying bird and sitting cat, examples of drawing formulae often taught to Western children

apparent naturalness and diversity of the expressions and poses of the figures depicted in many traditional Western paintings can be seen to be illusory. Careful analysis reveals the deployment of a relatively limited range of schemata, used with skill, but which were essentially production routines to create particular visual effects. By comparison, the range of poses and expressions to be found in a selection of snapshot photographs will be very much greater. In practice, even artists who self-consciously try to resist the influence of traditional styles and techniques, as Constable did, for example, cannot avoid using pictorial schemata derived originally from previous pictures (Gombrich, 1960; 1977).

In relation to children's drawing, the importance of having a schema in order to make a picture is nicely illustrated by Phillips, Inall and Lauder (1985). In this study, 6–7-year-olds were asked to make a drawing in perspective of a pyramid and a cube which they viewed in oblique projection through a sighting tube. The children's first attempts at drawing oblique views of these relatively unfamiliar topics were generally quite inadequate. Subsequently, some of the children were explicitly taught a sequence of pencil strokes for creating an appropriate perspective drawing of one of the solids (cube or pyramid), the other children were given instruction on the visual properties of that solid. Teaching on making a drawing produced significant improvements in the drawing of the solid on which the instruction had been based. There was no appreciable generalization to drawings of the other solid. There was no significant effect on drawing quality of instruction on the visual properties of either of the solids.

To sum up, better visual knowledge of the object to be depicted had no effect on quality of drawings. Specification of a sequence of pencil strokes to generate a drawing was helpful, but did not generalize to drawings of another topic. Phillips *et al.* suggest that making a drawing requires not visual knowledge of an object, but a specific 'graphic description' for making a picture of that object. The particular problem posed by geometrical solids is that it is not easy to derive an effective graphic description from knowledge of the three-dimensional solid. In the language of the present chapter, I would say that this study nicely illustrates that a picture is not a straightforward copy of its referent but has to be constructed using a pictorial schema – what Phillips *et al.* have termed a graphic description.

Early drawing schemata

Kellogg (1970) has recorded many examples of children's early drawings. Between the ages of 18 months and 3 years, many children begin to make marks on paper and progress to a variety of more complex patterns and combinations of forms. Kellogg herself did not consider these drawings to be representations of anything, although this conclusion may be premature. Both Matthews (1984; 1990) and Campbell and Harrison (1990) have argued that at least some of these early scribbles, though not easily recognizable to adult observers, may have been intended as representations by the child artist who produced them.

With very young children the evidence for this conclusion is often indirect and not decisive. With slightly older children, the representational character of their drawing is less in doubt. The child declares that the drawing is a picture, and nominates the topic that it represents. The visual resemblance between picture and nominated referent is often fairly minimal. The looseness of this relation allows the child to change her interpretation of the same drawing from one occasion to the next (see, for example, Luquet, 1927/1977; Freeman, 1987). Indeed, 3-year-old children often complete a drawing before declaring what it is a picture of, a phenomenon termed 'fortuitous realism' by Luquet (1927/1977).

Although the nominated topics of such drawings can be very varied, the range of forms comprising the drawings themselves is relatively limited. Kellogg (1970), for example, identified only 20 basic types of scribble in her collection of over 8,000 children's drawings. It seems reasonable to suppose that the child develops a limited set of drawing procedures which yield a graphic vocabulary of simple shapes. These shapes – the ubiquitous circle, for example – are then used for a wide variety of representational purposes. (See Figure 8.2 of a house, man and dog – all drawn with circles.)

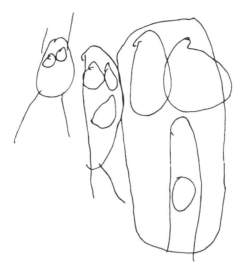

Figure 8.2 Drawings of a house, a man and a dog by a 4-year-old girl, showing the use of a common schema for each topic (from Thomas and Silk, 1990)

Arnheim (1956/1972; 1974) and subsequently Golomb (1992) have argued that there are perceptual and aesthetic reasons for the child's selection of these shapes to make pictures. This may be so, but the fact that these shapes appear regularly in children's drawings is not good evidence that children find them aesthetically satisfying (see Freeman, 1980). As Thomas and Silk (1990) have argued, circles may be ubiquitous in children's early drawing simply because they are pictorially useful shapes which are *easy to make*. The production decisions for drawing a circle, for example, are where to start, which direction to take and how big. The mechanical movements in circle drawing seem to be smooth and relatively easy for most people, in comparison to, say, drawing a diamond (see Laszlo and Broderick, 1985).

The development of schemata for pictures of people

First drawings of a human figure are often the primordial circle already referred to, sometimes with the addition of scattered marks within the perimeter to represent facial features or other details. The subsequent development of this form into better articulated and more accurately detailed figures is well known (see Figure 8.3). Briefly, the first step beyond a simple circle is normally the addition of two trailing legs to produce the classic 'tadpole' drawing. Sub-

Figure 8.3 Drawings of a man and a dog (from Silk and Thomas, 1986)

sequently, a differentiated head and trunk will be drawn, sometimes with arms added, and progressively in older children the figure will become more detailed and better proportioned.

There are several pointers to what may be needed to construct a drawing in the characteristic sequence of development illustrated in Figure 8.3.

Figure 8.4 Drawings of (a) Santa Claus; and (b) a policeman made by a girl aged 4
years

First, it seems rather unlikely that children's knowledge or mental description
of a human figure develops in the way that these drawings develop. It is scarcely
to be conceived, for example, that 4-year-olds actually believe that there are
people with arms on the sides of their heads (see Freeman 1980; 1987). Indeed,
when confronted with these anomalies, children will happily admit that their
drawing does not always accurately reflect the way they know things are (see
Gardner, 1980; Freeman, 1987). These facts suggest that factors other than the
underlying mental description may be responsible for the peculiarities we have
noted.

Second, just like the circle formula, the later, more elaborated drawings are
often used as general purpose pictures. Sometimes a differentiating 'marker' –
such as a hat – to identify the figure will be included (Figure 8.4), but otherwise
the standard formula is used to depict everyone (again, see Figure 8.4). The
obvious use of general-purpose forms for a variety of pictures has been widely
commented on and reflected in the term 'schematic', which is often used to
describe the drawings of children aged from 3 up to 8 years. The argument in the
present chapter is that all pictures are schematic; but in some pictures the
underlying schema is more obvious than in others.

Culture, schema and copying

I have suggested that the schemata children use for drawing pictures become
more elaborated and better proportioned with increasing age and experience of

the drawer. Some of this development is likely to be a result of improved motor control and planning ability. This seems an unexceptional conclusion. More controversial, however, is the suggestion that much of children's drawing development is based on copying pictures made by others.

As noted above, children seldom, if ever, choose to draw from life. Although their pictures are often generated in the absence of an immediate external model, some investigators have reported that the principal sources of inspiration for most children's drawing can be traced back to other pictures the children have seen and copied (see, for example, Wilson and Wilson, 1977). In this study, drawings made by a sample of teenagers were in almost every case found to be based on some other picture that the drawer had seen previously and then copied and adapted.

Further evidence obtained by Wilson and Wilson suggests that the same conclusion is true for younger children. Children in an Egyptian village studied by Wilson and Wilson (1984), for example, used a very restricted graphic vocabulary. They made drawings of people consisting of a few distinctive shapes for head and trunk, and standard ways for drawing the limbs. In another study, Wilson and Ligtvoet (1992) found distinctively different formulae and styles adopted for drawing trees by children aged 7–9 years in several different cultures. Such differences must reflect differences in culture and education. Wilson and Ligtvoet argue that the most significant cultural influences were the different pictures available in the different cultures, as models for the children to copy.

It must be said that the notion that children learn drawing skills by copying other people's pictures is contrary to a tradition of art education that values children's art primarily as self-expression (see Duncum, 1988; Wilson, 1992). While slavish copying might well be stultifying, children who are discouraged from copying altogether may be missing an important route to the acquisition of drawing skills.

To sum up this section, several studies confirm the conclusion that children's drawing is significantly influenced by the pictures that are available in their environment. This evidence reinforces the argument that schemata, copied from past pictures or discovered and developed by trial and error, are the essential basis for picture-making in both children and adults.

How the schema constrains the picture

It could be argued that children make simple schematic drawings because that is the way they like their drawings. I shall argue, on the contrary, that the character of early drawings arises principally from production limitations, although children's aesthetic and pictorial preferences for particular configurations should not be dismissed altogether.

I have argued that a schema is needed to get started at all on the process of making a picture. To that extent, knowing how to produce a schema makes it possible to create a picture. It is inherent in the use of schemata, however, that they introduce constraints on the kinds of picture that result.

Children's drawing is constrained principally because they have at their disposal only a small range of schemata, and because they are relatively limited in their ability to adapt these schemata to make different pictures. One line of evidence that reveals children's limitations in both these ways comes from their attempts to draw something which they have seldom if ever attempted to draw before.

Some years ago, Angèle Silk and I asked children of different ages to make drawings of a man and a dog (Silk and Thomas, 1986). The youngest children made man and dog drawings to the same basic formula; older children progressively differentiated them. The influence of the same basic schema used for both man and dog is quite evident. In an analysis of detailed features we were able to show that dog drawings – even quite well-developed ones – displayed many human features. The human eyebrows in one of the dogs shown in Figure 8.3 are a good example of this. In contrast, drawings of a man seldom if ever displayed any dog features. This asymmetry in shared features strongly suggests that early dog drawings are based on the children's formula for drawing a human figure. Presumably, the youngest children, who lacked a specific schema for drawing a dog, simply borrowed and adapted the already familiar schema for drawing a human figure (see Graewe, 1935; Goodnow, 1977). The perpetuation of inappropriate human features in the dog drawing can be considered an example of 'conservatism' (see van Sommers, 1984).

The occurrence of conservatism is interesting because it reflects the influence of the drawing procedure rather than the underlying mental description children have of dogs. (Most children must be very familiar with dogs, and know that they do not really possess the human features which appear in their dog drawings.) When drawing the dog the child artist has to begin by using the already known schema for a more familiar subject matter, and adapts it where possible to fit the new topic. A drawing schema generally has a momentum of its own, with the result that features of the old topic are conserved in the picture of the new.

The same phenomenon can be seen in adult art. Gombrich (1960; 1977) records how medieval drawings and woodcuts of exotic animals 'drawn from life' often contained features of contemporary domestic animals which the artists already knew how to depict.

The constraints on differentiation imposed by the schema can also be seen in a study of size differentiation. In the man and dog study just described (Silk and Thomas, 1986) we found that even the youngest children were able to differentiate their man and dog drawings by size of figure; dogs were drawn smaller than men. This differentiation contrasts with the lack of difference between the man and dog drawings in other respects. What is interesting is that the size difference could be implemented without modifying the basic schema for the figure. We take this result to indicate that the general lack of differentiation of the youngest children's man and dog drawings does not necessarily indicate a lack of desire to make the drawings distinguishable, but rather reflects the constraints imposed by adopting the same basic schema for both the figures.

A striking feature of children's drawing up to about the age of 6 years is the predominance of canonical views (views that best display the characteristic or defining features of the object). Ives and Rovet (1979), for example, report that children will often persist in drawing canonical views regardless of the orientation of the model they have been asked to draw. It is often claimed that this tendency to draw canonical views of objects reflects a preference for such views, perhaps based on an implicit conception that good pictures should display the typical and defining features of the objects portrayed. While this interpretation may be partly correct (see Davis, 1983), it seems to me that another powerful factor must be children's ability (or lack of it) to produce other views.

Children's early drawing development seems to consist more of the acquisition of discrete graphic formulae (schemata) for specific topics than of the development of generic drawing skills which can be deployed for drawing pictures of a range of topics. Recall that Phillips *et al.* found that teaching children to draw a cube failed to transfer to their drawings of a pyramid. The study of man and dog drawings (Silk and Thomas, 1986) illustrates that the availability of graphic formulae can be more important than preferences for particular views.

In this study we found that the youngest children drew dogs in front view rather than in the side view favoured by older drawers and which provides a canonical picture of a quadruped. It seems unlikely that the younger children had not yet acquired a preference for canonical views, because in their drawings of other topics – such as the human figure – the canonical bias was almost universal. The obvious answer is that canonical views are attractive for unskilled artists because the resulting pictures are more likely than noncanonical views to be easily recognizable. Consequently, when all other considerations are equal, the schemata children acquire will provide canonical views. When the drawing is of an unfamiliar topic for which the child has no established schema, then the view that emerges will depend on the schema that is borrowed and adapted. Young children will draw dogs in a noncanonical front view if the schema on which the dog drawing is based is an adaptation of the front view schema for drawing a human figure. Similarly, where canonical views are technically hard to produce – in drawing a cube, for example, the canonical oblique projection is notoriously difficult – then other solutions will be adopted (Freeman, 1986; Thomas and Silk, 1990).

Executing a drawing

A drawing has of necessity to be constructed in a linear sequence, one step at a time. The planning and execution of the various steps in a drawing sequence are a complex skill, and one which cannot necessarily be derived from just looking at the topic to be drawn.

In the nature of things some drawing sequences are easier than others. Van Sommers (1984) has discussed how, for example, in drawing a sun with radiating rays it is inherently easier to draw the disc of the sun first and then add the rays than to draw the rays first and subsequently draw in the disc of the sun. Similarly, when children make a drawing of a human figure, most will first draw the outline of the head before adding details of eyes, nose and mouth. These considerations comprise what van Sommers (1984; 1991) has called the 'practical logic' of drawing. I shall present next an example of the influence of sequencing decisions on the structure of the final picture.

Most children adopt a top-to-bottom sequence in making a drawing. This procedure has the advantage that the parts of the drawing already completed are not obscured by the drawing hand, and are thus available as positioning cues for the remainder of the drawing. The adoption of this top-to-bottom sequence in drawing procedure can have a crucial influence on the configuration of the final picture.

Thomas and Tsalimi (1988) examined the well-known exaggeration of the size of the head relative to the trunk in children's drawings of a human figure (see Figures 8.3 and 8.4). Most of the children in their sample began by drawing the head and then added the trunk and legs. In their initial positioning of the head, however, many of the children left insufficient space on the paper for a visually correct rendering of the rest of the body. When some of the children were persuaded to start their drawings with the trunk then in every case the resulting figure was more accurately proportioned (see Figure 8.5). What these results suggest is that a notable feature of young children's drawing – exaggeration of the relative size of the head – is due at least in part to a space planning problem inherent in a procedure in which one of the smaller elements is drawn first.

Changing the drawing sequence

The results of the Thomas and Tsalimi experiment also indicate that some aspects of the drawing procedure – in this case order of executing the steps – can be modified, but with significant consequences for the configuration of the final picture. Golomb (1992) has also reported that the order of drawing the parts of the human figure can be modified, on request, in children aged 5 years and older.

The extent to which the sequence in which children execute their drawings can be varied is a matter of some debate. Freeman (1980) has reported that children younger than about 4 years are generally unable or unwilling to vary the sequence in which they draw the head and trunk of a human figure drawing.

Additional support for the view that children will not or cannot readily vary the sequence of their drawing comes from arguments and evidence presented by

Figure 8.5 Effects of order of drawing head and trunk on their relative proportions (from Thomas and Tsalimi, 1988)

Karmiloff-Smith (1990). In this paper she presented data from a study in which children aged between 5 and 6 years and between 8 and 9 years were asked to make drawings of a house, a man and an animal, and then of a house, a man and an animal 'which does not exist'.

Older children successfully produced a variety of solutions to this unusual request, but it is the responses of the younger children that are of more relevance to the present discussion. Nearly all the younger children made drawings of houses, men or animals 'which do not exist' by reproducing their characteristic drawing for each topic, and then adding some novel feature afterwards to make it different. An implication of this result is that the children's production formulae for making the pictures were inflexible and resistant to change.

Figure 8.6 Man with two heads, drawn by 3-year-old girl

Karmiloff-Smith argued that children's performance on these drawing tasks illustrates some general constraints on representational change and flexibility in young children. Karmiloff-Smith proposed that both drawings and internal representations develop from sequentially fixed lists into flexibly ordered sets of manipulable elements. The important point for our discussion is the conception of the origins of picture-making that Karmiloff-Smith presents; that is, the production of schematic pictures by means of a habitual sequence of actions which cannot be changed, but has to be run off in its entirety.

As further evidence for the immutability of the younger children's drawing sequence, Karmiloff-Smith described what happened when some of these children were asked to draw a man with two heads. In nearly all cases the children first drew a conventional man with one head and then added a second head beside the first. Karmiloff-Smith found that most of her small group of 5- and 6-year-old children could not then prevent themselves from adding a second body, arms and legs and so forth to go with the second head (see Figure 8.6). It was as if once started on the sequence by drawing the second head the children were unable to interrupt it. While this result seems convincing, further work on this question at Birmingham has found more flexibility in young children's drawing procedures than that suggested by Karmiloff-Smith's results.

More research seems to be needed to explore the flexibility of drawing procedures at different stages of children's drawing development. Some interesting results reported by van Sommers (1984) seem to suggest that children attempting to draw something they have seldom, if ever, drawn before show more variability from one drawing to the next than do children following well-practised procedures for drawing familiar topics. This finding suggests that apparent inflexibility may sometimes arise from habit rather than limits to cognitive capabilities.

Concluding remarks

This chapter presents ideas, evidence and arguments drawn largely from Peter van Sommers' studies of graphic skill (van Sommers, 1984), Norman Freeman's work on strategies of representation in children (Freeman, 1980) and Ernst Gombrich's analysis of picture-making in art (Gombrich, 1960; 1977). While there is admittedly an underlying perceptual basis for perceiving pictures in blotches and lines on a flat surface, the main focus of the present chapter has been on the graphic formulae and motor skill required to make them.

Chapter 9

Children's understanding about pictures

Rebecca Nye, Glyn V. Thomas and Elizabeth Robinson
University of Birmingham

It may at first seem strange to suggest that young children could have difficulty understanding pictures. From the earliest age, most children – at least those in Western cultures – are surrounded by pictures and appear to have little difficulty identifying their topics. Moreover, many children devote much time and energy to producing pictures in their painting and drawing. On reflection, however, perhaps this early apparent facility with pictures should arouse our suspicions. There are conceptual complexities in pictures that might well be difficult for young children to understand. In particular, a picture has two identities, being both a thing in itself (e.g. a page of a magazine, a painting in a gallery or an advertising poster) but at the same time also referring to something else (its referent).

As Gregory puts it: 'Pictures are unique among objects; for they are seen both as themselves and as some other thing, entirely different from the paper or canvas of the picture' (Gregory, 1970, p. 32). Therefore, while young children might readily recognize what a picture is of (the referent), they could be expected to have difficulty appreciating the *two* identities of pictures and the relation between them.

The dual identity of a picture is, perhaps, most salient when a picture has an immediate physical referent – a portrait of a real person, for example. Nevertheless, even a picture which has no 'real' referent – a picture of unicorns, perhaps – has a dual identity in essentially the same way. Most adults have no trouble grasping this dual identity of pictures. Although they frequently attend only to the referent of a picture and overlook its identity as a thing in itself, adults can normally attend to either aspect of a picture when required to do so, and have no difficulty keeping separate the properties peculiar to each of these identities. The holding of these distinctions is, of course, required for a full understanding

123

of all forms of representation, including verbal symbols and mental representations, as well as pictures.

Given that the distinctions required for a full understanding of pictures are quite complex, it would not be too surprising to discover that the apparent ease with which even very young children respond appropriately to pictures masked a conception of pictures rather different from that held by most adults. Some early studies of the development of understanding about representations have in fact suggested that preschool children experience difficulty in distinguishing between representations and their referents in the way adults are able to (Piaget, 1926/ 1929; Kohlberg, 1969; Broughton, 1978). Piaget (1926/1929), for example, concluded that young children have 'a spontaneous and immediate tendency to confuse the sign and the thing signified'. This confusion in children's thinking came to be known as 'childhood realism'. In the same vein, but more specifically, confusion between pictures and their referents has also been termed 'iconic realism' (Beilin and Pearlman, 1991) and 'syncretism' (Liben and Downs, 1992).

More recently, however, the prevalence of the phenomenon of childhood realism has been strongly challenged by Wellman and Estes and their associates (Wellman and Estes, 1986; Estes, Wellman and Woolley, 1989). In their studies they focused, as Piaget had done, on children's abilities to distinguish between mental and physical entities (e.g. distinguishing the properties of a thought of an icecream from the properties of a real icecream), and concluded that realist confusion was virtually nonexistent in preschool children.

It is against this background that we shall review research into children's conceptions about pictures. In particular, we shall consider whether Wellman and Estes' dismissal of childhood realism in their studies can be extended to children's understanding about pictures.

There are at least three areas in which children might be expected to display confusion (realist thinking) concerning pictures and their referents. Specifically, young children who confuse picture and referent might:

1. Expect a picture to *share the nonvisual properties* of its referent (e.g. a picture of the sun to feel warm).
2. Expect a picture to *share the fate* of its referent, and possibly the referent to share the fate of the picture (e.g. the milk in a picture of a glass of milk to disappear if the milk from the real glass is drunk, or a flower to die if its picture is destroyed).
3. Have difficulty when required explicitly to attend to the *dual identity* of a picture (e.g. collapsing the appearance and reality of a picture of a flower, by stating that the picture both looks like and really is a flower).

Shared properties

Understanding about pictures as representations can be thought of as arising out of a number of subsidiary accomplishments (see, for example, Thomas, Nye and Robinson, 1994). These accomplishments emerge at successive points in development. First, it is necessary to recognize some degree of *correspondence* between a picture and its referent. There is now a considerable body of evidence that very young infants will respond similarly to realistic pictures and their referents (see, for example, a review by Beilin, 1991). As Hochberg and Brooks (1962) have argued, early recognition of a picture could be based largely on its perceptual similarity to its referent, but we can also allow for the learning of conventional correspondences (Goodman, 1976). Whatever the basis of the recognition, infants might simply regard the picture as identical to its referent, or perhaps a substitute for it.

Such children might not distinguish at all between picture and referent and thus would be displaying an extreme form of what Piaget (1926/1929) described as childhood realism. As we have noted, adults can and do normally distinguish between pictures and their referents. To establish that children understand pictures as representations, therefore, it is necessary (but not sufficient) to show that in addition to recognizing a correspondence between pictures and their referents they can also *discriminate* between the two. A number of studies using habituation techniques have tested the ability of infants to distinguish between photographs and their referents, and in general it appears that an ability to make this discrimination normally develops between 3 and 6 months of age (see DeLoache, Strauss and Maynard, 1979; Beilin, 1991). It is possible, however, that realist thinking is not outgrown abruptly but evolves gradually, so that children show progressively more discrimination between representations and referents as they grow older. Given Wellman and Estes' (1986) challenge to the existence of realist confusion concerning mental representations, it may well also be the case that some discriminations are more easily mastered and appear earlier for some situations and forms of representation than for others.

With regard to pictures, it is only a very basic and simple achievement to detect that there are differences between pictures and their referents. The mastery of such a discrimination in infancy does not, of course, amount to a full reflective understanding about pictures as representations. As Woolley and Wellman (1990) and Perner (1991), amongst others, have pointed out, children who discriminate between pictures and referents might simply treat pictures as a variety of the real thing they represent, perhaps a substandard version of it.

Consistently with this argument, Thomas, Nye and Robinson (1994) found that 3- and 4-year-olds generally make few errors when asked to sort mixed sets of pictures and real things into the appropriate categories (e.g. when asked to point to all the pictures in such a set they made no more errors than when asked to pick out all the items in some other category, such as toys).

Moreover, there is little evidence that very young children have difficulty discriminating between the specific *properties* of referents and pictures in their everyday encounters with them. There are, however, a few anecdotal accounts which suggest that children may not always distinguish pictures and their referents. Perner (1991), for example, cites a toddler, aged 16 months, who tried to 'put on' a picture of a shoe.

Further evidence that confusion may sometimes occur comes from a longitudinal study by Ninio and Bruner (1978) of the responses to pictures of a child between the ages of 8 months to 18 months. In the early stages of the period studied, the child tried to manipulate, grasp or scratch pictured objects on a page, but as he grew older these behaviours became steadily less frequent. This report suggests that very young children have difficulty in regarding a picture as 'standing for' its referent, rather than being another example of it, and that the development of the ability to treat them in this way may in fact be facilitated by experience of pictures which highlights the distinctiveness of the picture's properties from those of the referent. Against the background of these limited reports, Beilin and Pearlman (1991) carried out several studies *explicitly* to investigate the extent of young children's confusion of the properties of pictures and their referents. They presented children aged from 3 to 5 years with real objects (such as a baby's rattle, a wristwatch) and life-size colour or black and white photographs of the same object. The children were asked a series of questions about the properties of each item. Concerning *physical properties*, for example, children were asked: 'If you shook this picture, would you hear the rattle?' Or concerning *functional properties*, they were asked: 'Can you eat this picture of an icecream cone?' As necessary, they encouraged children to clarify their answers, so that if a child said she could eat a picture of an icecream cone, she was asked additionally: 'How would the picture taste? Would the picture taste like strawberry icecream?'

Five-year-olds almost never confused functional properties of pictures and their referents, and rarely confused the physical properties. The younger children were significantly less clear about the separation of picture and referent properties. While none of the 3-year-olds displayed confusion about every picture–referent pair, most made some errors. Like the older group, they had significantly more difficulty with questions about physical properties than with questions about functions.

Finally, after a short break, children who had shown confusion over the properties of some picture–referent pairs were further challenged to investigate how deeply held this misconception was. For example, with regard to physical properties the child was reminded of her earlier realist answer: 'You told me you thought that the picture [of an icecream] would feel cold if you touched the picture here. You can touch the picture here to see how it feels. How does the picture feel? Does the picture feel as cold as icecream from the candy store?' Just over a third of the initial physical property confusion persisted in children's responses following these challenges. When earlier confusion about functional property was challenged, however, even children who had said they could eat a picture of an icecream declined to try to eat it when they were presented with the picture.

Beilin and Pearlman therefore concluded that believing that pictures share their referents' physical properties is a feature of some 3-year-olds' thinking which is 'robust and resistant to counterevidence', but conceded that as such it is relatively weak, since it affects some but by no means all children's responses to questions about the properties of pictures.

It is possible, however, that Beilin and Pearlman underestimated the prevalence of 'realist' thinking for properties and functions, because they excluded from their study children who failed on a pretest to check, amongst other things, whether they could distinguish between pictures and their referents at all. A quarter of Beilin and Pearlman's sample of 3-year-olds were excluded from the study for failing this pretest. Because this pretest screened for a more extreme form of 'realist' confusion (identity confusion), Beilin and Pearlman may have excluded from consideration some of the children most likely also to have shown property and functional realism.

Shared fates

Children who know that a picture of an icecream cannot be eaten and know that the picture will not feel wet and cold as real icecream does, may nevertheless confuse the visual properties of pictures and their referents. Beilin and Pearlman tested for this possibility by asking children what would happen, for example, to a picture of a flower if the real rose it depicted were changed in some way. In other words, children were asked whether the picture would change if the appearance of its referent were altered. The data reported by Beilin and Pearlman suggest an incidence of 'realist' thinking with regard to the fate (existence) of pictures and referents which was intermediate between those for property and functional realism.

Again, the results obtained by Beilin and Pearlman may underestimate the extent of realist thinking among preschool children, this time because of an ambiguity in their questions. Specifically, when Beilin and Pearlman altered the rose, the picture of the rose had been removed from sight, and the child was then asked whether 'anything has happened' to the picture. Children might well judge (correctly) that nothing had been *done* to the picture – perhaps even that the picture had not changed – but nevertheless still confuse in memory the appearance of the picture with that of its referent (see Robinson, Nye and Thomas, 1994).

A procedure developed by Zaitchik (1990) is not subject to this objection, and produces a much higher estimate of the incidence of iconic realism. In Zaitchik's procedure, children saw a polaroid photograph being taken of a particular scene (e.g. Rubber Duckie lying on a bed) which then changes (Rubber Duckie is transferred to a bath) while the photograph develops. Children are asked to predict what the photograph will depict, and many 3-year-olds answer wrongly that it will depict current reality rather than the original scene (a realist error).

Zaitchik (1990) reported that as many as 40 per cent of children aged 3–4 years made this realist error, and her results have been replicated by Leekam and Perner (1991), Leslie and Thaiss (1992) and Charman and Baron-Cohen (1992).

On the face of it, these results indicate that a significant misconception about pictures is held by some preschool children, and thereby constitute a dramatic vindication of Piaget's claims for childhood realism in the domain of pictures.

One possible objection to this interpretation is that the children who apparently made realist errors had in fact misunderstood the test question. Specifically, in Zaitchik's procedure the test question was 'In the picture, where is Rubber Duckie?' At this stage we cannot rule out the possibility that children may have simplified the question, and construed it simply as a request for information on Rubber Duckie's current location – overlooking the conditional clause 'In the picture . . .' from the test question (see Perner *et al.*, 1993).

To examine this possibility, and to explore further children's conceptions of picture–referent relationships, we performed a series of studies of this 'updating effect' (Robinson, Nye and Thomas, 1994). In the first study we used a procedure similar to one originally devised by Perner *et al.* (1993). In our procedure, children were shown a doll wearing a T-shirt, watched a picture being drawn of the doll and then witnessed a change to the T-shirt (either on the doll or in the picture). In the *change doll* condition, children were shown a doll and were asked to choose a sticker to put on her T-shirt. Once the sticker had been chosen, named and placed on the T-shirt, the experimenter then drew a picture of the doll with the appropriate sticker on her T-shirt. After the child had scrutinized the picture and identified the sticker, the picture was turned over. The sticker on the doll's T-shirt was then changed for a different sticker, which the child was also asked to identify. Finally, the doll too was turned away so that her sticker was no longer visible, and the child was asked the following questions:

The changed item: Remember Anne (pointing to the doll), what sticker is on Anne's T-shirt?

The unchanged item: Remember this picture (pointing briefly), what sticker is drawn on the T-shirt?

The procedure in the *change picture* condition was the same until the drawing of the doll was finished. At this point the doll (not the picture) was turned away. Then the sticker drawn on the picture was erased and a different sticker was drawn in its place. The child identified the new sticker as before, the picture was turned away and the following test questions were asked:

The changed item: Remember this picture (pointing briefly), what sticker is drawn on the T-shirt?

The unchanged item: Remember Anne (pointing to the doll), what sticker is on Anne's T-shirt?

The pointing procedure was, of course, included to minimize the risk that children would misinterpret the test questions. Preschool children in the change doll condition made more errors when asked about the picture (the unchanged item) than when asked about the doll. In the change picture condition, however, there were also more errors to the picture than to the doll (although the doll was now the unchanged item). These results confirm the earlier findings by Zaitchik and others that some preschoolers make realist errors and appear to judge that a picture will update to match a change in its referent. More precisely, the children who make errors judge that the picture will show the current rather than the original appearance of the referent. It is not clear whether these children believe the picture has actually *changed*, or whether they are just confusing the properties of the picture and its referent in memory (see Robinson, Nye and Thomas, 1994). In either case, unlike the previous results, the errors cannot readily be attributed to misunderstanding of the test questions. Furthermore, the present results also demonstrate another form of realist error: some preschoolers seem to judge that a changed picture will backdate to restore a match with an unchanged referent.

This last result is of particular interest because it confirms that while some preschool children confuse pictures and their referents, the confusion is asymmetrical. Children who make realist errors on these tasks nevertheless appear to consider the real object as the primary member of the picture–referent pair. They attribute to the picture visual properties possessed only by its referent, and not vice versa.

It is not possible to determine from the presently available evidence precisely why children should assign this kind of priority to objects rather than to their pictures. One mundane possibility is that pictures are often less perceptually salient and functionally less interesting than their three-dimensional referents, and therefore less stable in memory. Nevertheless, even if it is only this feature of memory which gives rise to asymmetrical updating (updating of the picture but not of the referent), it is possible that this in itself might contribute to the child's developing a more explicit understanding of the conceptual priority of the referent in the picture–referent relationship.

The issue of dual identity

Pictures have a dual identity: they are both things in themselves and repres-entations of something quite different. Childhood realism is manifest when children display confusion between these two identities and their respective properties. One possible explanation for this confusion is that it simply results from children overextending the correspondence between sign and significate which is fundamental to all representations. Another factor, however, which may contribute to confusion – and thus to realist errors – is young children's supposed inability to hold in mind two interpretations of the same input (Flavell, 1988).

Children who are unable to accept that a single entity can be interpreted in more than one way will obviously have difficulty responding to pictures both as things in themselves and as representations. There is now considerable evidence collected by DeLoache and others (e.g. DeLoache, 1991; Dow and Pick, 1992) to suggest that this is indeed the case. In DeLoache's studies children were tested on their ability to use a picture as a clue to the location of a hidden item. In these studies, children aged from 2 to 3 years were normally able to use a picture as a clue successfully, but were unable to do so under conditions which predisposed them to attend to the picture as a thing in itself.

In the original studies, the object retrieval game involved searching for a toy dog (Snoopy) which had been hidden behind a piece of furniture in a model room. A clue was provided for each child to help in the search. In one study by DeLoache (1991), the clue for some children was a scale model of the piece of furniture behind which Snoopy was hidden, for other children the clue was a picture of that piece of furniture. Children aged 30 months were quite unable to exploit the clue provided by the scale model of the furniture. In contrast, children who were shown the picture of the same piece of furniture were dramatically more successful in using the picture as a clue to Snoopy's hiding place.

DeLoache (1991) interpreted the substantial difference in performance with the model and with the picture in terms of what she described as the dual representation hypothesis (see also DeLoache, 1989). She reasoned that to use either the model or the picture as a clue, children had to identify (represent) it as a symbol for Snoopy's hiding place. Children who find it hard to hold two interpretations of the same thing can either treat the proffered clue as a symbol for Snoopy's hiding place or as a thing in itself, but not both. For something as attractive and as salient as the scale model of a piece of furniture, the 30-month-old children were inclined to see it as a thing in itself and so were unable to use it as a symbol. In contrast, a picture is much less salient as a thing in itself, and so the children were able to see it as a symbol and use it as a cue to Snoopy's whereabouts.

In support of this analysis, DeLoache also found that hiding a miniature Snoopy behind one of four pictures (rather than pointing to that picture) rendered the 30-month-olds unable to use even a picture as a cue. The actual placing of a toy behind the picture apparently had prompted the children to think of the picture, like the model furniture, as a thing in itself, and thus left them unable to consider it as a symbol.

To sum up, when required to consider either one of the identities of a picture, even very young children appear to have little difficulty. The results of our own sorting studies (described above) confirm this: children were able to pick out 'all the pictures', showing they could focus on pictures as things in themselves without difficulty, when this was the only requirement in their treatment of the picture. Similarly, DeLoache and Burns (1993) report success in children as young as 27 months when the task requirement is only to focus on the referent, as when they use the picture as a clue in the hiding tasks just described. Nevertheless, studies of young children's performance on the hiding task also confirm that they may have difficulty combining these two accomplishments because they have difficulty understanding that a picture (or a model) is at the same time both a thing in itself and a representation of something else. In other words, these tasks, which elicit children's ability to attend to just one of a picture's two identities, may not in fact require the child to understand the conceptual distinction at all.

Another way to examine the extent of children's understanding of the dual identity of pictures is to ask them explicitly to attend in turn to each of the identities. In a recent series of studies (Thomas, Nye and Robinson, 1994) we attempted to do this by investigating children's ability to judge that pictures are not actually the real objects they represent but nevertheless can look like them. In this regard children's responses to the dual identity of pictures can be compared to their performance on appearance–reality tasks (Flavell, Green and Flavell, 1986). In the latter, the child sees a trick object; for example, something that looks like a rock but feels like a sponge. The test questions are: 'Is it really and truly a rock or really and truly a sponge?' and 'Does it look like a rock or does it look like a sponge?' The error made by many 3-year-olds is to claim that it really is a sponge and that it *looks* like a sponge, even though on first sight, they thought it was a rock. It is held to be difficult for these children to understand that a particular object can be represented in different ways.

In our procedure (Thomas, Nye and Robinson, 1994), each child was shown a set of two trick objects (plastic fruit and flowers), two real (nondeceptive) objects (fruit and flowers) and two matched colour photographs of the real objects. (This use of 'real' is a little odd, because pictures and trick objects are real too; but for brevity we will keep to this usage for the present chapter.)

The stimulus items were presented one at a time, and the child asked to name them. Once an item had been correctly identified the child was allowed to handle it and the alternative identity was pointed out in the case of trick items and pictures. The experimenter said: 'It's just a trick/picture. Feel it, it doesn't feel like a ———. You couldn't eat it, could you?' or 'It couldn't grow in the ground, could it?' as appropriate. For real items, the experimenter pointed out that the item *could* be eaten or grown in the ground, as appropriate. The item was then placed in front of the child and the two test questions about appearance and reality were posed (order counterbalanced across children). The appearance question was: 'Now tell me, does it *look* like a ———?' The reality question was: 'Now tell me, is it *really* a ———?' The name supplied earlier by the child was used for these questions.

The results indicated that there were no significant differences in correct responding to pictures and to trick objects, but that both elicited significantly fewer correct responses than did the real objects. To examine the relation between scores on pictures and tricks, a multiple regression analysis was performed on the scores for picture items, using scores on real objects, trick objects and age in months as predictor variables. The only significant coefficient was that for trick items, suggesting a common source of difficulty on both pictures and tricks.

In most cases the errors to both pictures and tricks were of the kind in which children judged, for example, that a picture of an apple – or a plastic trick apple – both looked like an apple and really was an apple.

Our finding that tricks and pictures seem to be equally difficult for children at about 4 years is consistent with the preceding analysis of the conceptual problems that the dual identity of pictures might present. None the less, this result appears to conflict with the outcome of an examination of children's performance on pictures and tricks reported by Woolley and Wellman (1990). These authors found significantly fewer errors to pictures than to tricks, whereas we found no difference (if anything, we found slightly more errors to pictures). We conducted a number of follow-up experiments (comparing question phrasing, coloured photographs versus coloured line drawings, and so on) in an attempt to identify possible procedural differences that might account for this discrepancy. The results all confirmed our earlier finding that the incidence of errors in response to appearance–reality questions about pictures is similar to that for appearance–reality questions about trick objects. Consequently, it appears to us that Woolley and Wellman (1990) overestimated the ability of preschool children to make appearance–reality distinctions with pictures (for further details, see Thomas, Nye and Robinson, 1994).

We conclude that children who make errors on trick objects also make errors on pictures, and that the errors have a common source. The significance of these results for the present discussion is that not only do a number of preschool children make errors when asked to attend to the two identities of a picture, but that these errors can be construed as confusion of the picture as a thing in itself with the referent of the picture.

Discussion and conclusion

Despite their apparent facility in recognizing what pictures are of, many preschool children appear to conceptualize pictures rather differently from adults. In particular some – but not all – preschool children make statements about pictures which display confusion between pictures and their referents.

First, some judge that a picture may share some of the nonvisual properties of its real referent, and this confusion persists even when challenged. Some preschoolers, for example, state that a picture of an icecream will feel cold and wet, although they do not attempt to eat the picture.

Second, a number of children make realist errors when asked about a picture whose referent has changed in appearance. These children judge that a picture will show its referent in its new rather than its original state. They also judge that a picture that is changed will backdate to restore its match to an unchanged referent. We cannot be sure that these errors derive from a belief that a picture can actually change to match its referent, or simply reflect confusion in memory between the properties of picture and referent.

Third, some children make errors – confusing picture and referent – when asked to attend to both identities of a picture. In particular, this confusion can be revealed by asking children appearance–reality questions about pictures.

All this evidence taken together constitutes convincing confirmation of what Piaget referred to as childhood realism in relation to pictures. Childhood realism may not, however, be a unitary phenomenon; it is not at all clear at present that all instances of children confusing pictures and their referents have a common cause. There are, in fact, a number of potential sources of confusion which could plausibly explain the different sorts of realist errors described above.

Specifically, some of children's errors in discriminating the properties of pictures from those of their referents could arise simply from a lack of *experience* with pictures, rather than a more deep-seated conceptual misunderstanding. As Ninio and Bruner (1978) and Beilin and Pearlman (1991) suggest, it may be that children gradually learn to differentiate the properties possessed by pictures and their referents respectively on the basis of their explorations of the pictures they encounter. This learning account of development out of childhood realism would certainly be consistent with the variations in the incidence of realist errors obtained in the studies reviewed above. Accordingly, children with the greatest exposure to pictures of the objects in their everyday environment might be expected to learn to differentiate the properties and functions of pictures and their referents at an earlier age than other children do.

The realist expectation that pictures will share the fates of their referents can also be set in the context of early experience. In this case, however, there may be elements in children's typical experience with pictures which exacerbate rather than dispel any confusion of picture and referent. Much of children's experience with pictures, for example, has little to do with picture–referent relationships. It is quite likely that, as far as children are concerned, many of the pictures they see in picture books, on the television screen, in magazines and on posters have no identifiable tangible referents. A picture of a horse, for example, need not be construed as a representation of a particular horse, but rather as a symbol for horses in general (Dow and Pick, 1992), or as a kind of pretend horse. Walton (1990) has argued that in fact much adult pictorial art functions in this way; that is, a painting serves as a prop to guide viewers in a game of make-believe that they are seeing the scene depicted.

Consequently, if most of children's encounters with pictures have more in common with pretend games than with the accurate presentation of specific information about a particular referent, then it may not be too surprising that many children are ill-prepared for tasks such as those described above which are used to test for understanding of picture–referent relationships.

Children's linguistic experiences can also be considered to influence their vulnerability to realist errors. Adults habitually talk about pictures in ambiguous terms, particularly with children, often referring to a picture simply as its referent. Some extreme examples of this can be found in an art book designed for adults to discuss paintings with their young children (Blizzard, 1990). In this work, children are frequently invited to respond to the pictures in a realist way: 'How do you think these clothes would feel if you touched them?' (referring to unusual velvet trousers), and 'Do you think the boy's arrows are real?' (distinguishing toy arrows from real arrows).

It is interesting to note that in Wellman and Estes' (1986) demonstration of the rarity of realist thinking in childhood for mental entities, the careful use of disambiguating language in the test questions played an acknowledged part in the children's success. In the case of pictures, however, our everyday discourse about them is seldom clear and unambiguous, and actually seems likely to dispose children to make realist statements about pictures in a variety of contexts.

Although there are a number of ways in which realist errors may depend on the extent and nature of children's experiences with pictures, the difficulty children have understanding that a picture has two, coexisting identities points to a deeper underlying conceptual confusion in at least some cases. Much evidence now indicates that children as young as 2 years can use a picture as a clue in a hiding task (DeLoache, 1991) or can attend to a picture as a thing in itself, but cannot do both at once. Furthermore, direct questions about the two identities of pictures seem to be as conceptually difficult for many children aged about 4 years as appearance–reality questions about trick objects (Thomas, Nye and Robinson, 1994). Finally, some of the updating and backdating errors may also have a conceptual basis; namely, an inability to keep distinct in memory the different properties of a picture and a referent which has changed in appearance. It is possible that these conceptual difficulties are all a manifestation of a more general conceptual problem in holding two interpretations of the same input, rather than a misconception about the nature of pictures particularly.

To conclude, it seems that preschool children's apparent facility with pictures may mask a conceptual misunderstanding about them which is shared by a number of children up to the age of about 4 years. Nevertheless, the difficulties created by this misunderstanding may not normally be very serious. Children's everyday encounters with pictures rarely require them to attend to both identities. Indeed, for much of the time even adults overlook the identity of pictures as things in themselves. The dual identity of pictures appears to cause confusion only when special circumstances direct children's attention to both aspects of a picture.

Chapter 10

The emergence of a framework theory of pictorial reasoning

Norman H. Freeman *University of Bristol*

A framework theory of something is a general way of thinking about that thing. Thus, folk psychology is a general way of thinking about people and their mentality; folk biology is a general way of thinking about the living world. Do adults have a general framework theory of how pictorial properties arise? And if they do, is there a turning point in middle childhood in the development of the framework theory? We shall examine the dramatic change in Western children's conception of pictures, which occurs in middle and late childhood.

Background considerations: from aesthetics to criticism

If 'Folk astronomy is a general way of thinking about the heavens', what term should fill the blank in 'Folk ———— is a general way of thinking about pictures'? The term 'art' will not do here, for 'folk art' is reserved for picture production, the products that are put on display. The term 'aesthetics' is a possible contender. Thus it has been suggested that children 'inherit aesthetic attitudes from their parents' reactions to photography, snapshots especially . . . a belief in verisimilitude is taken for granted by the majority of the population' (Taylor, 1989, p. 104). Let us follow up that comment briefly. Although photography is only one type of image-making, rather a special type, photography is actually an amalgam of art, documentary and personal imaging; an amalgam that poses severe problems in 'getting it right' (see Beloff, 1985). It is certainly the case that photography influences people's ideas about picturing, and it is certainly the case that people have general ideas about photography itself and how photographs seem to capture a likeness. Ziller (1990) asked undergraduates in the United States to take photographs and to write a brief caption explaining 'what the photographs are intended to portray'. Indigenous Americans tended to depict themes such as 'patriotism' and 'freedom', presumably attesting to the assimilation of photography within ideological obedience. Foreign students tended to depict 'sports', 'food' and 'security'. Ziller (1990, p. 119) commented that the outsiders 'have their own nations with which to compare and contrast images . . . food and sports . . . are on greater display in the United States than in the comparison nations'. The study attests to the assimilation to general ideas of one type of image-making. Presumably, the assimilation could be traced to some conception of verisimilitude, some conception of what it is to image a social truth. If that is the case, it should be possible to investigate people's conception of more general pictorial truth. What function is it that people think is peculiar to pictorial truth-telling? Posing that question might be acceptable as an approach to folk aesthetics; but a great deal would be left out. Revealingly, Ziller (1990, p. 143) left as a mere suggestion that 'differences in the meaning of "What is beauty?" should be explored'.

It would be a peculiar formulation of folk aesthetics if no statement on pictorial beauty were included, as the folk description of something being 'as pretty as a picture' attests. Folk aesthetics has also adopted the formulation 'Beauty is in the eye of the beholder.' The former slogan sets up the category of pictures as a criterion of beauty, the latter slogan assigns the beholder the role of 'beautifier'. Are the two contradictory? Folk conceptions are indeed generally characterized by inconsistency. To be more charitable, folk wisdom seems to specialize in hedging its bets – witness 'Look before you leap' and 'He who hesitates is lost'. It is not at all clear that one can distil the common sense of folk aesthetics into an orderly statement of a general framework of thinking about pictures, a general way of thinking about how qualities get into pictures and are thereby available on inspection to a beholder.

We need to take one step further, to enquire into what it is that makes it possible for folk aesthetics to develop into a set of ideas (around verisimilitude and beauty) that is integrated into a wider framework of relating to the world. Such a step can be taken for all types of imaging. Thus, van Sommers (1984, p. 242) commented on his study of Australian adults' everyday drawing (vernacular sketching) that 'the graphic output of any social group will to a large degree mirror their general sociology and psychology'. It is interesting that one of the main reasons the Australians gave for not working further on their drawing was 'lack of talent'. It is a notion embedded in folk aesthetics that picture production involves a special talent. One wonders where such a notion comes from, and when children pick up the idea (see Gardner, Winner and Kircher, 1975). It is immaterial whether the notion is true or false or confused. The point of interest is that if a folk aesthetics contains a notion, some developmental process must have made it possible for that particular notion to be preserved in adult awareness, perhaps against the pressure of competing notions, perhaps inconsistently coexisting with competing notions.

In sum, folk aesthetics can be regarded as a general way of thinking which is shaped by general social and psychological constraints as the prevailing culture provides them (including any taboos prevalent in any particular society, such as pressure against depiction of the human form or the gods); but the pressing issue to investigate is what develops to provide the psychological material for that cultural shaping. Here we can take a leaf from the book of research on non-art domains. Research on children's construction of astronomy or of physics involves enquiry into what distinctions children recognize and respect, and how they reason about those distinctions. It is thus profitable to enquire into whether children hold a concept of 'physical momentum' as a mysterious quality that is passed on when a moving body collides with a stationary body. By direct analogy, it is hard to think of a more mysterious quality than beauty. One would enquire whether children believed that beauty passes from artist to picture (the artist as beautifier) or from world to picture (a picture as mirror of the beauty in a scene), or from beholder to picture (beauty seen as being in the eye of the beholder), or perhaps all of those. Figure 10.1 shows the 'pathways' along which a child might conceive of beauty passing as a property. If children do think in that way, and we have yet to establish that they do, is it plausible to suppose that great developmental shifts in the pattern will occur? These questions will be dealt with later.

Such an approach has its virtues. It is based on a thought experiment whereby one regards a picture as initially devoid of all properties but with the potential to acquire properties. One then asks children whence a property could come if a picture is actually to acquire that property. If we knew what properties to enquire into, we could build up an account of how children gradually enrich their aesthetic judgements by drawing finer distinctions between properties and distinguishing between the artist, beholder and world as sources of these properties. At some point one would expect children to be able to segregate judgements, to be able to say that a picture can simultaneously be ugly yet be a good picture, or that the topic in the world may be ugly (e.g. war) yet *Guernica* is not a bad picture.

Such an approach, laid out in the next sections, is designed to bring to light the changing patterns of children's pictorial reasoning. Such reasoning is what makes folk aesthetics possible. Accordingly, we can categorize what we are after as exposure of conceptual change within the child's theory of pictures. Another way of formulating the endeavour is to say that early pictorial reasoning is what makes it possible for people to develop art criticism. The study would thereby be the study of the emergence of art criticism in the child.

In one sense, the theory approach is narrower than the traditional aesthetics approach, and in another sense it is broader. Let us first note how it is broader. Traditionally, children are shown pictures and are invited to verbalize their reactions and to give justifications (as in Parsons, 1987). That follows the traditional view of the development of aesthetic judgement as the developing sophistication of the child as a beholder. The traditional view can be categorized

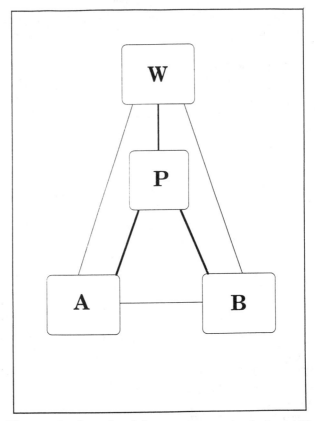

Figure 10.1 The intentional net that defines a representational picture (P) as being at the centre of relations with artist (A), beholder (B) and world (W)

as centring on the child's awareness of the aesthetic uses to which beholders can put pictures. Another traditional approach to the child's pictorial understanding is to focus on the child as producer of pictures, trying to infer from the children's solution of pictorial problems (e.g. how to draw a church tower with a steeple) how the child conceives of pictures as mapping onto the world so as both to be right and to look right (Willats, 1984; Freeman and Cox, 1985). It is known that children readily get ideas for their own picture production from experience with other children's pictures (see Thomas, this volume) – children willingly adopt a pictorial culture. Such information is generally informative of the child's taking up her own role as an artist. It is interesting that Golomb (1992) argued that only after the age of 7 years or so would children normally agree that they could improve a picture they had just produced along with some insight into how their picture might appear to a nonprivileged beholder. Both approaches, putting the child in the role of beholder or of artist, are narrower than the proposed approach, since they confine the child to a role in contact with a particular picture. The emergence of general pictorial reasoning involves being able to step out of both those roles and to survey the net of relations among artist, beholder, picture and world, independently of current involvement.

Yet while my study of child's theory of pictures is broader than traditional approaches to pictorial judgement, it is also narrower in the sense that it does not extend to capturing the complexity and force of the child's involvement with pictures (see Karpati, 1991). Pictures arouse passions and enable artists to express passions. Pictures address vital issues in life and stretch the imagination. The price to be paid for a method of research that detaches the child from first-hand involvement is a degree of pallidness in the exposition. Is that too high a price to pay? It may be. Yet it is a price that scientists are, for better or worse, accustomed to pay. The study of the child's theory of biology says nothing about how children will interact with pets and pests, but does inform us about how children categorize the animal kingdom. The study of the child's theory of physics says nothing about how children will play snooker or enjoy deploying the rules of fielding when watching cricket, but does inform us about how children explain dynamics. The study of critical pictorial reasoning has just the same status, affording insight into what pictorial inferences and causal arguments children of different ages regard as legitimate. Once that is known, children can be engaged in a more informed debate about pictures. Just as not all art education is centred on studio work, so not all research into the child's pictorial theory need be centred on picture production and on reactions to pictures in immediate view. A general framework theory of pictorial reasoning is built on critical distinctions which are put to broad cultural use. We now take the further step of enquiring into what purpose is served by acquiring the critical distinctions.

An intentional theory of pictures

In the previous section the traditional topics of beauty and of verisimilitude were mentioned as part of the study of the child's theory. Beauty was mentioned as a mysterious transferable property along paths in the concept map of Figure 10.1. Verisimilitude was mentioned as a vague matter of capturing some truth about a state of affairs. Both topics need now to be given more consideration. In order to do so, it is useful to put forward a proposition that might have the requisite unifying force. The proposition is that every theory is organized around some central fact that the theory purports to explain. The rise of modern linguistic theory, for example, initially focused on the proposition that 'The central fact to which any significant linguistic theory must address itself is this: a mature speaker can produce a new sentence of his language on the appropriate occasion, and other speakers can understand it immediately, though it is equally new to them' (Chomsky, 1964, p. 7). Reassuringly, there is no substantive Tower of Babel problem in pictures – even remote cultures can come to understand pictures after very little familiarization (see Deregowski, 1989). It should be relatively straightforward, therefore, to characterize the central fact for which one searches. As so often, a clue has been given by Wollheim (1993) in the context of discussing whether (1) pictorial meaning is there to be discovered in the picture and the task of the beholder is to retrieve it, or (2) pictorial meaning is constructed and imposed by an act of judgement. Wollheim (1993, p. 134) commented that the constructivist position is 'an appropriate response to the central fact about art: that it is an intentional manifestation of mind'. From now on, the child's mental resource for emerging as an art critic will be treated as the child's acquisition of an intentional theory of pictures. The focus of the child's theory will be taken to be an explanation of that central intentional fact, whereby an artist can produce a new picture of a state of affairs, and a member of the same cultural community who can recognise the state of affairs can recognize what the picture is about. That formulation is a generalization from the functional account of Schier (1986). The child comes to hold a theory of beholders' uptake and artists' productive investment, linked by a theory of mind. The child comes to see that pictures are vehicles of representation, mediating communication from one mind (artist) to another (beholder) about a state of affairs (world) real or imaginable in some sense.

As a preliminary to discussing how the formulation serves to make sense of some existing data and to predict new data, let us briefly take note of a pair of experiments that show how it can be difficult for children to work out what meaning a beholder will impose on a picture. That evidence will then be taken as information on why children may find it difficult to address Wollheim's central fact about intentionality.

The first study was reported by Pillow (1993). Children were shown a fragment of a picture, for example a triangle, and were asked 'What do you think this is?' Then they were shown the full picture, whereupon they saw that the triangle represented the roof of a house, say. The procedure was repeated with a second, identical picture. On the third trial, the triangle turned out to be a shark's fin. The whole series was repeated with a puppet as the fresh observer, and at the moment when the puppet 'saw' the third triangle the child was asked how the puppet interpreted the triangle. The correct answer was 'roof' or 'house', not 'shark', since the fresh beholder would have built up the same false interpretation as had the child originally. Success at inferring the fresh beholder's false interpretation was only around 50 per cent even for children as old as 5 or 6 years of age. The finding suggests that before the age of 7 years or so one cannot rely on children considering beholders' pictorial interpretation as being a function of their mental activity applied to the picture.

The second study was reported by Chandler and Lalonde (1994). Children were shown droodles, cryptic drawings that at first sight defy interpretation. A pair of concentric circles can be interpreted as a bird's eye view of a Mexican sombrero or of a fried egg, a rectangle aligned with a circle can be interpreted as an elephant's trunk smelling a grapefruit or a car approaching a pot-hole. A group of 30 children (ten aged 5, ten aged 6 and ten aged 7) were shown a droodle and after they had guessed what it might be were told, 'That's a good guess, now guess again.' The procedure was repeated with two more droodles. All but one child (a 5-year-old) gave alternative interpretations to each droodle which were nontrivially different. So children do grasp that a drawing warrants interpretation in a way that legitimates diversity of interpretation. Yet in further studies of children of the same ages, where children interpreted droodles and then saw the full drawings, only the 7-year-olds showed reliable evidence of grasping that it would be something of a miracle if a pair of fresh observers always made the same interpretations of the droodles. Again, the evidence suggests that before the age of 7 years or so one cannot rely on children considering that beholders can spontaneously diversify in their interpretations of ambiguous drawings.

It may be objected that the studies are remote from art and aesthetics, and that is true in an obvious sense. But there is an intimate connection with the central fact of art, whereby the posing of an explicit pictorial puzzle reveals young children's lack of dexterity in deploying an interpretative theory of mind. Young children are constrained by their forgetting that alternative interpretations are legitimate, and are readily seduced by their conception of what the droodle 'really' represents into imposing the same mentality on fresh observers. A second objection is that the studies violate one of the considerations of which much was previously made, namely forcing children into the role of beholder rather than leaving them free to reason about pictures in general. That is true. Clearly one will have to go beyond the methods and find a way of posing conceptual pictorial puzzles. But the evidence does serve three purposes here. First, we gain a pointer to the age range to work with – we expect to find an advance in the years after the age of 7 years once children have had a chance to apply their theory of mind to the more challenging manifestations of mind in pictures. Second, the data give a pointer to a possible weakness in children's theory after age 7. If it is difficult for children to think about the mind of the beholder, it may be that children will reason well about some of the relations in Figure 10.1 before they can do so for those particular relations that beholders contract (to anticipate the data noted below, that indeed appears to be the case). Finally, the studies demonstrate how recent research into the child's theory of mind has set the tone for investigating children's inferences about pictures. If the central fact about art is that it is an intentional manifestation of mind, the emergence of a theory of art should be bound up with the emergence of an interpretative theory of mind. It only remains briefly to consider the term 'intentional' in the formulation of the central fact.

There are two senses to 'intentional'. One sense corresponds to the common-sense 'purposeful'. Artists have their purposes. Representational pictures are meant to trigger a recognition of a scene and to provide a pictorial comment. That sense of intentional is embedded in people's general way of thinking about art. A pile of bricks might suggest a face, but if the configuration has not been set up on purpose by an artist it is difficult to regard the product as an artwork. The random pile of bricks had no reason to adopt a face configuration.

The studies of van Sommers (1984) and of Ziller (1990) on sketching and photography were mentioned earlier as revealing something of people's conception of pictorial purposes in this first sense of intentional. The second sense of the term intentional is even more fundamental and is necessary for interpreting the purposeful aspect. Searle (1983, p. 1) formulated the matter thus:

> As a preliminary formulation we might say: Intentionality is that property of many mental states and events by which they are directed at or about or of objects and states of affairs in the world. If, for example, I have a belief it must be a belief that such and such is the case . . . if I have a desire, it must be a desire to do something or that something should happen or be the case . . .

The relations in Figure 10.1 are intentional relations in that sense. People desire things, and believe things, of pictures and of each other. Beholders desire artists to do certain things; artists desire beholders to use their pictures in certain ways. The study of the emergence of a framework theory of pictures is the study of the emergence of a theory of intentional pictorial reasoning. For such a theory to get off the ground, the child has to come to make crucial distinctions, fundamentally to distinguish between the properties of a picture and the role of a picture as a vehicle for the beliefs and desires of the producer (artist) and the user (beholder). The common ground between those two agents is the fact of (1) belonging to the same culture (A–B link in Figure 10.1), (2) having the same world available (A–W, B–W) and (3) some common link between picture and world (P–W) whereby the picture is about, or of, or directed towards a state of affairs.

It may have been noticed that the intentional approach to child development serves naturally to focus on verisimilitude – how a picture ought to be made to depict states of affairs so that the community can use the depiction. But the problem of beauty readily falls into the study in the following way. Langer (1957, p. 61) commented that 'symbols are not proxy for their objects, but are vehicles for the conception of objects . . . . It is the conceptions, not the things, that symbols directly "mean" ' (emphasis in original). There is no reason for confining 'conception' to a solely intellectual affair, a pictorial symbolization can mean that the referent is beautiful or a cause for wonderment or extremely loveable. Symbols can be viewed as instructions on how to think of something, or what to desire of it, or of oneself in relation to that thing. To take up an artist's instruction to admire something that before seemed banal (think of a still life picture of a cup and apple) is a great achievement for a beholder.

To sum up this section, the emergence of a theory of pictures is the emergence of a theory of mind applied to pictures. There should be a conceptual shift to be found whereby children progress from merely attributing properties to pictures ('that is a beautiful picture') and from seeing the world as the source of those properties ('only beautiful things will yield beautiful pictures of those things') to understanding the relations of production (artist–picture) and of use (beholder–picture) as the generators of pictorial significance. Similarly, the question of verisimilitude should shift from a direct mapping from the world ('a picture should look like what it portrays') to an interpretative theory ('a picture shows the artist's pictorial vision of the world').

There are data available from studies of children as beholders that tally with the above proposals. Feinberg (1987) asked children to undertake pictorial reasoning: she showed 18 drawings and asked children if they could infer the ages of the artists. From age 4 years upwards, the prime criterion of judgement was clarity – the more clearly the scene could be recognized in the picture the older the artist must have been, in the eyes of the children. As children passed the age of 9 or 10 years, a further criterion was how the picture triggered recognition of a scene (e.g. distance was represented by perspective scaling). So primary school children are ready to use themselves as beholders to make an inference from picture to artist on the basis of a conception of verisimilitude. The data tally with Taunton's (1980) study of reasons children give for liking pictures (i.e. for giving a positive evaluation to the beholder–picture relation). Let us now proceed to new studies of children reasoning about the relations in Figure 10.1.

A conceptual shift in childhood

Parsons (1987, p. 39) summed up his reconstruction of children's earliest attitude to pictures as 'A painting is best if it is about beautiful things and if it pictures them realistically.' Parsons gave no age-related breakdown of the results of his interviews about reactions to a small set of pictures. On the basis of pilot work and on the sort of evidence cited in the sections above, it seemed probable that the age of 9 years or so would see a decisive shift from absolute beauty and verisimilitude to an interpretative theory. Freeman and Sanger (1993) interviewed 24 children who attended a rural Sunday school in Anguilla, asking 'Would an ugly thing make a worse picture than a pretty thing?' Ten of the 12 in the 11-year-old group answered 'Yes' compared with only 3 of 12 in the 14-year-old group, a significant difference ($p = 0.01$, Fisher Exact Probability). The reasons given by the younger children were that something ugly can only give an ugly picture, and that is a bad picture. The older children argued that whether a picture is good or not depends on the skill of the artist and her enthusiasm. Thus, given an inference to make about the world–picture relation of Figure 10.1, the younger children accepted that beauty flows from world to picture, while the older children spontaneously rerouted their reasoning through artist. That spontaneous recruitment of an entity shows children's mastery of relations in the intentional net within which a picture acts as a vehicle. Perhaps one could say that children progress from regarding (1) a picture as picking up beauty from the world that it is about, to regarding (2) an artist as beautifier by virtue of her agency in controlling what the picture is to be about. A follow-up study on 24 metropolitan English children gave even clearer results, with 11 of 12 of the 7-year-old and 1 of 12 of the 11-year-old children holding to the world-as-source-of-beauty position (Freeman and Brown, 1993).

All but one of the children in the follow-up metropolitan study agreed that an artist can shape a picture to make a beholder happy. Pictures have power to give pleasure or pain, and the intentional relation A–P points an artist towards exercising that power. But what is the beholder's role in that process? Are all beholders equally passive recipients of whatever hedonic qualities the artist has symbolically invested in the picture? Only 2 of 12 of the 7-year-olds broke away from such a view. When asked if the way you are feeling affects the way you look at a picture, 10 of 12 in the 7-year-old group said that a beholder's prior feelings were irrelevant, since what mattered was what was in the picture. In contrast, 9 of 12 of the 11-year-olds explained that how you felt determined how you would regard a picture. Again, the shift to an interpretative theory of intentional relations was significantly evident.

One wonders whether the younger children regard an artist as a passive copier of what is there. Accordingly, we asked whether an artist's feelings would affect how good the picture was. Here 10 of 12 of the 7-year-olds said that the artist's feelings were indeed relevant; and that judgement contrasts with their view of the beholder's feelings. But it was noticeable that the children regarded happiness as directly transferred to the picture: a happy artist would make a 'happy picture' and a sad artist would make a 'sad picture'. As one would expect, only 1 of 12 of the 11-year-olds held to such a view: the rest explained that the artist's skill determined picture quality. Again then, an early reasoning pattern based on absolute qualities to be transferred gave way to reasoning about appropriate intentional relations.

In sum, a change in pictorial reasoning was evident in most of the children around the middle of middle childhood. It may, perhaps, be no accident that that is the period when children's drawings often lose flexibility in favour of a concern with mapping the picture onto the world by means of great precision on the picture surface and of systems such as linear perspective (see Gardner, 1980). In our studies, children developed a new freedom to make inferences over the intentional net, instead of being confined to transporting properties mechanically along the intentioned relations. But the question arises of how robust the children's theory may be. Do children readily apply their insights in the face of conceptual puzzles? That is what we are currently working on by means of a game I call 'dilemmas'. A preliminary study (with Melanie King) revealed a dramatic collapse in 11-year-olds' use of their theory when confronted with a dilemma about a beholder, and I end with a brief description of that.

If you ask children whether they can tell if a picture is beautiful or not, they either think that it is a trick question or they answer that all you have to do is to look at a picture and you can directly see if it is beautiful. Accordingly, we devised a question that removed the world from the intentional net: we casually asked,

'How could you tell whether a picture of a unicorn is beautiful if you've never seen a real unicorn?' There were 16 children of 11 years of age, of whom only five gave a prompt reply about pictorial qualities (how the picture was drawn, what the configuration was). No fewer than five children said they did not know how one could tell, and another said, 'It's a bit hard.' Why should it be hard to see if a picture is beautiful? An answer might be gleaned from the replies of the remaining five children, who focused their answers on whether unicorns were beautiful rather than on pictures of unicorns. I suggest that even these sophisticated children regressed to transporting a property across a relation: if a picture is to be judged and you know what the picture is about yet cannot see the referent (i.e. no visual B–W relation is possible), imagine how W would look if it could be seen, transport the property from W to P and thence from P to B. That may seem laboured and/or implausible, but the analysis might nevertheless be on the right lines. One of the 7-year-olds we studied in fact pretty nearly articulated just such a chain of reasoning rather brightly: she said she would judge the beauty of the picture 'By the way I usually sort of think like you could say a princess is beautiful or like if you want you could say a tramp is ugly, then you could say a unicorn is sort of more beautiful than a tramp and it's an animal so it's sort of as beautiful as a princess.' Whatever one thinks of the child's philosophical aesthetics, this is a clear case of pictorial reasoning, along with a resolute justification. That is the work of an emerging critic.

Conclusions

The problem of the unicorn helps clarify the nature of the central fact to which a theory of pictures has to be directed. To adapt Searle's (1983) initial formulation, while pictures can be of or about unicorns, they are not directed towards unicorns. Pictures are directed towards beholders. So it is desirable to move away from talking about representational pictures, as though they simply were representations *tout court* (as did Perner, 1991), to talking about pictures as vehicles of intentional relations. Those pictorial vehicles cannot be understood unless subtle intentional distinctions are made. It is greatly to the credit of the primary school children we interviewed that they reasoned their way so well over the intentional net. That reasoning will stand them in good stead as they come to puzzle out how pictures can convey meaning about situations and about artistic minds, and how pictures can become invested with the qualities we value, such as beauty and interestingness. Eventually, one hopes that the children will come to understand how pictures challenge the mind. But that may be a further step that many children do not take without encounters with challenging art (see Parsons, 1987).

Finally, it is important to take note that preschool children make great advances in understanding intentionality, understanding that the mind is representational.

Preschool children struggle to apply that understanding to pictures, as shown by Nye, Thomas and Robinson (this volume). It would be worthwhile simplifying the present method and adapting it to somewhat younger children. What one would be looking for is some conception that pictures are realizations of mentality. We have a glimmer of such a possibility from a comment made by a 7-year-old. We asked 7-year-old children whether a picture can change your view of the world; whether someone who found snakes ugly would come to like snakes more if she saw a really beautiful picture of a snake (i.e. whether a P–B relation could alter a B–W relation). Eight children said that it was possible, seven said that it was impossible. That diversity encourages one to look to even younger children. But for present purposes, what is of interest is a 7-year-old who commented, 'Not exactly, because that's only a picture, that's someone's mind being put on paper.' That's perfectly correct. With the proviso that one should not say 'that's only a picture', the central fact of depicting is someone's mind being 'put on paper'. The elaboration of an intentional net theory of pictures merely works out the consequences of that epistemological advance.

Chapter 11

The psychological function of children's drawing: a Vygotskian perspective

Anna Stetsenko *University of Berne*

After being more or less on the sidelines for some years, children's drawings are now regaining the focus of attention of developmental psychologists. This has been a result of emerging new methodological techniques and theoretical approaches in psychology. On the one hand, new statistical methods allow us to assess multiple and complex age-related changes in the process of how children draw pictures and perceive them. On the other, modern information-processing theories and other models stemming from cognitivist approaches give rise to new questions regarding children's drawings, as well as help to explain and assimilate findings in this field. Psychology is now better equipped than ever before to deal with such seemingly simple – but in reality extraordinarily complicated and multifaceted – 'everyday life phenomenon' as drawing pictures and perceiving them in childhood.

One particular theoretical approach of as yet unappreciated significance to our understanding of children's drawings is the cultural-historical theorizing of Lev Vygotsky, which has since been adopted and developed by his many followers both in Western and in Russian psychology. Although Vygotsky did not create a fully fledged theory of how children perceive and produce drawings, his work provides an original metatheoretical perspective which can add a new dimension to our understanding of these activities. The originality of the Vygotskian approach to children's drawings, as we shall attempt to show in this chapter, is primarily that it addresses and clarifies the *functional role* of drawings in the overall development of the child – that is, in the entirety of cognitive, emotional, communicative and other aspects of this development. In other words, his cultural-historical approach focuses on the meaning of the child's achievements in the domain of drawing for his or her life in a real world, in a given socio-cultural context, as a member of a human community.

The issue of the functional role of children's drawings has been raised within other theoretical frameworks. The issue, however, is far from being resolved. In answering the question about why children draw pictures, researchers have pointed to several possibilities – that drawing may have a communicative function; or that this process can fulfil the purpose of expressing emotions; or that it can help the child to exercise control over an illusory world of pictures. Amidst this diversity of proposals, most researchers seem to agree that drawing satisfies important needs in many children. The basis for this view is that the majority of children experience a period in their development when nothing seems to be able to substitute for drawing in terms of its attractiveness and the amount of pleasure it gives the child. This period of childhood in fact is quite distinctive in its developmental timing: most children start drawing at the age of about 2 years but then lose interest at the age of about 10 years. It has even been given a romantic name – the 'golden period of children's drawings'.

It is interesting to note that very similar ways of academic reasoning characterize scholarly discussions about the role and place of art in the history of human civilization. Here too researchers have to account for the pervasive importance of art and its persistence throughout human history. Here also the most common answers focus on the expressively and aesthetically satisfying functions of art. However, as Rudolf Arnheim argued: one of the important functions of art is that it helps us to understand our world and ourselves.

What the cultural-historical theory strives at is a precise specification of the unique ways making and looking at pictures help a child both to understand the world and come to terms with it. In doing so, cultural-historical theory goes beyond identification of those important but too general purposes (i.e. communication, aesthetic satisfaction or exercise of control) which can be, and in fact often are, successfully achieved by processes other than drawing – for example, by language, symbolic play and imitation.

In this chapter I shall briefly present the Vygotskian approach in order to show why it capitalizes to a great extent on the functional role of the activities children perform (drawing among them) in attempt better to understand and explain child development. I shall then consider plausible instrumental features of drawing which make this process unique in the child's development. Finally, I shall present a number of studies conducted using a Vygotskian approach.

The cultural-historical approach is based on a number of general assumptions that are more or less explicitly present throughout the works of Vygotsky and his followers (Luria, Leontiev, Elkonin, Galperin, Zaporozhets – to name just some of the representatives of the Vygotskian school).

The first assumption concerns the instrumental function of the mind in the life of a human being. According to this point of view, the human mind in the complexity of its cognitive, emotional and communicational processes emerges for the purpose of meeting life demands and mastering the tasks that each individual is faced with in the course of his or her development. Practical activities performed in order to meet such demands define particular constellations of psychological processes which are the necessary conditions for these activities at each stage of an individual's development:

> Cognitive processes ... are not independent and unchanging 'abilities' or 'functions' of human consciousness; they are processes occurring in concrete, practical activity and are formed within the limits of this activity. (Luria, 1971, p. 226)

The second assumption concerns the nature of developmental tasks and life demands that are specific to human beings. Here, the cultural-historical approach argues that human life in its essential characteristics and from its very onset is fundamentally social; that is, it is based on interactions between people, organized as interactions between people and developed through interactions between people. The life of an individual is regarded as embedded in a social context which imposes its demands on the individual, and at the same time provides affordances for the realization of these demands. Social embeddedness of individual development means that environmental demands and developmental tasks are not preprogrammed; they vary with and depend on the concrete cultural and historical context.

Neither of these basic assumptions is taken for granted, but they are supported by evolutionary, phylogenetic and historical evidence, though I lack the space to discuss them here. It is also noteworthy that on both assumptions a Vygotskian approach has similarities with other psychological theories. There is a parallel between Vygotsky's approach and the epistemology of Jean Piaget in focusing on the adaptive role of the human mind as evolving in transactions with the environment. There is also a parallel between Vygotsky's approach and that of the French sociological school in stressing the social embeddedness of individual development. Important differences in approach remain, however, concerning concrete inferences about the nature of psychological processes and the ways of studying them.

From an assumption about the transactional dynamic nature of social demands and tasks varying with cultural and historical dimensions, the Vygotskian approach concludes that such demands cannot be successfully met with standardized, innate (and thus static and rigid) mechanisms only. Consequently, Vygotsky argued that cultural artefacts (signs and tools) must play a crucial role as accumulators and transmitters of human experience across generations. Cultural artefacts are appropriated by the child and serve as mediators of a progressive variety of practical activities. Here, an inference is made that the adults' role is not just to facilitate the child's development, but rather to provide the child with sufficient means to deal with the world through culturally patterned and shared activities. Thus, culturally patterned and mediated shared activity is regarded as the source and constituent of the child's developing mind. This thesis was succinctly formulated by Vygotsky in his 'general law of cultural development':

> Any function [i.e. psychological process], in the child's cultural development appears twice, or on two planes. First, it appears on the social plane, and then on the

psychological plane. First it appears between people as an interpsychological category, and then within the child as an intrapsychological category. (Vygotsky, 1981, p. 163)

It is not surprising that a strong emphasis is placed in the cultural-historical approach on the functional characteristics of psychological processes. Since these processes are instruments aimed at solving dynamic, contextually embedded and interactionally bounded, culturally mediated and socially significant tasks, they have to be studied in terms of their function, use, context and social significance.

What do these theoretical ideas and analytical principles mean when applied to children's drawings? As was alluded to before, it is important to define the unique and specific instrumental function of the processes of drawing, perceiving and understanding pictures. At the same time, the process of drawing should not be treated as isolated from other mental abilities of the child. On the contrary, relating drawing to such processes as language (in both its oral and written form), gestures and symbolic play is equally important since all these processes are aimed at an overarching task of mastering social-semiotic ways of communicating. In fact, such an approach corresponds to Vygotsky's dialectical claim that children's development is a dynamic system of unitary but not uniform, integral but not homogeneous processes.[1] It is by comparing and juxtaposing, finding similarities and differences, contrasts and analogies among various aspects of the child's developing mastery to participate in social life (i.e. in interactive, shared, meaningful activities with other people) that the ultimate uniqueness of children's drawing can be revealed. It is especially important to relate the process of drawing in early childhood with the development of oral and written forms of language at the same age. There are several reasons for hypothesizing that these processes are mutually interdependent and that they form a kind of 'dynamic unitary system' which imparts meaning to its elements.

First of all, empirical research as well as observations suggest that there is a period of development when the boundaries between drawing and writing are very fuzzy and arbitrary in terms of how children produce, utilize and interpret both forms of expression in their everyday activities. Young children do not radically differentiate between drawing and writing. The difference between the two is practically unknown to children and they tend to confuse what drawing is and what writing is (e.g. Luria, 1983; Martlew, 1988). As Luria (1983) showed, children between the ages of 3 and 5 when asked to write down a dictated sentence try very seriously to fulfil this task, believing that the scribbles they produce are real strings of words. Also, long before children acquire the ability to write, they try to imitate writing through drawing, sometimes even relating the length of their scribbles to the perceived length of the spoken words (e.g. De Goes and Martlew, 1983). Moreover, children seem to begin writing *through* drawing. Specifically, the first letters a child produces usually appear as spontaneous parts of drawings (see, for example, Kellogg, 1970; Martlew, 1988). At least part of this confusion must be due to the fact that children view both drawing and writing primarily as ways of communicating with others (see Rueda, 1988).

Only gradually do children learn to differentiate between picture drawing and writing, and that is usually through formal instruction received at school. But even after writing skills are acquired, the boundary between writing and depiction does not become absolute. Several researchers have pointed out that adults who are supposed to make such a differentiation still often fill handwritten texts with graphic elements such as arrows, circles and others (see Lemke, 1990; Witte, 1992). For some types of writing (e.g. in texts on chemistry, botany or mathematics) it is even accepted that nonlinguistic symbols such as diagrams, graphs and schemes will be used as an indispensable part of the written text (see Lemke, 1993). Further evidence of a similarity between writing and drawing can be found in the historical accounts of early writing, which originally closely resembled pictures and only gradually became emancipated from drawing over the course of history (see, for example, Foeldes-Papp, 1987).

It seems plausible to conclude that although adults are taught to distinguish between drawing and writing as completely discrete processes, this differentiation is to a large extent a developmentally late social convention, which is much less evident to children (see also Lemke, 1993). That is why it is rather unfortunate that the basic similarity between drawing and writing has been underestimated in the research on children's drawings.

Although it does not concern the process of drawing so directly, the relationship between oral and written forms of language is also of some relevance, since we want to draw a comparison between all these three elements of a presumably unified dynamic semiotic system, comprising various ways of making and communicating meanings. Surprisingly, most research on oral and written forms of language has capitalized primarily on the differences between the two. As Schneuwly (1989) has noted, in most studies these processes (writing and talking) were treated as even opposed to each other. This tendency is reflected in educational practices where writing is viewed as an isolated and purely motor skill, having little to do with the earlier developed skills of talking and drawing. This could account, at least in part, for why so many students encounter problems in learning to write (see Rueda, 1988).

An alternative approach to the study of writing is that of viewing writing as yet another facet of the child's general language development, embedded in social communication and interrelated with other forms (means) of carrying out such communication.

There is a growing body of research conducted in such an alternative framework (e.g. Elsasser and John-Steiner, 1977; McLane, 1988; Rueda, 1988; Schneuwly, 1989). In these studies the similarity between oral and written forms of discourse is emphasized, and the latter is defined as a speech production system adapted for specific but always meaningful and socially significant communicative situations. This approach has already been implemented in educational practices based on creating a meaningful environment for studying writing skills (see, for example, Rafoth and Rubin, 1988).

It is noteworthy that most of these studies explicitly borrow heavily from Vygotsky's cultural-historical theory, in which the principle of a dynamic unity of psychological processes is central to the analysis.

To complete the analysis of interrelations between various aspects of a dynamic semiotic system in service of communicative purposes, a comparison between drawing and oral language is needed. Again, surprisingly little research has been undertaken on the possible links between these two forms of meaning-making activity. Nevertheless, one study has been carried out within a Vygotskian framework and this has provided some evidence to suggest a strong interdependency between the development of language and drawing. The study in question was conducted by Obukhova and Borisova (1981) and Obukhova (1981). The main premiss of the study was that the process of acquiring and mastering the ability to draw pictures constitutes a necessary component of language development.

In this study Obukhova and Borisova traced the parallels between stages in the development of children's drawings and the types of language production corresponding to each of these stages. The method employed was to observe what kinds of pictures children draw at different ages and to document all the utterances produced by children immediately before they started to draw, during the process of drawing and immediately after they completed their pictures. Children aged 3–7 years from one of the preschool institutions in Moscow participated in the study.

The authors developed a simple classification scheme based on the analysis of graphic elements which children of different ages used in their drawings. Three stages in the development of drawings in preschool children were differentiated: (1) simple forms (circles, lines, squares), characteristic of children aged 3–4 years; (2) complex forms (combinations of graphic forms previously drawn apart into one complex design, such as a house or a tree), characteristic of children aged 4–5 years; (3) drawings by children aged 5–7 years, conceptualized as a stage of dynamic combinations (when combinations of graphic forms are used to depict episodes/scenarios, such as a visit to a circus, space travel and when dynamic aspects of these episodes are expressed by graphic means).

In terms of language development, a certain sequence was also observed which tended to correspond with the stages distinguished in the development of drawing. In the first stage – the stage of simple forms – children were rarely observed to talk about what they were drawing. The few verbal comments made by children in this age group were those produced after the drawing was completed, but not before or during the process of drawing. These concluding verbal comments were usually one-word names for the topic of the picture or emotionally expressive references to it. In other words, speech at this age did not anticipate or accompany the process of drawing. This stage of language development was conceptualized by Obukhova and Borisova as a stage of syncretic speech, characterized by an immediate link between the word and the object to which this word referred.

At the next stage of development (complex graphic forms) the child starts to accompany drawing with verbal comments. Children at this stage not only name the picture after completing it, they also talk while drawing, explaining what they are drawing and often adding new details to the picture. Words are now used to expand and enrich the content of a drawing; they refer now to something which cannot be seen in the picture but is only intended by the child. Thus, speech starts to fulfil a generalizing function which goes beyond a one-to-one correspondence with an object.

At the third stage of development (dynamic scenes) children were observed to talk mostly before they started to draw. Children first described what they were going to draw as if setting the plan for their further drawing, directing and organizing this process in advance. Thus, as the authors concluded, the planning and organizing function of language emerged in relation to the child's growing mastery in drawing.

Although Obukhova and Borisova did not present any statistical evidence for a relationship between language development and drawing development (the study rather was a qualitative observation), it did provide some preliminary observations to suggest that such a relationship might exist and should be further examined.

Summarizing what was discussed above about possible links between the processes of drawing, writing and language development, the following conclusion can be made. The use- and context-based analysis already applied to the study of these domains of cognitive development suggests their functional interrelatedness in what can be called a unique dynamic semiotic system. A number of empirical facts were presented above to support the argument that the basis for such interrelatedness is the functional similarity of talking, writing and drawing as instruments for achieving goals in a larger context of meaningful communication with the help of semiotic (metalinguistic) means. The co-construction of meaningful discourse in communicative settings of everyday life is an important developmental task in childhood. Children are encouraged and prompted to participate in communication with adults by the very nature of highly constrained and socially structured settings and activities shared with adults. Children need to master various means to meet the demands and requirements of these activities in order to perform them successfully. Specifically, children have to develop the abilities of signalling/expressing and extracting/interpreting meanings in progressively more complex communicative settings. To do this successfully, not only the learning of language, but also writing and drawing skills may be of crucial importance. It seems likely that these processes, each in its own way, enhance the child's mastery of discursive communicative skills.

It is important to return now to the question of the specific and unique instrumental function which the process of drawing might fulfil in children's development. We can reformulate the question about what it is in the drawing that helps the child to understand better about the world and him/herself. We can ask questions about the particular aspects of a metalinguistic, semiotic ability, aimed at solving communicative tasks, which children acquire through the mastery of drawing pictures – aspects that are similar but not identical to those acquired through talking and writing.

While learning spoken language the child makes the first great discovery that the combination of sounds can mean something, refer to something, that is, play a symbolic role in communication. Understanding the symbolic function of words is built on the child's knowledge of how to use communicative means, such as gestures and vocalizations, prior to language. A new linguistic medium – spoken words – equips the child with more sophisticated ways of thinking and communicating. The use of the verbal medium opens up new horizons for the child to express and interpret more complex and abstract meanings within communicative patterns.

Nevertheless, although through learning to talk the child masters perhaps the most important means of communication and symbolic representation available, this has certain limits imposed by specific characteristics of any spoken language.

Words (as well as means of symbolic representation prior to language, such as gestures and motion) are limited in that they cannot be freely and easily dissociated, detached by a child from the narrator as well as from the objects the words represent. Early periods of language development are characterized by what has been called the phenomenon of a word's transparency (Bühler, Stern, Vygotsky). At certain ages, children regard words as belonging to the things they describe, as inseparable elements or qualities of these things rather than their symbols. For example, children refuse to accept the idea that a word can refer in principle to anything and that a thing can in principle be named with any word. This phenomenon reflects the fact that from learning to talk (mastering oral forms of language) children are not necessarily able to grasp that words not only refer to things and events in the world, represent them, but also have their own independent and highly conventional mode of existence. To put it another way, children only gradually come to realize the dual nature of symbols, and in helping a child to make this next 'great discovery' drawing is likely to play a crucial role.

Indeed, pictures can be said to be more distanced from the painter than are words from the narrator. The very nature of pictures, which have a very clear and 'visibly' reified independence from those who produce them, might play a facilitating role in grasping the idea that symbols not only represent the world, but also exist on their own, have their own life with its own relatively independent rules. Children draw a picture and then can come back to it, change it, supplement it with new details, interpret it in different ways, as well as show it to other people and thus distance it from themselves. Symbols presented in graphic form on paper are more emancipated and available for rational scrutiny and reflection.

Moreover, through drawing children learn to use graphic elements and ways to combine them, as well as the rules of how and which of these elements best represent given aspects in the environment. This process has strong similarities to learning the lexical, syntactical and pragmatic rules of a spoken language, but with one important difference: in the case of pictures these rules and elements are presented to a child in a material, reified and thus objectivized form. Specifically, the material, reified form of drawings plays the role of an externalized 'third reality', which intervenes between the word and its referent and thus facilitates the word's progressive emancipation from a given speaker as well as from the word's referent. Such a third reality of graphic symbolization is needed for the child to understand the conventional and dual nature of symbols in general.

To summarize: mastering the process of drawing is an important step in the development of the child's symbolic competence; that is, the ability to represent symbolically the world in decontextualized ways. Drawing marks the child's 'second great discovery' about symbols (both linguistic and nonlinguistic ones) – about their potential to stand for the things as well as being things in their own right. This discovery leads to the further development of abstract thinking, imagination and logical reasoning, since it allows children to perform a much wider range of operations within a system of symbols.

As Nye, Thomas and Robinson (this volume) have argued, understanding pictures as symbols/representations is in itself an important developmental achievement and a process which unfolds gradually through childhood. Moreover, a full understanding of pictures is not limited to grasping their dual nature but, as Freeman (this volume) shows, it entails an understanding of the possible relations and distinctions between picture, artist, beholder and world as sources of a picture's properties.

Assigning a concrete psychological function to the process of drawing – that of establishing the dual nature of symbols – helps us to understand better why drawing is so attractive and important for children of a certain age. From such a perspective it is clear that drawing does not emerge and develop for its own sake; rather, it fulfils an important function in the overall development of the child, potentiating his or her ability to operate in a specific medium of symbols. This ability allows the child to communicate better within complex social settings, which demand not only the use of symbolic representations in reference to the world, but also a second-order ability to operate with the symbols themselves.

From the functional role of drawing conceptualized in this way, the role of this process as an intermediate step between oral and written forms of language can also be elucidated. As it is known from the literature, writing can be characterized as more abstract and isolated than oral forms of discourse, 'as an algebra of oral language' (Vygotsky, 1935/1978). Indeed, an ability to write presumes that prior to mastering the skill the child has successfully acquired several important ideas. The first is that words can be used not only to refer to other things, but can themselves be designated with the help of other symbols, such as letters. The prerequisite for this – the knowledge that symbols have their own material existence – becomes evident through drawing graphic substitutes for words and objects. The second idea is that things can be designated by a variety of symbols, not just a certain particular combination of sounds. The prerequisite for this –

the knowledge that a visual object on paper can stand for very different things in reality – is also explored through drawing. In both cases, drawing clearly can play a facilitating role in preparing the child for a highly abstract idea of 'drawing' letters and words.

Theoretical analysis of the relationship between drawing, talking and writing does not imply that drawing is only and exclusively linked to these two forms of language development. From a Vygotskian perspective, language development itself is only a part – and far from being an entirely independent one – of a broader process of the child's overall development. The differentiation of aspects in this development makes sense to the extent that it allows us to highlight the relative functional specificity of each of these processes in individual development. Otherwise, mastering an ability to draw pictures is by no means abstracted from a larger context of practical activities of a child with a variety of non-linguistic purposes.

The idea of the embeddedness of drawing in the child's overall individual development has been explored in another line of research conducted in the framework of a cultural-historical approach. This research does not investigate drawings *per se*, but examines the particular ways in which drawings are used by children of different ages in the context of performing other activities. I shall present here two empirical studies on the differentiated role of drawings in performing memory and other cognitive tasks.

The first (Leontiev, 1931/1983; see also Luria, 1979) is quite well known in the field of memory research, but is rarely referred to in studies on drawing. Indeed, the experiment conducted by Leontiev referred to the development of memory. But given that the mediating tools employed by the subjects in performing the memory task were drawings (used as reminders), this study also has relevance to children's understanding about pictures.

Specifically, Leontiev showed that when asked to memorize as many words as possible (1) directly, and (2) with the help of picture-reminders, subjects of different ages employed very different strategies. Young children (aged 4–5 years) relied more on spontaneous memory: they did not use picture-reminders in order to perform the task successfully, but rather tried to memorize the words directly. At the next age level (6–12 years) children successfully used pictures in recalling words. The results of natural/direct memory (without the support of pictures) were lower than that of remembering mediated by pictures. As for adults, the results of their performance on both tasks were generally higher then at the younger age levels, but they did not differ significantly from each other: adults recalled the words equally successfully with and without the help of picture-reminders. Leontiev explained this finding by postulating a gradual internalization of mnemonic tools. Thus, the study revealed age-related changes in the functional role of drawings in memory: (1) an increasing ability to use mediating tools (drawings) as mnemonics, and (2) a gradual internalization of these mediating tools (from using external, material tools/pictures to using internal cognitive tools).

Although interpretations of this experiment might differ, in my view it does represent an important strategy for studying the development of drawing in its functional characteristics. The same research strategy was pursued in a study by Obukhova and Minina (1986) to examine possible differences in perception, drawing, use and interpretation of pictures between a group of normal children and a group of language-impaired children. The subjects were normal children aged 7–11 years from a primary school, and children of the same age diagnosed as language-impaired. Four drawing-related tasks included (1) a 'free drawing task' (children are asked to draw as many pictures as they can on a sheet of paper divided into cells); (2) drawing pictures in association with words to be memorized and then using these pictures as reminders (cf. Leontiev's study described above); (3) interpreting the content of drawings (children are asked to describe what they think is presented in a given picture); and (4) drawing on a given topic ('My favourite hobby') with subsequent expert evaluation of the pictures. In a supplementary task testing free verbal association, children were asked to produce as many words as came to their mind.

As expected, children from the primary school group performed better on the free verbal association task than the language-impaired children. The latter group produced fewer words and these words were less thematically organized (i.e. there were fewer semantically similar words). This finding served as a validity test for the diagnosis of language impairment in this group of children.

On the 'free drawing task' no differences were revealed between the two groups of children. Both the number of drawings produced and the graphic characteristics of the drawings were similar across the two groups.

More interesting findings were obtained on other drawing-related tasks. On the task to draw picture-reminders in order to remember the words better children from the primary school group performed better than the language-impaired children. The normal children had no difficulties in finding graphic equivalents for words and later in using picture-reminders to recall these words. Children with language impairment also could find graphic equivalents for the words but these equivalents were often too concrete and full of irrelevant details. As a result, children with language impairment produced picture-reminders, but often failed to make use of them when trying to recall the words. Pictures did not serve the function of a mnemonic tool successfully enough in this group of children.

Differences between the two groups were also revealed on the task where children had to describe the content of a picture. Children from the primary school group mostly interpreted pictures in terms of 'what is going on the picture', especially focusing on the meaning of the situation and on the intentions of the personages. In contrast, children with language impairment mostly described the details of pictures, rarely trying to refer to the meaning of the situation in general, or to the intentions of those shown in a picture.

Finally, on the task to draw a picture on a given topic ('My favourite hobby'), some interesting differences emerged. The main problem which language-impaired children seemed to have in performing this task was that of keeping to the chosen topic while drawing the picture. Such a child might say, for example, 'I like to watch TV', start to draw a television set, but then become preoccupied with drawing another part of the room and forget about the initial intention. As a result, according to expert evaluation, their pictures often lacked topicality, that is, they did not present a story or scenario. Children from the primary school group had virtually no problems of this kind; they kept to their initial plan in drawing the picture, using graphic means to construct a story on a given topic. Importantly, language seemed to play a planning and organizing role in this process.

To summarize: the main difference revealed between the two groups was that whereas drawings produced in both groups were basically similar in their graphic characteristics, they differed in terms of their instrumental properties, that is, in how well they served the purposes of a broader activity such as memorizing words, expressing ideas or concepts, interpreting and composing a story.

The research strategy employed in this study can provide an important additional dimension to those studies where the development of drawing is treated mostly from the point of view of how graphic competence in children develops. As we have already mentioned, studying pictures *per se* may be an indispensable but not the only possible dimension of studying the process of drawing.

The brief exposition of some applications of the cultural-historical approach to the domain of children's drawings does not provide conclusive answers to the questions of why, how and what for children draw pictures. Nevertheless, the approach outlines directions of enquiry which can substantially broaden our understanding of children's drawings in their functional role in individual development.

Note

1. This metatheoretical claim was elaborated by Vygotsky (1934/1962) in relation to the processes of thinking and speech. Using these processes as an illustration, Vygotsky formulated the so-called principle of a 'systematic structure of consciousness'. This principle indicates that psychological processes are internally linked in a dynamic system such that they reciprocally constitute each other and are mutually interdependent.

Chapter 12

The contribution of social factors to the development of graphic competence

Christiane Lange-Küttner *Free University Berlin*
Wolfgang Edelstein *Max Planck Institute for Human Development and Education, Berlin*

This chapter deals with individual differences in the development of graphic competence related to social factors such as gender and the socioeconomic status of the family of the child. In the first section the universalist position will be described as well as views that are critical of this position. Universalists basically assume a parallel development of culture and individual. The opposite stance is taken when arguing that there is more variety than development. An intermediate position claims that cognitive styles of groups may account for individual differences, thus bearing in mind that individual development can be constrained without rejecting the notion of development completely. In the second section we present evidence from a longitudinal study of children's performance on a drawing task for a change of factors responsible for the variation of the degree of graphic elaboration in middle childhood, but also for a constant gender difference. In the third section we discuss the results and draw conclusions on possible implications for fostering development of graphic competence.

The development of societies and of individuals: history of art and the acquisition of graphic competence

We have quite clear-cut and straightforward accounts of the sociological structure of a society that is more or less supportive of artistic production and development. In comprehensive studies the role of economic and political factors (for Europe: Hauser, 1953/1975; for the United States: Ashton, 1972/1979) as well as of gender and family systems (Greer, 1979) for pictorial production have been described. It is perhaps not surprising that the contribution of these sociological variables to the development of graphic and artistic competence has rarely been studied in children. Various reasons for this can be posited. First, in societies of equal opportunities it would not make much sense to look at children within a sociological framework. It is assumed that, ideally, well-behaved, intelligent and gifted children will overcome any socioeconomic handicap of their parents. Therefore, it becomes more important to assess children's behaviour and performance on tests than the income and professional status of their parents. Second, even if sociological factors can be considered to play a role in childhood, the dedication children show with regard to drawing and the ability to draw are assumed not to depend on financial or cultural support, but instead show the freshness, creativity and pleasure derived from the voluntary engagement in the business of drawing without the experience of schooling and the drawing tasks imposed by the school (Gardner, 1980; Krauss, 1986a).

These arguments are reasonable from an educational perspective. To improve the conditions required for the optimal development of the graphic language of the child, we have to make the educational environment more attractive, being aware of appealing tasks and helpful cues the child needs from early on. And indeed, Luquet (1927/1977) pointed out that young children may have a visually realistic intention (*une intention de réalisme visuel*). An American girl aged 4 years 3 months of his acquaintance drew a cat with just one ear and claimed that one could not see the other one. Another girl aged 4 years 7 months, before starting to draw a bee, asked for advice with regard to the problem of whether the bee's legs were visible in flight. On the other hand, Luquet encountered a 20-year-old, well-educated Bolivian woman drawing a house in the same way as a 7-year-old would have done (ibid., p. 203). We can assume from these examples that we do not necessarily have to study illiterate (Deregowski and Strang, 1986) or tribal (Nanda, Das and Mishra, 1965) communities when we are concerned with individual differences. But to assume that only individual differences and individual styles (Hagen, 1985; 1986) cause variety, and that there is no development at all, is just another extreme view of the problem which we would not wish to share either.

For a more detailed account of universal development and individual differences let us recall what the universalist position really maintains. We can observe certain analogies between individual development and the cultural development of societies. Thus, in the course of the development of graphic competence, graphic constructions are initially two-dimensional and only later become three-dimensional and illusory, a phenomenon comparable to the development from religious medieval to later secular Renaissance art (Almgren, 1971; Gardner, 1980, pp. 208–34; Edgerton, 1991, pp. 27–9). Again, the latest accomplishments in contemporary European and American art correspond to the earliest achievements of children, the difference between artist and child being that the child is trying to acquire new knowledge while the artist is trying to abandon his old knowledge while striving for innovation (Gardner, 1980, pp.

138–42). That we can find these analogies in the two directions of the time-scale does not mean that they are accidental. Hagen (1986, p. 271) has explained that it was only during the twentieth century that painters have made a self-conscious use of the depiction styles of other times and cultures, liberated from the burden of documenting visual reality through the emerging technique of photography. These surface similarities between cultural and individual development of pictorial and spatial construction systems, respectively, should not be taken to support the universality of the stage system of development. In this case, Gardner (1980, pp. 252–69) would be justified in suspecting a closed theory that is not sensitive to subtle but important differences between cognitive processes leading to the same pictorial constructions in children's drawings and artistic production. Yet, modern artists, when citing infantile graphic constructions, follow the same method as Piaget when he used children's argumentation and explanation of concepts. Considering children's types of reasoning, Piaget was able to determine systems of cognitive processes more precisely and distinctly than most other developmental psychologists of his time. Paradoxically, universalists who claim a correspondence between cultural and child development do so by explaining what is specific about children's cognitive systems in different domains: Only through the children's conceptual glasses do we understand that the adult conception of space, time, morality or pictures is neither obvious nor self-explanatory, and perhaps even neither appealing nor desirable; perhaps it is just necessary.

But is the world of the child so entirely infantile or is it influenced by the pre-existing culture?; and if so, in what way? Golomb (1992, pp. 325–39), in her reflections on cultural variables, argued that, historically, children's drawings were seen as culture-free products in the same way as primitive art in tribal communities. However, she argued that during the past decades theorizing about pictorial perception and depiction has been challenged in the same way as the prevailing models of language development (see Piatelli-Palmarini, 1980). Beyond the description of the development of graphic competence we want to know what factors can be held responsible for it. Is it an internal logic of development that triggers new functions when the mistakes of an ineffective cognitive system accumulate unacceptably (Inhelder, 1980)? Or is it an innate programme that determines biased behaviour and remains relatively automatic and closed to modification unless the imitation of publicly accepted models offers a reward for overcoming old habits (Fodor, 1980)? Keil (1990) extends these two possibilities to four approaches, combining them in logical multiplication. First, an extreme nativist perspective holds the view that cognition is domain-specific and innate. Second, a moderate nativist position claims that only domain-general knowledge, consisting of biases, heuristics, and so forth, is innate, while domain-specific procedures may be acquired. Third, the extreme empiricist position concedes only the human physical 'hardware', like sensory transducers, as innate and every other ability as acquired. Fourth, a moderate empiricist perspective claims that there are innate constraints imposed by sensation and perception as well as innate domain-general learning procedures, heuristics and biases but acquired expertise constraints. Thus, sorting theoretical approaches to development of graphic competence into two categories, development either understood as a cultural convention or as an outcome of internal mental activity, represents a false dichotomy. Following Keil's suggestion (1990) of four theoretical approaches about the relation between the development of internal cognitive structure and external factors we conceive that the moderate positions share the position of assuming innate domain-general heuristics and biases. Still, in none of these approaches do we find acquired domain-general knowledge. In this chapter, we shall suggest how general learning heuristics might become necessary and acquired.

In studies about children's drawings, style has been understood like personal handwriting. The existence of a personal style was proved by the result that individual drawings were attributable to individual subjects with a likelihood beyond chance (Hartley *et al.*, 1982; Somerville, 1983; Trautner, Lohaus and Schorsch, 1989; Trautner *et al.*, 1989). However, we would like to suggest that style is not a notion that refers to the individual only. It would be a gross exaggeration to attribute style exclusively to individuals, although individuals may play a role as trendsetters. In art history we find that individuals may belong to an avant-garde that invents new modes of pictorial depiction. But referring to the twentieth-century notion of avant-garde already implies reference to a new group norm, i.e. becoming explicit about the nonfigurative, honest, transparent and structured matter of painting itself and the material used (Krauss, 1986b). Krauss suggests that the originality of the artist is a modernist myth because modern art, like traditional art, also relies on selectively varying one topic. Taking up the example of the grid as a common issue of modern art, she claims that the grid is a badge of freedom because it is supposed to be independent of figures and narratives about them. At the same time, she believes the grid to be extremely restrictive in the actual exercise of freedom: 'structurally, logically, axiomatically, the grid *can only be repeated*' (Krauss, 1986b, p. 160; emphasis in the original). Thus, originality and repetition are understood as a pairing which cannot exist separately, being logical halves, or sister notions. Therefore, we suggest that individual style should also be considered as a group phenomenon.

Turning now to children's drawings, we find that although style is claimed to determine individual differences in graphic performance (Hagen, 1985; 1986), the effect of the stylistic biases of groups has very rarely been studied. We hypothesize that social factors influence children's drawing styles. Detecting primary style preferences of groups of subjects gives us an idea of domain-specific biases and heuristics in drawing. Further, correcting and controlling for these special biases and heuristics might need more than just teaching skills and expertise. A modification of domain-general learning procedures might be important for progress within one domain.

A longitudinal study of the effects of social factors for performance on a drawing task

Within the longitudinal research project 'Individual development and social structure' (Edelstein, Björnsson and Kreppner, 1977; Edelstein, 1983; Edelstein, Keller and Schröder, 1990) an attempt has been made to test Piaget's model of the child as an epistemic subject. It is assumed that there are universal structures in cognitive development, but that their transformations are constrained by social factors, which channel, limit or otherwise impact on life experience. Thus, we presume that children are offered a selected, restricted or rich choice of tasks which they could consider worthwhile solving. This selection of tasks is more often conceived as a freedom of will (Planck, 1936) by the subjects, perceiving one's own direction instead of perceiving possible options. This is the reason why we would not predict a direct effect of the socioeconomic context on children's development. A poor background may not inevitably lead to poor performance; likewise, children who perform well may not necessarily come from affluent families. For an empirical test of the assumption that social variables and children's ability may interact in development, the relatively homogeneous society of Iceland appeared to be a good testing field. A quasi-experimental, balanced design was used to test for social class, gender and ability.

The sample consisted of two subsamples, one urban, one rural. In the rural sample complete age groups of communities were assessed, without balancing membership of social class. Results from this sample will be reported elsewhere (Lange-Küttner, in preparation). In the urban subsample, the sociological variables, social class and gender, and the developmental variable, ability as assessed by the school teacher at the onset of school at age 7, were used as stratifying variables in the design. Drawings on the topic 'Draw yourself and your friends at school or home' were collected repeatedly on three (rural) and two (urban) measurement occasions, when the children were 7, 9 and 12 years old.

Based on the stage models of Luquet (1927/1977), Piaget and Inhelder (1948/1956) and recent studies on the development of graphic competence in the child (see the overviews of Freeman, 1980; Freeman and Cox, 1985; Thomas and Silk, 1990; Cox, 1992) the dimensions of space and human figure were analyzed. Criteria for assessing the graphic space concept and the graphic human figure concept were listed in a code manual as pictograms (see appendix, pp. 170–2). The elaboration of the graphic space concept and the human figure was rated by three judges drawn from a group of expert art students. Average interrater agreement was 85 per cent. For the purpose of comparing means between groups, the scores of the space and human figure variables were aggregated to sum scores.

The social variables had an impact, only, on the drawing of the human figure. Thus, individual differences did not emerge in the performance of graphic representation of inanimate spatial objects. This replicates the results of an earlier study (Lange-Küttner, 1989) showing that a clinical group differed from a comparison group only in the quality of the graphic representation of the human figure, but not with respect to inanimate spatial objects such as furniture.

We assume that the property of animatedness of the object has an important effect on the interaction between subject and object. Hollos (1974; 1975; Hollos and Cowan, 1973) found that children with little exposure to social interaction, living in isolated dwellings, nevertheless developed well-functioning cognitive processes, although their social cognition was less developed compared to children who lived in a more entertaining and discursive urban environment. The fact that children develop cognitive functions in silent interaction with objects, despite a restricted social context, is in line with the finding that properties of the designer do not impact on the variation of the performance of graphic signs for inanimate physical objects. Further, as described by Lange-Küttner and Reith (this volume), proprioceptive feedback of the object, understood as a physical Gestalt, is a major facilitator of performance, especially in young children. In this case the real objects to be depicted had different proprioceptive properties. Why did the properties of the designer play a role only when the object to be depicted was animate? We assume that proprioceptive feedback of inanimate objects is far more uniform, predictable and universal than the proprioceptive feedback of an animate object such as the human figure. Therefore, with regard to inanimate objects the specific information to be processed is more uniform and thus opportunities to build a theory about graphic depiction were more or less similar for all children.

The contribution of social factors, therefore, only refers to the human figure drawing. The depiction of the profile of the human figure drawing, i.e. the decentration of the body axis, was not affected by any of the sociol factors, but only by the developmental variable of ability. However, the modification of the shape of graphic segments and the depiction of volume and movement varied both as an effect of social class and gender, and of ability. Thus, it was possible to tease apart the contribution of both social and developmental factors on the graphic construction of the human figure in middle childhood.

As differentiation of a natural shape of segments and depiction of volume are both graphic constructions of internal parts of a figure, these were aggregated in a composite variable 'differentiation of dimensions and details'. Multivariate and multifactorial analysis of variance was used for each measurement occasion. Figure 12.1 shows that for both differentiation and depiction of movement the degree of elaboration of the human figure depended on ability status at the onset of school at age 7 years, as rated by the class teacher. In particular, this was the case two years later, at age 9 (F (1, 92) = 9.02, p = 0.004), with ability as the only significant main effect. However, at age 12 this effect was less impressive (F (1, 92) = 4.43, $p < 0.04$), while as can be seen in Figure 12.2, social class emerged as a new main effect (F (1,92) = 10.33, p = 0.002), exceeding the significance of ability.

While at age 9 individual differences still depended on the ability as assessed by a teacher at the onset of school, at age 12 the degree of elaboration of the

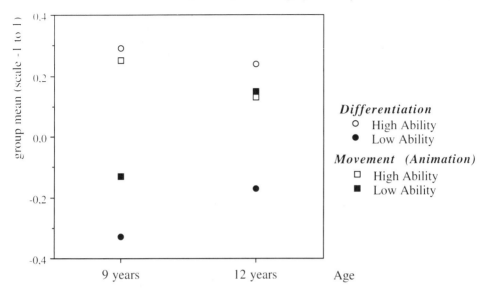

Figure 12.1 Effects of *ability* on graphic differentiation and animation of children's human figure drawings. Open circles: differentiation scores of high-ability children. Filled circles: differentiation scores of low-ability children. Open squares: movement depiction scores of high-ability children. Filled squares: movement depiction scores of low-ability children

human figure drawing depended on the socioeconomic background of the designer. To control for ability, the score of the Raven Progressive Matrices Test was introduced as a covariate in a second analysis of variance. Again, the relevant factors changed. The main effect of ability did not reach statistical significance and was replaced by the Raven score (9 years: F (1, 92) = 17.59, p < 0.000; 12 years: F (1, 92) = 4.54, p < 0.04). But, again, at 12 years the effect of social class surpassed the effect of the Raven (F (1, 92) = 7.39, p = 0.008). Thus, we could say that the Raven as a measure for intelligence validated the more intuitive teacher's judgement at school entrance at 7, an effect superseded by social class as development progressed: while ability appears to influence graphic perfor-mance in the early years of school, socially mediated and class-related experience increasingly appears to affect development in later childhood and adolescence.

The finding that socioeconomic background is important only later in the development of graphic competence is supported by a longitudinal study by John-Winde (1981) who did not find individual differences due to socioeconomic background in drawing performance at 7 years, but did find such differences at age 11. Why would factors impacting on performance of graphic differentiation and animation processes change from more individual properties such as developmental status to sociocultural variables such as social class? Recently,

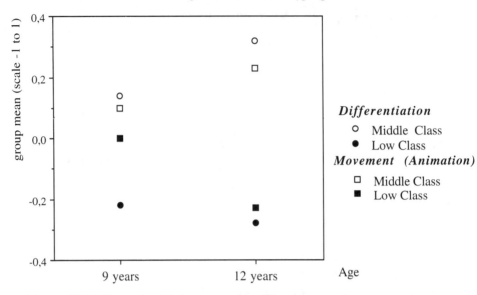

Figure 12.2 Effects of *social class* on graphic differentiation and animation of children's human figure drawings. Open circles: differentiation scores of middle-class children. Filled circles: differentiation scores of lower-class children. Open squares: movement depiction scores of middle-class children. Filled squares: movement depiction scores of lower-class children

Karmiloff-Smith (1990) has discussed the influence of endogenous and exogenous factors on representational change in children's drawings. She describes the mind of the child as an increasingly flexible set of manipulable core features. These components are supposed to be quite rigidly represented primarily, but later can be related and controlled. Elaborate graphic constructions also imply the flexible modification and composition of segments and axial systems, one main issue modern art is reflecting. Bourdieu (1979), in his empirical studies on aesthetic judgement, found that lower-class individuals hold a negative opinion about laborious metareasoning on pictorial methods. Instead, they prefer simple depictions of familiar objects, as children do spontaneously (Gardner, 1973). Thus, differentiation and animation of the human figure appear as a matter of personal development for younger children, but a question of cognitive style in older children and adults. This finding is supported by a study by Globerson (1983), who found that the more age-sensitive a developmental test was, the less variation occurred in social class, and vice versa.

A somewhat similar effect of social variables was shown for the same sample at the same age (Schröder and Edelstein, 1991). In a verbal classification task an interaction of ability and social class was found at age 9 and 12, but not at age 7 years: high-ability children showed the best group means independent of their

Figure 12.3 Effects of sex of drawer on graphic differentiation and animation of children's human figure drawings. Open circles: differentiation scores of girls. Filled circles: differentiation scores of boys. Open squares: movement depiction scores of girls. Filled squares: movement depiction scores of boys

socioeconomic background. Low-ability subjects from a low social class background showed the lowest performance, while the mean of low-ability, middle-class subjects was between these two groups. Thus, the effect of social variables also emerges in other domains of cognition in middle childhood, although in interaction with ability and not as conspicuously as in performance of graphic competence.

Analysis of variance did not only show a change over age in factors responsible for the variation of graphic performance, but also a constant gender by concept interaction (9 years: $F (1, 92) = 33.61$, $p = 0.000$; 12 years: $F (1, 92) = 8.38$, $p = 0.005$). Figure 12.3 shows that boys more often depicted movement and were less likely to differentiate the human figure. Girls, on the other hand, more often differentiated dimensions and details while they depicted movement less frequently. While the gender difference remained stable with regard to differentiation processes, subjects of both sexes tended to converge in depicting movement.

In studies of drawing of the human figure gender differences in drawing have been found at a very early age (Goodenough, 1926). Goodenough reported that girls were generally better than boys in drawing the human figure. However, close inspection reveals that boys depicted movement three times more often than girls (Goodenough, 1926, p. 60). Goodenough assumes that the tendency of the boys in her sample to exaggerate the size of the feet and the length of the arms can be explained by their interest in physical movement. However, this finding cannot be directed at sports alone in the light of Goodenough's result that boys draw transparent trousers four times more often than girls. Girls were more likely to differentiate features of the face of the human figure. Koppitz (1968) replicated these results and considered them as an outcome of gender-specific education and gender prototypes.

We may conclude that boys are more likely to depict movement because it relates to their interest in movement as this has been reinforced or introduced to them by a significant other. We could also presume that the selectively better performance of the two genders on graphic dynamization or differentiation of the human figure, respectively, seems to reflect a basic temperamental difference: boys do explore more actively, while girls are more clinging and passive (Herman, Shiraki and Miller, 1985). Thus, it seems reasonable that children concentrate on features of the graphic object which exhibit some relation to their own properties. But we favour an explanation which takes into consideration the cognitive dimension of the task. We know that both selection and drawing of correct depictions of a mobile object such as a liquid are more difficult to perform than those of immobile objects such as houses or trees (Perner, Kohlmann and Wimmer, 1984). The better performance of the boys on the more difficult task corresponds to the findings Maccoby (1966) reported: boys were more likely to respond to an intellectual challenge, while girls were more likely to retreat from it. For the present study this implies that boys do not give up trying to depict movement, although the graphic depiction of a mobile human figure is a difficult problem to solve.

We do not wish, however, to suggest that girls are more likely to retreat from intellectual challenges. Another part of the study provided some evidence that this is not the whole truth. When following subject's individual pathways in drawing the human figure (Lange-Küttner, 1994) we found that two tendencies prevail in middle childhood: reduction and differentiation. Especially at the end of middle childhood the pin man phenomenon emerges: subjects draw the human figure composed of one-dimensional strokes only, which nevertheless may be depicted in profile or movement. Statistical analysis of individual differences in the human figure drawing at age 12 years, introducing the pin man factor as an independent variable and the design factors as covariates showed that subjects who drew pin men were more likely to be male and to live in a lower-class family. Further, the lower-class male subjects were more likely to draw the pin men in groups of more than four individuals, as compared to other subjects who preferred to represent themselves with just one friend at age 12 years. Accordingly, the pin man type drawing of the human figure seems adequate for the depiction of public group activities of peers – for instance, soccer. We also know that it is common in public to use diagrams of the human figure for instant communication, for instance, at airports. Thus, the only peculiarity seems to be that lower-class males seem to define friendship graphically in public rather than in private terms.

We can conclude that gender differences in drawing do not merely relate to the biological differences between the sexes. The present study shows that girls were more likely to differentiate the human figure while boys more often reduced complexity or depicted movement. Thus, boys chose either a very easy drawing task, as the pin men drawers did, or a very difficult task, like the depiction of movement; while girls, differentiating the human figure, selected a task of medium difficulty. This effect was not limited to the domain of drawing. The gender difference was found in the same sample as a constant and even increasing effect in the performance on syllogistic inferences and Piagetian classification tasks. The distribution of the girls showed the same group means but significantly less variance than the boys (Schröder, 1992). Thus, gender differences found in drawing the human figure related both to biological and psychological differences, and were not limited to just the domain of drawing. First, children selectively depicted features of the human figure which referred to gender-specific behaviour in everyday life. Second, subjects focused on graphic problems of extreme or average level of difficulty corresponding to their gender-specific level of aspiration or achievement motivation.

Conclusions

The fact that we found effects of social variables in drawing performance, the late emergence of the significance of social class in middle childhood, and the extreme achievement level of boys, phenomena not restricted to this domain but also obtained in cognitive tasks such as classification and inference, leads to the concept of cognitive style when exploring individual differences in graphic performance. Selective task definition by the subjects does not necessarily result in good or bad performance. On the contrary, while having the same level of performance, different implicit aspects of the task are made explicit.

The concept of cognitive style originally had the advantage of accounting for differences between impulsive and field-dependent or reflective and field-independent subjects at the same stage of development or at the same age (Witkin *et al.*, 1954/1975; Kagan, Moss and Sigel, 1963; Brodzinsky, 1985; Globerson, 1989). Thus, the concept of cognitive style was contrasted with the notion of a universal and pure cognitive development. We saw, however, that differences in cognitive style also arise from social factors, as Kagan, Moss and Sigel (1963, p. 111) assumed. From this perspective, the development of graphic competence does not only imply a new understanding of graphic forms and their relations, but a disregard for earlier idiosyncratic cognitive styles. Overcoming constraints of social class or gender may not mean abandoning their styles in a false separation or deformation, but trying other approaches. Thus, we suggest that girls may be confronted with more extreme cognitive affordances, boys might be encouraged to relax, middle-class subjects might enrich their style approaching real objects in a more straightforward manner, and lower-class individuals might give up their contempt for apparently useless and time-consuming speculations about (pictorial) methods and material. In conclusion, we found that modification of domain-general heuristics and biases might become necessary and may be acquired. Findings about the contribution of social variables demonstrate that children may need social support for development of graphic competence and teachers may need to extend their instructional fantasy.

Appendix

Graphic space concept

1. Overall space concept (creating the illusion of depth with axes systems)

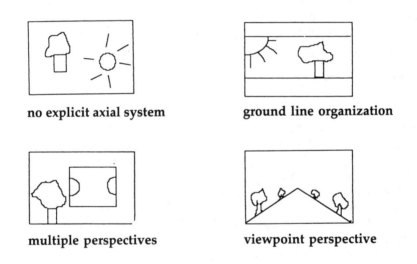

no explicit axial system   ground line organization

multiple perspectives   viewpoint perspective

2. Figurative space concept (creating the illusion of depth with single objects)

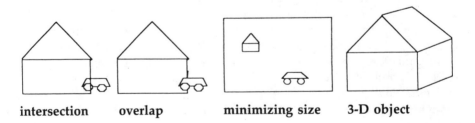

intersection   overlap   minimizing size   3-D object

Human figure drawing

3. Volume of the human figure

**one-dimensional
elements**

**two-dimensional
organization**

**three-dimensional
elements**

4. Perspective of the human figure

central body axis

motile body axis

part view

5. Shape of the human figure

**geometric shape
segments**

**single irregular
segments**

**natural shape
segments**

6. Depiction of movement in the human figure

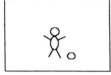   

static body   **movement of body**

References

Ackermann-Valladao, E. (1987) 'Que deviennent les idées à propos d'un phénomène une fois retraduites à travers différentes medias? Le rôle du dessin, du récit et du geste dans la construction d'une connaissance', *Archives de Psychologie*, vol. 55, pp. 195–218.

Almgren, A. (1971) *Die umgekehrte Perspektive und die Fluchtachsenperspektive. Eine Untersuchung der Zeichen für Körper und Raum in Kinderzeichnungen und anderen Bildern*, unpublished dissertation, Uppsala.

Alp, I. E. (1994) 'Measuring the size of working memory in very young children: The imitation sorting task', *International Journal of Behavioral Development*, vol. 17, pp. 125–41.

Arnheim, R. (1954) *Art and Visual Perception: A psychology of the creative eye*, University of California Press, Berkeley.

Arnheim, R. (1956/1972) *Art and Visual Perception: A psychology of the creative eye*, Faber & Faber, London.

Arnheim, R. (1969) *Visual Thinking*, University of California Press, Berkeley.

Arnheim, R. (1974) *Art and Visual Perception: A psychology of the creative eye. The new version*, University of California Press, Berkeley and Los Angeles.

Arnheim, R. (1980) 'The puzzle of Nadia's drawings', *The Arts in Psychotherapy*, vol. 7, pp. 79–85.

Arnold, C. and Johnson, J. (1991) 'Cognitive and developmental factors in learning Logo graphics programming'. Paper presented at the biennial meeting of the Society for Research in Child Development, Seattle, April.

Ashton, D. (1972/1979) *The New York School: A cultural reckoning*, Penguin Books, New York.

Atlas, J. A. (1985) 'Sociality and exceptional drawing ability: Review of "Normal and anomalous representational drawing ability in children" by L. Selfe', *New Ideas in Psychology*, vol. 3, pp. 341–4.

Barnes, E. (1894) 'The art of little children', *Pedagogical Seminary*, vol. 3, pp. 302–7.

Barrett, M. D. and Bridson, A. (1983) 'The effect of instructions upon children's drawings', *British Journal of Developmental Psychology*, vol. 1, pp. 175–8.

Bartlett, F. C. (1932) *Remembering: A study in experimental and social psychology*, Cambridge University Press, London.

173

Basso, A., Bisiach, E. and Luzatti, C. (1980) 'Loss of mental imagery: A case study', *Neuropsychologia*, vol. 18, pp. 435–42.

Bataille, G. (1963) *Der heilige Eros*, Ullstein Materialien, Darmstadt.

Bauer, R. M. (1982) 'Visual hypoemotionality as a symptom of visual–limbic disconnection in man', *Archives of Neurology*, vol. 39, pp. 702–8.

Bauer, R. M. (1984) 'Autonomic recognition of names and faces in prosopagnosia', *Neuropsychologia*, vol. 22, pp. 457–69.

Beilin, H. (1991) 'Developmental aesthetics and the psychology of photography', in R. M. Downs, L. S. Liben and D. S. Palermo (eds), *Visions of Aesthetics, the Environment and Development*, Lawrence Erlbaum, Hillsdale, NJ.

Beilin, H., Kagan, J. and Rabinowitz, R. (1966) 'Effects of verbal and perceptual training on water level representations', *Child Development*, vol. 37, pp. 317–28.

Beilin, H. and Pearlman, E. G. (1991) 'Children's iconic realism: Object versus property realism', in H. W. Reese (ed.), *Advances in Child Development and Behavior*, vol. 23, Academic Press, San Diego, CA.

Beloff, H. (1985) *Camera Culture*, Basil Blackwell, Oxford.

Biederman, I. (1987) 'Recognition-by-components: A theory of human image understanding', *Psychological Review*, vol. 94, pp. 115–47.

Binford, T. O. (1981) 'Inferring surfaces from images', *Artificial Intelligence*, vol. 17, pp. 205–44.

Blizzard, G. S. (1990) *Come Look With Me: Enjoying art with children*, Thomasson-Grant, Charlottesville, VA.

Borke, H. (1975) 'Piaget's mountains revisited: Changes in the egocentric landscape', *Developmental Psychology*, vol. 11, pp. 240–3.

Bourdieu, P. (1979) *La Distinction. Critique social du jugement*, Les Éditions de Minuit, Paris.

Bremner, J. G. and Moore, S. (1984) 'Prior visual inspection and object naming: Two factors that enhance hidden feature inclusion in young children's drawings', *British Journal of Developmental Psychology*, vol. 2, pp. 371–6.

Brodzinsky, D. M. (1985) 'On the relationship between cognitive style and cognitive structures', in E. D. Neimark, R. de Lisi and J. L. Newman (eds), *Moderators of Competence*, Lawrence Erlbaum, Hillsdale, NJ, pp. 147–74.

Brooks, L. R. (1968) 'Spatial and verbal aspects of the act of recall', *Canadian Journal of Psychology*, vol. 22, pp. 349–50.

Brooks, M. R., Glenn, S. M. and Crozier, W. R. (1988) 'Pre-school children's preferences for drawings of similar complexity to their own', *British Journal of Educational Psychology*, vol. 58, pp. 165–71.

Broughton, J. (1978) 'Development of concepts of self, mind, reality and knowledge', in W. Damon (ed.), *Social Cognition*, Jossey-Bass, San Francisco.

Bryant, P. (1982) 'The role of conflict and of agreement between intellectual strategies in children's ideas about measurement', *British Journal of Psychology*, vol. 73, pp. 243–51.

Bühler, K. (1930) *The Mental Development of the Child*, Kegan Paul, London.

Butterworth, G. and Grover, L. (1988) 'The origins of referential communication in human infancy', in L. Weiskrantz (ed.), *Thought without Language*, Clarendon Press, Oxford, pp. 5–24.

Butterworth, G. and Jarrett, N. (1991) 'What minds have in common is space: Spatial mechanisms serving joint visual attention in infancy', *British Journal of Developmental Psychology*, vol. 9, pp. 55–72.

Campbell, R. N. and Harrison, A. (1990) 'The representational status of early child drawings', Poster presented at IVth European Conference on Developmental Psychology, Stirling.

Caron-Pargue, J. (1985a) *Le Dessin du cube chez l'enfant: Organisations et réorganisations de codes graphiques*, P. Lang, Berne.

Caron-Pargue, J. (1985b) 'Coding processes and units of processing in children's drawings of regular solids', Paper presented at the Meeting of the Society for Philosophy and Psychology, Toronto.

Caron-Pargue, J. (1987) 'Analyse d'instructions graphiques pour faire un nœud: La filiation des significations dans des dessins d'enfants', *Archives de Psychologie*, vol. 55, pp. 153–73.

Caron-Pargue, J. (1992) 'A functional analysis of decomposition and integration in children's cylinder drawing', *British Journal of Developmental Psychology*, vol. 10, pp. 51–69.

Carothers, T. and Gardner, H. (1979) 'When children's drawings become art: The emergence of aesthetic production and perception', *Developmental Psychology*, vol. 15, pp. 570–80.

Case, R. (1978) 'Piaget and beyond: Toward a developmentally based theory and technology of instruction', in R. Glaser, (ed.), *Advances in Instructional Psychology*, Lawrence Erlbaum: Hillsdale, NJ, pp. 167–228.

Case, R. (1985) *Intellectual Development: Birth to adulthood*, Academic Press, New York.

Case, R. (1992) *The Mind's Staircase*, Lawrence Erlbaum, Hillsdale, NJ.

Casson, H. (1987) Introduction, in *Stephen Wiltshire, Drawings*, J. M. Dent, London, pp. 5–6.

Chandler, M. and Lalonde, C. (1994) 'Shifting to an interpretive theory of mind: 5- to 7-year olds' changing conceptions of mental life', in A. Sameroff and M. Haith (eds), *Reasons and Responsibility: The passage through childhood*, University of Chicago Press, Chicago.

Charman, T. and Baron-Cohen, S. (1992) 'Understanding drawings and beliefs: A further test of the metarepresentation theory of autism', *Journal of Child Psychology and Psychiatry*, vol. 33, pp. 1105–12.

Charman, T. and Baron-Cohen, S. (1993) 'Drawing development in autism: The intellectual to visual realism shift', *British Journal of Developmental Psychology*, vol. 11, pp. 171–85.

Chen, M. J. and Cook, M. (1984) 'Representational drawings of solid objects by young children', *Perception*, vol. 13, pp. 377–85.

Chomsky, N. (1964) *Current Issues in Linguistic Theory*, Mouton, The Hague.

Costall, A. P. (1985) 'How meaning covers the traces', in N. H. Freeman and M. V. Cox (eds), *Visual Order*, Cambridge University Press, Cambridge.

Costall, A. P. (1990) 'Picture perception as "indirect" perception', in K. Landwehr (ed.), *Ecological Perception Research, Visual Communication and Aesthetics*, Springer-Verlag, New York, pp. 15–22.

Costall, A. (1993) 'Beyond linear perspectives: A cubist manifesto for visual science', *Image and Vision Computing*, vol. 11, no. 6, pp. 334–41.

Cox, M. V. (1985) 'One object behind another: Young children's use of array-specific representations', in N. H. Freeman and M. V. Cox (eds), *Visual Order*, Cambridge University Press, Cambridge.

Cox, M. V. (1986) 'Cubes are difficult things to draw', *British Journal of Developmental Psychology*, vol. 4, pp. 341–5.

Cox, M. V. (1992) *Children's Drawings*, Penguin Books, Harmondsworth.

Cox, M. V. (1993) *Children's Drawings of the Human Figure*, Lawrence Erlbaum, Hove.

Crook, C. (1985) 'Knowledge and appearance', in N. H. Freeman and M. V. Cox (eds), *Visual Order*, Cambridge University Press, Cambridge, pp. 248–65.

Davidoff, J., Matthews, W. B. and Newcombe, F. (1986) 'Observations on a case of prosopagnosia', in A. W. Ellis, M. A. Jeeves, F. Newcombe and A. W. Young (eds), *Aspects of Face Processing: A NATO symposium*, Martinus Nijhoff, Dordrecht.

Davis, A. M. (1983) 'Contextual sensitivity in young children's drawings', *Journal of Experimental Child Psychology*, vol. 35, pp. 478–86.

Davis, A. M. (1985) 'Conflict between canonicality and array-specificity in young children's drawings', *British Journal of Developmental Psychology*, vol. 3, pp. 363–72.

De Goes, C. and Martlew, M. (1983) 'Young children's approach to literacy', in M. Martlew (ed.), *The Psychology of Written Language*, John Wiley, Chichester.

DeLoache, J. S. (1989) 'The development of representation in young children', in H. W. Reese (ed.), *Advances in Child Development and Behavior*, vol. 22, Academic Press, New York, pp. 1–39.

DeLoache, J. S. (1991) 'Symbolic functioning in very young children: Understanding of pictures and models', *Child Development*, vol. 62, pp. 736–52.

DeLoache, J. S. and Burns, N. M. (1993) 'Symbolic development in young children: Understanding models and pictures', in C. Pratt and A. F. Garton (eds), *Systems of Representation in Children: Development and use*, John Wiley, Chichester.

DeLoache, J. S., Strauss, M. S. and Maynard, J. (1979) 'Picture perception in infancy', *Infant Behaviour and Development*, vol. 2, pp. 77–89.

Dempster, F. N. (1992) 'The rise and fall of the inhibitory mechanism: Toward a unified theory of cognitive development and aging', *Developmental Review*, vol. 12, pp. 45–75.

Dennis, S. (1992) 'Stage and structure in the development of children's spatial representations', in R. Case (ed.), *The Mind's Staircase*, Lawrence Erlbaum, Hillsdale, NJ, pp. 229–45.

Denny, P. J. (1978) 'The "extendedness" variable in classifier semantics: Universal features and culture variation', in M. Mathiot (ed.), *Boas, Sapir and Whorf Revisited*, Mouton, The Hague, pp. 97–119.

Denny, P. J. (1979a) 'Semantic analysis of selected Japanese numeral classifiers for units', *Linguistics*, vol. 17, pp. 317–35.

Denny, P. J. (1979b) 'Two notes on Ojibway shape roots', *Algonquian Linguistics*, vol. 4, pp. 26–7.

Deregowski, J. B. (1989) 'Real space and represented space', *Behavioural and Brain Sciences*, vol. 12, pp. 51–87.

Deregoswki, J. B. and Strang, P. (1986) 'On the drawing of a cube and its derivates', *British Journal of Developmental Psychology*, vol. 4, pp. 323–30.

Derousne, J. and Beauvois, M-F. (1985) 'The "phonemic" stage in the non-lexical reading process: Evidence from a case of phonological alexia', in K. E. Patterson, J. C. Marshall and M. Coltheart (eds), *Surface Dyslexia: Cognitive and neuropsychological studies of phonological reading*, Lawrence Erlbaum, London.

Dow, G. A. and Pick, H. L. (1992) 'Young children's use of models and photographs as spatial representations', *Cognitive Development*, vol. 7, pp. 351–63.

Dubery, F. and Willats, J. (1972) *Drawing Systems*, Studio Vista, London.

Dubery, F. and Willats, J. (1983) *Perspective and Other Drawing Systems*, Herbert Press, London.

Duncum, P. (1988) 'To copy or not to copy: A review', *Studies in Art Education*, vol. 29, no. 4, pp. 203–10.

Edelstein, W. (1983) 'Cultural constraints on development and the vicissitudes of progress', in F. S. Kessel and A. W. Siegel (eds), *The Child and Other Cultural Inventions: Psychology and society*, Praeger, New York, pp. 48–81.

Edelstein, W., Björnsson, S. and Kreppner, K. (1977) *Explorations in Social Inequality: Stratification dynamics in social and individual development in Iceland*, Max Planck Institute for Human Development and Education, Studien and Berichte 38, Berlin.

Edelstein, W., Keller, M. and Schröder, E. (1990) 'Child development and social structure: A longitudinal study of individual differences', in P. B. Baltes, D. L. Featherman and R. M. Lerner (eds), *Life-span Development and Behavior*, vol. 10, Lawrence Erlbaum: Hillsdale, NJ, pp. 152–87.

Edgerton, S. Y. (1991) *The Heritage of Giotto's Geometry: Art and science on the eve of the scientific revolution*, Cornell University Press, Ithaca, NY.

Edwards, B. (1979) *Drawing on the Right Side of the Brain: A course in enhancing creativity and artistic confidence*, J. P. Tarcher, Los Angeles.

Elsasser, N. and John-Steiner, V. P. (1977) 'An interactionist approach to advancing literacy', *Harvard Educational Review*, vol. 47, pp. 355–69.

Estes, D., Wellman, H. M. and Woolley, J. D. (1989) 'Children's understanding of mental phenomena', in H. W. Reese (ed.), *Advances in Child Development and Behavior*, vol. 22, Academic Press, New York.

Fabricius, W. V. and Wellman, H. M. (1993) 'Two roads diverged: Young children's ability to judge distance', *Child Development*, vol. 64, pp. 399–414.

Feinberg, S.G. (1987) 'Children's awareness of aspects of competence in drawing: Level or representation and level of spatial integration', *Visual Arts Research*, vol. 13, pp. 80–93.

Fischer, K. W. (1980) 'A theory of cognitive development: The control and construction of hierarchies of skills', *Psychological Review*, vol. 87, pp. 477–531.

Flavell, J. H. (1988) 'The development of children's knowledge about the mind: From cognitive connections to mental representations', in J. W. Astington, P. L. Harris and D. R. Olson (eds), *Developing Theories of Mind*, Cambridge University Press, New York, pp. 244–71.

Flavell, J. H., Green, F. L. and Flavell, E. R. (1986) 'Development of knowledge about the appearance–reality distinction', *Monograph of the Society for Research in Child Development*, vol. 51, no. 1 (Serial No. 212).

Flavell, J. H., Green, F. L. and Flavell, E. R. (1993) 'Children's understanding of the stream of consciousness', *Child Development*, vol. 64, pp. 387–98.

Fodor, J. (1980) 'On the possibility of acquiring "more powerful" structures', in M. Piatelli-Palmarini (ed.), *Language and Learning: The debate between Jean Piaget and Noam Chomsky*, Harvard University Press, Cambridge, MA, pp. 142–62.

Fodor, J. (1983) *The Modularity of Mind*, MIT Press, Cambridge, MA.

Foeldes-Papp, K. (1987) *Vom Felsbild zum Alphabet. Die Geschichte der Schrift*, Belser, Stuttgart-Zürich.

Foucault, M. (1979) *Sexualität und Wahrheit. Der Wille zum Wissen*, Suhrkamp, Frankfurt/ M.

Franklin, S., van Sommers, P. and Howard, D. (1992) 'Drawing without meaning? Dissociations in the graphic performance of an agnosic artist', in R. Campbell (ed.), *Mental Lives: Case studies in cognition*, Basil Blackwell, Oxford.

Freeman, N. H. (1972) 'Process and product in children's drawing', *Perception*, vol. 1, pp. 123–40.

Freeman, N. H. (1980) *Strategies of Representation in Young Children: Analysis of spatial skills and drawing processes*, Academic Press, London.

Freeman, N. H. (1986) 'How should a cube be drawn?', *British Journal of Developmental Psychology*, vol. 4, pp. 317–22.

Freeman, N. H. (1987) 'Current problems in the development of representational picture-production', *Archives de Psychologie*, vol. 55, pp. 127–52.

Freeman, N. H. and Brown, N. M. (1993) 'The emergence of a theory of pictures: Intentional net analysis', working paper in the Department of Psychology, University of Bristol.

Freeman, N. H. and Cox, M. V. (eds) (1985) *Visual Order*, Cambridge University Press, Cambridge.

Freeman, N. H., Eiser, C. and Sayers, J. (1977) 'Children's strategies in producing three-dimensional relationships on a two-dimensional surface', *Journal of Experimental Child Psychology*, vol. 23, pp. 305–14.

Freeman, N. H. and Sanger, D. (1993) 'Language and belief in critical thinking: Emerging explanations of pictures', *Exceptionality Education Canada*, vol. 3, pp. 43–58.

Friederici, A. D. (1990) 'On the properties of cognitive modules', *Psychological Research*, vol. 52, pp. 175–80.

Friederici, A. D. and Levelt, W. J. M. (1986) 'Cognitive processes of spatial coordinate assignment: On weighing perceptual cues', *Naturwissenschaften*, vol. 73, pp. 455–8.

Friederici, A. D. and Levelt, W. J. M. (1990) 'Spatial reference in weightlessness: Perceptual factors and mental representations', *Perception and Psychophysics*, vol. 47, pp. 253–66.

Gardner, H. (1973) *The Arts and Human Development*, John Wiley, New York.

Gardner, H. (1980) *Artful Scribbles: The significance of children's drawings*, Basic Books, New York.

Gardner, H., Winner, E. and Kircher, M. (1975) 'Children's conception of the arts', *Journal of Aesthetic Education*, vol. 9, pp. 60–77.

Gibson, J. J. (1950) *The Perception of the Visual World*, Houghton-Mifflin, Boston.

Gibson, J. J. (1966) *The Senses Considered as Perceptual Systems*, Houghton-Mifflin, Boston.

Gibson, J. J. (1973) 'On the concept of "formless invariants" in visual perception', *Leonardo*, vol. 6, pp. 43–5.

Gibson, J. J. (1979) *The Ecological Approach to Visual Perception*, Houghton-Mifflin, Boston.

Globerson, T. (1983) 'Mental capacity and cognitive functioning: Developmental and social class differences', *Developmental Psychology*, vol. 19, pp. 225–30.

Globerson, T. (1989) 'What is the relationship between cognitive style and cognitive development?', in T. Globerson and T. Zelniker (eds), *Cognitive Style and Cognitive Development*, Ablex, Norwood, NJ, pp. 71–85.

Golomb, C. (1973) 'Children's representation of the human figure: The effects of models, media and instructions', *Genetic Psychology Monographs*, vol. 87, pp. 197–251.

Golomb, C. (1992) *The Child's Creation of a Pictorial World*, University of California Press, Berkeley.

Gombrich, E. H. (1960) *Art and Illusion*, Pantheon, London.

Gombrich, E. H. (1965) 'Visual discovery through art', *Arts Magazine*, November.

Gombrich, E. H. (1977) *Art and Illusion: A study in the psychology of pictorial representation*, 5th edition, Phaidon Press, London.

Goodenough, F. L. (1926) *Measurement of Intelligence by Drawings*, Harcourt, Brace and World, New York.

Goodman, N. (1976) *Languages of Art*, 2nd edition, Hackett, Indianapolis.

Goodnow, J. (1977) *Children's Drawing*, Harvard University Press, Cambridge, MA.

Goodnow, J. (1978) 'Visible thinking: Cognitive aspects of change in drawings', *Child Development*, vol. 49, pp. 637–41.

Graewe, H. (1935) 'Das Tierzeichnen der Kinder', *Zeitschrift für Pädagogische Psychologie*, vol. 36, pp. 25–256, 291–300.

Greer, G. (1979) *The Obstacle Race: The fortunes of woman painters and their work*, Secker & Warburg, London.

Gregory, R. L. (1970) *The Intelligent Eye*, Weidenfeld & Nicolson, London.

Habermas, J. (1981), *Theorie des kommunikativen Handelns*, Suhrkamp, Frankfurt/M.

Habib, M. (1986) 'Visual hypoemotionality and prosopagnosia associated with right temporal lobe isolation', *Neuropsychologia*, vol. 24, pp. 577–82.

Hagen, M. A. (1985) 'There is no development in art', in N. H. Freeman and M. V. Cox (eds), *Visual Order*, Cambridge University Press, Cambridge, pp. 59–77.

Hagen, M. A. (1986) *The Varieties of Realism*, Cambridge University Press, Cambridge.

Halford, G. S. (1978) 'Towards a working model of Piaget's stages', in J. A. Keats, K. F.

Collis and G. S. Halford (eds), *Cognitive Development: Research based on a neo-Piagetian approach*, John Wiley, London, pp. 169-220.

Halford, G. S. (1982) *The Development of Thought*, Lawrence Erlbaum, Hillsdale, NJ.

Harris, D. B. (1963) *Children's Drawings as Measures of Intellectual Maturity*, Harcourt, Brace and World, New York.

Hartley, J. L., Somerville, S. C., von Cziesch Jensen, D. and Eliefja, C. C. (1982) 'Abstraction of individual styles from the drawings of five-year-old children', *Child Development*, vol. 53, pp. 1193-214.

Hatfield, G. C. and Epstein, W. (1979) 'The sensory core and the medieval foundations of early modern perceptual theory', *ISIS*, vol. 70, pp. 363-84.

Hauser, A. (1953/1975) *Sozialgeschichte der Kunst und Literatur*, Beck, München.

Hayes, J. (1978) 'Children's visual descriptions', *Cognitive Science*, vol. 2, pp. 1-5.

Herman, J. F., Shiraki, J. H. and Miller, B. S. (1985) 'Young children's ability to infer spatial relationships: Evidence from a large, familiar environment', *Child Development*, vol. 56, pp. 1195-203.

Hochberg, J. and Brooks, V. (1962) 'Pictorial recognition as an unlearned ability: A study of one child's performance', *American Journal of Psychology*, vol. 73, pp. 624-8.

Hollos, M. (1974) *Growing up in Flathill: Social environment and cognitive development*, Universitetsforlaget, Oslo.

Hollos, M. (1975) 'Logical operations and role-taking abilities in two cultures: Norway and Hungary', *Child Development*, vol. 46, pp. 638-49.

Hollos, M. and Cowan, P. A. (1973) 'Social isolation and cognitive development: Logical operations and role-taking abilities in three Norwegian social settings', *Child Development*, vol. 44, pp. 630-41.

Howe, M. J. A. (1989) *Fragments of Genius: Investigating the strange feats of idiots savants*, Routledge, London.

Hume, D. (1878), *Treatise on Human Nature*, Green and Grose, London.

Humphreys, G. W. and Riddoch, M. J. (1987) *To See But Not to See: A case study of visual agnosia*, Lawrence Erlbaum, London.

Ingram, N. and Butterworth, G. (1989) 'The child's representation of depth in drawing: Process and product', *Journal of Experimental Child Psychology*, vol. 47, pp. 356-69.

Inhelder, B. (1980) 'Language and knowledge in a constructivist framework', in M. Piatelli-Palmarini (ed.), *Language and Learning: The debate between Jean Piaget and Noam Chomsky*, Harvard University Press, Cambridge, MA, pp. 132-41.

Ives, S. W. and Rovet, J. (1979) 'The role of graphic orientations in children's drawings of familiar and novel objects, at rest and in motion', *Merrill Palmer Quarterly*, vol. 25, pp. 281-92.

Jaensch, E. R. (1911) *Über die Wahrnehmung des Raumes. Eine experimentell-psychologische Untersuchung nebst Anwendung auf Ästhethik und Erkenntnislehre*, Barth, Leipzig.

James, W. (1983) 'Are we automata?', in W. James, *Essays in Psychology*, Harvard University Press, Cambridge, MA. (First published in 1879).

Johnson, J. and Kane, K. (1992) 'Developmental and task factors in Logo programming', *Journal of Educational Computing Research*, vol. 8, pp. 229-53.

John-Winde, H. (1981) '*Kriterien zur Bewertung der Kinderzeichnung*', Empirisch-pädagogische Längsschnittuntersuchung zur Entwicklung der Kinderzeichnung vom 1. bis zum 4. Schuljahr unter Berücksichtigung des Sozio-ökonomischen Status, Bouvier, Bonn.

Jones, S. (1972) 'An investigation into the conservative nature of children's drawings', unpublished honours thesis, University of New South Wales, Australia.

Juckes, T. J. (1991) 'Equilibration and the learning paradox', *Human Development*, vol. 34, pp. 261-72.

Just, M. A. and Carpenter, P. A. (1985) 'Cognitive coordinate systems: Accounts of mental rotation and individual differences in spatial ability', *Psychological Review*, vol. 92, pp. 137–71.

Kagan, J., Moss, H. A. and Sigel, I. E. (1963) 'Psychological significance of styles of conceptualization', in J. C. Wright and J. Kagan (eds), *Basic Cognitive Processes in Children*, Monographs of the Society for Research in Child Development, vol. 28 (Serial No. 86).

Kanizsa, G. (1979) *Organisation in Vision: Essays on Gestalt perception*, Praeger, New York.

Kant, I. (1787/1926) *Kritik der reinen Vernunft*, Meiner, Leipzig.

Karmiloff-Smith, A. (1988) 'The child is a theoretician, not an inductivist', *Mind and Language*, vol. 3, pp. 183–95.

Karmiloff-Smith, A. (1990) 'Constraints on representational change: Evidence from children's drawing', *Cognition*, vol. 34, pp. 57–83.

Karmiloff-Smith, A. (1992) *Beyond Modularity: A developmental perspective on cognitive science*, MIT Press: Cambridge, MA.

Karpati, A. (1991) 'Hungarian national assessment of critical skills of 6- to 14-year olds in art', *Visual Arts Research*, vol. 17, pp. 11–27.

Keil, F. C. (1990) 'Constraints on constraints: Surveying the epigenetic landscape', *Cognitive Science*, vol. 14, pp. 135–68.

Kellogg, R. (1970) *Analysing Children's Art*, National Press Books, Palo Alto, CA.

Kennedy, J. M. (1983) 'What can we learn about pictures from the blind?', *American Scientist*, vol. 71, pp. 19–26.

Kennedy, J. M. (1993) *Drawing and the Blind: Pictures to touch*, Yale Press, New Haven, CT.

Kerschensteiner, G. (1905) *Die Entwicklung der zeichnerischen Begabung*, Gerber, Munich.

Kohlberg, L. (1969) 'Stage and sequence: The cognitive-developmental approach to socialisation', in D. A. Goslin (ed.), *Handbook of Socialisation Theory and Research*, Rand-McNally, Chicago, pp. 347–480.

Koppitz, E. (1968) *Psychological Evaluation of Children's Human Figure Drawings*, Grune & Stratton, London.

Kornblum, S., Hasbroucq, T. and Osman, A. (1990) 'Dimensional overlap: Cognitive basis for stimulus–response compatibility. A model and a taxonomy', *Psychological Review*, vol. 97, pp. 253–70.

Kosslyn, S. M., Heldmeyer, K. H. and Locklear, E. P. (1977) 'Children's drawings as data about internal representations', *Journal of Experimental Child Psychology*, vol. 23, pp. 191–211.

Krauss, R. (1986a) 'No more play', in R. Krauss (ed.), *The Originality of the Avant-Garde and Other Modernist Myths*, MIT Press, Cambridge, MA, pp. 42–85.

Krauss, R. (1986b) 'The originality of the avant-garde and other modernist myths', in R. Krauss (ed.), *The Originality of the Avant-Garde and Other Modernist Myths*, MIT Press, Cambridge, MA, pp. 151–72.

Lange-Küttner, C. (1989) *Raumbegriff und Objektbeziehungen beim Kind. Die Entwicklung des perspektivischen Zeichnens bei verhaltengestörten und normalen Kindern*, Lang, Frankfurt.

Lange-Küttner, C. (1994) *Gestalt und konstruktion. Die Entwicklung der grafischen Kompetenz beim Kind*, Huber, Bern.

Lange-Küttner, C. (in preparation) 'Drawing the human figure in spatial context: Long-term effects of selective differentiation'.

Langer, S. K. (1957) *Philosophy in A New Key*, 3rd edition, Harvard University Press, Cambridge, MA.

Laszlo, J. L. and Broderick, P. A. (1985) 'The perceptual-motor skill of drawing', in N. H. Freeman, and M. V. Cox (eds), *Visual Order*, Cambridge University Press, Cambridge.

Lee, M. and Bremner, J. G. (1987) 'The representation of depth in children's drawings of a table', *The Quarterly Journal of Experimental Psychology*, vol. 39A, pp. 479–96.

Leekam, S. R. and Perner, J. (1991) 'Does the autistic child have a metarepresentational deficit?', *Cognition*, vol. 40, pp. 203–18.

Lemke, J. (1990) *Talking Science: Language, learning, and values*, Ablex, Norwood, NJ.

Lemke, J. (1993) 'Intertextuality and educational research', *Linguistics and Education*, vol. 4, pp. 257–68.

Leontiev, A. (1931/1983) 'Development of higher forms of memorizing', in A. N. Leontiev, *Selected Psychological Works*, vol. 1, Pedagogkia, Moscow (in Russian).

Leslie, A. M. and Thaiss, L. (1992) 'Domain specificity in conceptual development: Neuropsychological evidence from autism', *Cognition*, vol. 43, pp. 225–51.

Liben, L. S. (1978) 'Perspective-taking skills in young children: Seeing the world through rose-colored glasses', *Developmental Psychology*, vol. 14, pp. 87–92.

Liben, L. S. and Belknap, B. (1981) 'Intellectual realism: Implications for investigations of perceptual perspective taking in young children', *Child Development*, vol. 52, 921–4.

Liben, L. S. and Downs, R. M. (1992) 'Developing an understanding of graphic representations in children and adults: The case of GEO-graphics', *Cognitive Development*, vol. 7, pp. 331–49.

Light, P. (1985) 'The development of view-specific representations considered from a socio-cognitive standpoint', in N. H. Freeman and M. V. Cox (eds), *Visual Order*, Cambridge University Press, Cambridge.

Light, P. and Nix, C. (1983) ' "Own view" versus "good view" in a perspective-taking task', *Child Development*, vol. 54, pp. 480–3.

Light, P. and Simmons, B. (1983) 'The effects of a communication task upon the representation of depth relationships in young children's drawings', *Journal of Experimental Child Psychology*, vol. 35, pp. 81–92.

Lopera, F. and Ardila, A. (1992) 'Prosopamnesia and visuolimbic disconnection syndrome: A case study', *Neuropsychology*, vol. 6, pp. 3–12.

Lorant, G. and van Eeckhout, P. (1980) *L'Homme qui ne savait plus parler*, Nouvelles Editions Baudinière, Paris.

Lowe, D. G. (1985) *Perceptual Organisation and Visual Recognition*, Kluwer, Boston.

Lowenfeld, V. (1951) 'Psycho-aesthetic implications of the art of the blind', *Journal of Aesthetics and Art Criticisms*, vol. 10, pp. 1–9.

Lowenfeld, V. (1952) *The Nature of Creative Activity: Experimental and comparative studies of visual and non-visual sources of drawing, painting, and sculpture by means of artistic products of weak sighted and blind subjects and of the art of different epochs and cultures*, 2nd edition, Routledge & Kegan Paul, London. (First published in English in 1939).

Lowenfeld, V. and Brittain, W. L. (1975) *Creative and Mental Growth*, Macmillan, New York.

Luquet, G. H. (1913) *Les Dessins d'un enfant. Thèse pour le Doctorat Présenté à la Faculté des Lettres de L'Université de Lille*, Librarie Félix Alcan, Paris.

Luquet, G. H. (1922) 'La méthode dans l'étude des dessins d'enfants', *Journal de Psychologie*, vol. 19, pp. 193–221.

Luquet, G. H. (1924) 'La narration graphique chez l'enfant', *Journal de Psychologie*, vol. 21, pp. 183–218.

Luquet, G. H. (1927/1977) *Le Dessin enfantin*, Alcan, Paris. (Third edition reprinted by Delachaux and Niestlé, Lausanne and Paris, 1977).

Lurçat, L. (1985) 'Réalisme et modèle interne: A propos du dessin de l'enfant', *Bulletin de Psychologie*, vol. 38, pp. 231–41.

Luria, A. (1971) 'Towards the problem of the historical nature of psychological processes', *International Journal of Psychology*, vol. 6, pp. 259–72.

Luria, A. (1979) *The Making of Mind*, Harvard University Press, Cambridge, MA.

Luria, A. (1983) 'The development of writing in the child', in *Development and Educational Perspectives*, John Wiley, New York.

Maccoby, E. E. (1966) 'Sex differences in intellectual functioning', in E. E. Maccoby (ed.), *The Development of Sex Differences*, Stanford University Press, Stanford, CA, pp. 22–55.

Machover, K. (1949) *Personality Projection in the Drawings of the Human Figure*, C. C. Thomas, Springfield, IL.

Marr, D. (1982) *Vision: A computational investigation into the human representation and processing of visual information*, W. H. Freeman, San Francisco.

Martlew, M. (1988) 'Children's oral and written language', in A. D. Pellegrini (ed.), *Psychological Bases for Early Education*, John Wiley, Chichester.

Matthews, G. B. (1980) *Philosophy and the Young Child*, Harvard University Press, Cambridge, MA.

Matthews, J. S. (1984) 'Children drawing: Are young children really scribbling?', *Early Child Development and Care*, vol. 18, pp. 1–39.

Matthews, J. S. (1990) 'The first drawing'. Poster presented at IVth European Conference on Developmental Psychology, Stirling.

McLane, J. B. (1988) 'Writing as a social process', in J. Moll (ed.), *Vygotsky and Education: Instructional implications and applications of sociohistorical psychology*, Cambridge University Press, New York, pp. 304–19.

Metzger, W. (1936/1975) *Gesetze des Sehens*, Kramer, Frankfurt/M.

Metzger, W. (1956) 'Die Entwicklung der Gestaltauffassung in der Zeit der Schulreife', *Westermann Pädagogische Beitrage*, vol. 8, pp. 531–43, 603–15.

Miller, G. A. (1956) 'The magical number seven, plus or minus two', *Psychological Review*, vol. 63, pp. 81–97.

Mitchelmore, M. C. (1978) 'Developmental stages in children's representation of regular solid figures', *Journal of Genetic Psychology*, vol. 133, pp. 229–39.

Mooney, C. M. (1957) 'Age in the development of closure ability', *Canadian Journal of Psychology*, vol. 11, pp. 219–26.

Moore, V. (1986a) 'The use of a colouring task to elucidate children's drawings of a solid cube', *British Journal of Developmental Psychology*, vol. 4, pp. 335–40.

Moore, V. (1986b) 'The relationship between children's drawings and preferences for alternative depictions of a familiar object', *Journal of Experimental Psychology*, vol. 42, 187–98.

Morra, S. (1994) 'Issues in working memory measurement: testing for M capacity', *International Journal of Behavioural Development*, vol. 17, pp. 143–59.

Morra, S., Caloni, B. and D'Amico, M. R. (in press) 'Working memory and the intentional depiction of emotions', *Archives de Psychologie*.

Morra, S., Moizo, C. and Scopesi, A. (1988) 'Working memory (or the M operator) and the planning of children's drawings', *Journal of Experimental Child Psychology*, vol. 46, pp. 41–73.

Morra, S., Pascual-Leone, J., Johnson, J. and Baillargeon, R. (1991) 'Understanding spatial descriptions: A test of a mental capacity model', in R. Logie and M. Denis (eds), *Mental Images in Human Cognition*, North Holland, Amsterdam, pp. 241–54.

Morra, S. and Perchinenna, R. (1993) 'Thinkable images: Cognitive accounts of change in drawings'. Poster presented at the IV European Conference on Developmental Psychology in the workshop, 'Form and function of children's drawings' (Org. G. V. Thomas and C. Lange-Küttner), Bonn.

Morss, J. R. (1990) *The Biologising of Childhood: Developmental psychology and the Darwinian myth*, Lawrence Erlbaum, London.

Nanda, P. C., Das, J. P. and Mishra, H. K. (1965) 'Discrimination of geometrical patterns in tribal, rural and urban children', *The Journal of Social Psychology*, vol. 67, pp. 197–200.

Nicholls, A. L. and Kennedy, J. M. (1992) 'Drawing development: From similarity of features to direction', *Child Development*, vol. 63, pp. 227–41.

Nicolaides, K. (1941) *The Natural Way to Draw: A working plan for art studies*, Houghton-Mifflin, Boston.

Ninio, A. and Bruner, J. (1978) 'The achievement and antecedents of labelling', *Journal of Child Language*, vol. 5, pp. 1–15.

Obukhova, L. (1981) *Theory of Jean Piaget: Pros and contras*, Moscow University Press, Moscow.

Obukhova, L. and Borisova, V. (1981) *Relationship between Speech and Drawing*, unpublished manuscript, in Russian.

Obukhova, L. and Minina, S. (1986) *Relationship Between Verbal and Visual Components in Imagery: The case of children's drawing*, unpublished manuscript, in Russian.

Pariser, D. (1981) 'Nadia's drawings: Theorising about an autistic child's phenomenal ability', *Journal of Studies in Art Education*, vol. 22, pp. 20–9.

Parsons, M. J. (1987), *How We Understand Art*, Cambridge University Press, Cambridge.

Pascual-Leone, J. (1970) 'A mathematical model for the transition rule in Piaget's developmental stages', *Acta Psychologica*, vol. 63, pp. 301–45.

Pascual-Leone, J. (1976) 'On learning and development, Piagetian style', *Canadian Psychological Review*, vol. 17, pp. 270–97.

Pascual-Leone, J. (1980) 'Constructive problems for constructive theories: The current relevance of Piaget's work and a critique of information processing simulation psychology', in R. Kluwe and H. Spada (eds), *Developmental Models of Thinking*, Academic Press, New York, pp. 263–96.

Pascual-Leone, J. (1983) 'Growing into human maturity: Towards a metasubjective theory of adulthood stages', in P. Baltes and O. Brim (eds), *Life-span Development and Behavior*, vol. 5, Academic Press, New York, pp. 117–56.

Pascual-Leone, J. (1984) 'Attention, dialectics and mental effort: Towards an organismic theory of life stages', in M. L. Commons, F. L. Richards and G. Armon (eds), *Beyond Formal Operations: Late adolescence and adult cognitive development*, Praeger, New York, pp. 182–215.

Pascual-Leone, J. (1987) 'Organismic processes for neo-Piagetian theories: A dialectical causal account of cognitive development', *International Journal of Psychology*, vol. 22, pp. 531–70.

Pascual-Leone, J. (1989) 'An organismic process model of Witkin's field dependence–independence', in T. Globerson and T. Zelniker (eds), *Cognitive Style and Cognitive Development*, Ablex, Norwood, NJ, pp. 36–70.

Pascual-Leone, J. and Goodman, D. (1979) 'Intelligence and experience: a neo-Piagetian approach', *Instructional Science*, vol. 8, pp. 301–67.

Pascual-Leone, J., Goodman, D., Ammon, P. and Subelman, I. (1978) 'Piagetian theory and neo-Piagetian analysis as psychological guides in education', in J. Gallagher and J. A. Easley (eds), *Knowledge and Development*, vol. 2, Plenum Press, New York, pp. 243–89.

Pascual-Leone, J. and Johnson, J. (1991) 'Psychological unit and its role in task analysis: A re-interpretation of object permanence', in M. Chandler and M. Chapman (eds), *Criteria for Competence: Controversies in the assessment of children's abilities*, Lawrence Erlbaum, Hillsdale, NJ.

Pascual-Leone, J., Johnson, J. and Benson, N. (1989) 'Mental capacity constraints on symbolic processing: The case of language acquisition and of metaphor comprehension'. Paper presented at the 10th Biennial Meeting of the ISSBD, Jyvaskyla.

Pascual-Leone, J. and Morra, S. (1991) 'Horizontally of water level: A neo-Piagetian developmental review', in H. W. Reese (ed.), *Advances in Child Development and Behavior*, vol. 23, Academic Press, Orlando, FL, pp. 231–76.

Perner, J. (1991) *Understanding the Representational Mind*, MIT Press, Cambridge, MA.

Perner, J., Kohlmann, R. and Wimmer, H. (1984) 'Young children's recognition and use of the vertical and horizontal in drawings', *Child Development*, vol. 55, pp. 1637–45.

Perner, J., Leekam, S. R., Myers, D., Davis, S. and Odgers, N. (1993) 'Misrepresentations and referential confusion: Children's difficulty with false beliefs and outdated photographs', unpublished manuscript, University of Sussex.

Phillips, W. A., Hobbs, S. B. and Pratt, F. R. (1978) 'Intellectual realism in children's drawings of cubes', *Cognition*, vol. 6, pp. 15–33.

Phillips, W. A., Inall, M. and Lauder, E. (1985) 'On the discovery, storage and use of graphic descriptions', in N. H. Freeman and M. V. Cox (eds), *Visual Order*, Cambridge University Press, Cambridge.

Piaget, J. (1924/1928) *Judgement and Reasoning in the Child*, Routledge & Kegan Paul, London.

Piaget, J. (1926/1929) *The Child's Conception of the World*, Routledge & Kegan Paul, London.

Piaget, J. (1936/1952) *The Origins of Intelligence in Children*, International Universities Press, New York.

Piaget, J. (1946) 'La formation du symbole chez l'enfant', It. transl. *La formazione del simbolo nel bambino*, (1972) La Nuova Italia, Florence.

Piaget, J. (1971) *Psychology and Epistemology*, Grossman, New York.

Piaget, J. (1977) 'The role of action in the development of thinking', in W. F. Overton and J. MacCarthy Gallagher (eds), *Knowledge and Development*, Plenum Press, New York, pp. 17–42.

Piaget, J. and Inhelder, B. (1948/1956) *The Child's Conception of Space*, Routledge & Kegan Paul, London.

Piaget, J. and Inhelder, B. (1966/1971) *Mental Imagery in the Child*, Routledge & Kegan Paul, London.

Piaget, J. and Inhelder, B. (1969) *The Psychology of the Child*, Routledge & Kegan Paul, London.

Piaget, J., Inhelder, B. and Szeminska, A. (1948/1960) *The Child's Conception of Geometry*, Routledge & Kegan Paul, London.

Piatelli-Palmarini, M. (ed.) (1980) *Language and Learning: The debate between Jean Piaget and Noam Chomsky*, Harvard University Press, Cambridge, MA.

Pillow, B. (1993) 'Do 4-year-olds understand biased interpretation?'. Poster presented at the Biennial Meeting of the Society for Research in Child Development, New Orleans.

Planck, M. (1936) *Vom Wesen der Willensfreiheit*, Barth, Leipzig.

Preyer, W. (1888) *The Mind of the Child*. Part 1: *The Senses and the Will: Observations concerning the mental life of the human being in the first years of life*, trans. H. W. Brown, D. Appleton, New York. (Translation of 2nd edition, 1884; first edition, 1881).

Quirk, R., Greenbaum, S., Leech, G. and Svartvik, J. (1985) *A Comprehensive Grammar of the English Language*, Longman, London.

Rafoth, B. and Rubin, D. (1988) *The Social Construction of Written Communication*, Ablex, Norwood, NJ.

Rasmussen, E. T. and Vejleskov, H. (1986) 'Visually experienced parallelity', in I. K. Moustgaard and A. F. Patterson (eds), *Vision or Illusion*, Dansk Psykologisk Forlag, Copenhagen.

Read, H. (1956) *Education through Art*, 3rd rev. edition, Pantheon, New York.

Reith, E. (1987) 'Attitude intellectuelle et attitude visuelle dans la copie de modèles tridimensionelles et bidimensionelles chez des enfants de 4 à 10 ans', unpublished dissertation, Geneva.

Reith, E. (1988) 'The development of use of contour lines in children's drawings of figurative and non-figurative three-dimensional models', *Archives de Psychologie*, vol. 56, pp. 83–103.

Reith, E. (1990) 'Development of representational awareness and performance in drawing production', *Archives de Psychologie*, vol. 58, pp. 369–79.

Reith, E., Steffen, C. and Gillèrion, C. (in press) 'Children's drawings of water level: Operatory knowledge, attention to visual image, and depiction skills', *Revue Suisse de Psychologie*.

Ricci, C. (1887) *L'arte dei bambini*, Zanichelli, Bologna.

Robinson, E. J., Nye, R. and Thomas, G. V. (1994) 'Children's conceptions of the relationship between pictures and their referents', *Cognitive Development*, vol. 9, pp. 165–91.

Rubin, E. (1915) *Synsoplevede Figurer*, Gyldendals, Copenhagen.

Rueda, R. (1988) 'Assisted performance in writing instruction with learning-disabled students', in J. Moll (ed.), *Vygotsky and Education: Instructional implications and applications of sociohistorical psychology*, Cambridge University Press, New York, pp. 403–26.

Schier, F. (1986) *Deeper into Pictures*, Cambridge University Press, Cambridge.

Schneuwly, B. (1989) 'La conception Vygotskienne du langage écrit', *Etudes de Linguistique Appliqué*, vol. 73, pp. 107–17.

Schröder, E. (1992) 'Strukturbildung und Kontexte der kognitiven Entwicklung. Bedingungen und Kontexte der Selbstorganisation', in Center for Development and Socialization (eds), *Sozialer Konstruktivismus*, Max Planck Institute for Human Development and Education, Berlin, pp. 20–39.

Schröder, E. and Edelstein, W. (1991) 'Intrinsic and external constraints on the development of cognitive competencies', in M. Chandler and M. Chapman (eds), *Criteria for Competence: Controversy in the conceptualization and assessment of children's abilities*, Lawrence Erlbaum, Hillsdale, NJ, pp. 131–50.

Searle, J. R. (1983) *Intentionality*, Cambridge University Press, Cambridge.

Sedgwick, H. (1980) 'The geometry of spatial layout in pictorial representation', in M. Hagen (ed.), *The Perception of Pictures*, vol. 1, Academic Press, New York, pp. 33–89.

Selfe, L. (1977) *Nadia: A case of extraordinary drawing ability in an autistic child*, Academic Press, London.

Selfe, L. (1983) *Normal and Anomalous Representational Drawing Ability in Children*, Academic Press, London.

Selfe, L. (1985) 'Anomalous drawing development: Some clinical studies', in N. H. Freeman and M. V. Cox (eds.), *Visual Order*, Cambridge University Press, Cambridge, pp. 135–54.

Silk, A. M. J. and Thomas, G. V. (1986) 'Development and differentiation in children's figure drawings', *British Journal of Psychology*, vol. 77, pp. 399–410.

Silk, A. M. J. and Thomas, G. V. (1988) 'The development of size scaling in children's figure drawings', *British Journal of Developmental Psychology*, vol. 6, pp. 285–99.

Simó Teufel, S. and Lange-Küttner, C. (1993) 'What has the human figure drawing to do with the graphic space concept?'. Poster presented at the IVth European Conference on Developmental Psychology in the workshop 'Form and function of children's drawings'. (org. G. V. Thomas and C. Lange-Küttner), Bonn.

Somerville, S. (1983) 'Individual drawing styles of three children from five to seven years', in D. Rogers and J. A. Sloboda (eds), *The Acquisition of Symbolic Skills*, Plenum Press, New York, pp. 89–96.

Spelke, E. S. (1990) 'Origins of visual knowledge', in D. Osherson, S. M. Kosslyn and J. M. Hollerbach (eds) *Visual Cognition and Action*, vol. 2, MIT Press, Cambridge, MA, pp. 99–127.

Stanton, R. (1973) 'A further investigation into the conservative nature of children's drawings', unpublished honours thesis, Macquarie University, Australia.

Stern, W. (1930) *Psychology of Early Childhood*, George Allen & Unwin, London.

Sully, J. (1895) *Studies of Childhood*, Longman, Green and Co., London.

Taylor, B. (1989) 'Art history in the classroom: A plea for caution', in D. Thistlewood (ed.), *Critical Studies in Art and Design Education*, Longman, London.

Taunton, M. (1980) 'The influence of age on preferences for subject matter, realism, and spatial depth in painting reproductions', *Studies in Art Education*, vol. 21, pp. 40–52.

Thomas, G. V., Nye, R. and Robinson, E. J. (1994) 'How children view pictures: Children's responses to pictures as things in themselves and as representations of something else', *Cognitive Development*, vol. 9, pp. 141–144.

Thomas, G. V. and Silk, A. M. J. (1990) *An Introduction to the Psychology of Children's Drawings*, Harvester Wheatsheaf, Hemel Hempstead.

Thomas, G. V. and Tsalimi, A. (1988) 'Effects of order of drawing head and trunk on their relative sizes in children's human figure drawings', *British Journal of Developmental Psychology*, vol. 6, pp. 191–203.

Trautner, H. M., Lohaus, A., Sahm, W. B. and Helbing, N. (1989) 'Age-graded judgements of children's drawings by children and adults', *International Journal of Behavioral Development*, vol. 12, pp. 421–31.

Trautner, H. M., Lohaus, A. and Schorsch, S. (1989) 'The development of individual characteristics in drawings of 5–9 year old children', Berichte aus dem Psychologischen Institut III. no. 9, Universität Münster.

Trojano, L. and Grossi, D. (1992) 'Impaired drawing from memory in a visual agnosic patient', *Brain and Cognition*, vol. 20, pp. 327–44.

van Sommers, P. (1983) 'The conservatism of children's drawing strategies', in D. Rogers and J. A. Sloboda (eds), *The Acquisition of Symbolic Skills*, Plenum Press, New York, pp. 65–70.

van Sommers, P. (1984) *Drawing and Cognition*, Cambridge University Press, Cambridge.

van Sommers, P. (1989) 'A system for drawing and drawing-related neuropsychology', *Cognitive Neuropsychology*, vol. 6, pp. 117–64.

van Sommers, P. (1991) 'Where writing starts: The analysis of action applied to the historical development of writing', in J. Wann, J. A. Wing and N. Sovik (eds), *Development of Graphic Skills*, Academic Press, London.

Verworn, M. (1917) *Zur Psychologie der primitiven Kunst*, Fischer, Jena. (First published 1908).

Vygotsky, L. S. (1934/1962) *Thought and Language*, MIT Press, Cambridge, MA.

Vygotsky, L. S. (1935/1978). 'The prehistory of written language', in L. S. Vygotsky, *Mind in Society*, Harvard University Press, Cambridge, MA.

Vygotsky, L. S. (1981) 'The genesis of higher mental functions', in J. V. Wertsch (ed.), *The Concept of Activity in Soviet Psychology*, Sharpe, Armonk, NY.

Walton, K. L. (1990) *Mimesis as Make-Believe*, Harvard University Press, Cambridge, MA.

Wapner, W., Judd, T. and Gardner, J. (1978) 'Visual agnosia in an artist', *Cortex*, vol. 14, pp. 343–64.

Wellman, H. M. and Estes, D. (1986) 'Early understanding of mental entities: A re-examination of childhood realism', *Child Development*, vol. 57, pp. 910–23.

Willats, J. (1977a) 'How children learn to draw realistic pictures', *Quarterly Journal of Experimental Psychology*, vol. 29, pp. 367–82.

Willats, J. (1977b) 'How children learn to represent three-dimensional space in drawings', in G. Butterworth (ed.), *The Child's Representation of the World*, Plenum Press, London, pp. 189–202.

Willats, J. (1981) 'What do the marks in the picture stand for? The child's acquisition of systems of transformation and denotation', *Review of Research in Visual Arts Education*, vol. 13, pp. 18–33.

Willats, J. (1984) 'Getting the drawing to look right as well as to be right', in W. R. Crozier and A. J. Chapman (eds), *Cognitive Processes in the Perception of Art*, North Holland, Amsterdam.

Willats, J. (1985) 'Drawing systems revisited: the role of denotation systems in children's figure drawings', in N. H. Freeman and M. V. Cox (eds), *Visual Order*, Cambridge University Press, Cambridge.

Willats, J. (1987) 'Marr and pictures: An information processing account of children's drawings', *Archives de Psychologie*, vol. 55, pp. 105–25.

Willats, J. (1992a) 'What is the matter with Mary Jane's drawing?', in D. Thistlewood (ed.), *Drawing Research and Development*, Longman, London, pp. 141–52.

Willats, J. (1992b) 'The representation of extendedness in children's drawings of sticks and discs', *Child Development*, vol. 63, pp. 692–710.

Willats, J. (1992c) 'Seeing lumps, sticks, and slabs in silhouettes', *Perception*, vol. 21, pp. 481–96.

Wilson, B. (1992) 'Primitivism, the avant-garde and the art of little children', in D. Thistlewood (ed.), *Drawing Research and Development*, Longman, London.

Wilson, B. and Ligtvoet, J. (1992) 'Across time and cultures: Stylistic changes in the drawings of Dutch children', in D. Thistlewood (ed.), *Drawing Research and Development*, Longman, London.

Wilson, B. and Wilson, M. (1977) 'An iconoclastic view of the imagery sources in the drawings of young people', *Art Education*, vol. 30, pp. 5–11.

Wilson, B. and Wilson, M. (1984) 'Children's drawings in Egypt: Cultural style acquisition as graphic development', *Visual Arts Research*, vol. 10, pp. 13–26.

Wilson, B. and Wilson, M. (1985) 'The artistic tower of Babel: Inextricable links between culture and graphic development', *Visual Arts Research*, vol. 11, no. 1, pp. 90–104.

Winner, E. (1982) *Invented Worlds: The psychology of the arts*, Harvard University Press, Cambridge, MA.

Witkin, A. P. and Tennenbaum, J. M. (1983) 'On the role of structure in vision', in J. Beck, B. Hope and A. Rosenfeld (eds), *Human and Machine Vision*, Academic Press, New York, pp. 481–543.

Witkin, H., Lewis, H., Hertzman, M., Machover, K. *et al.* (1954/1975) *Personality Through Perception*, Greenwood Press, Westport, CT.

Witte, S. (1992) 'Context, text, intertext', *Written Communication*, vol. 9, pp. 237–308.

Wohlwill, J. F. (1962) 'From perception to inference: A dimension of cognitive development', in W. Kessen and C. Kuhlmann (eds), Thought in the Young Child, *Monograph of the Society for Research in Child Development*, vol. 27, no. 2, pp. 87–112.

Wollheim, R. (1993) *The Mind and its Depth*, Harvard University Press, Cambridge, MA.

Woolley, J. D. and Wellman, H. M. (1990) 'Young children's understanding of realities, nonrealities and appearances', *Child Development*, vol. 61, pp. 946–61.

Zagòrska, W. (1988) 'The schemes of facial emotional expression drawn by Polish and Portuguese pre-school age children'. Paper presented at the 3rd European Conference on Developmental Psychology, Budapest.

Zaitchik, D. (1990) 'When representations conflict with reality: The preschooler's problem with false beliefs and "false" photographs', *Cognition*, vol. 35, pp. 41–68.

Ziller, R. C. (1990) *Photographing the Self*, Sage, Newbury Park, CA.

Subject index

Name index